Palgrave Politics of Identity and Citizenship Series

Series Editors
Varun Uberoi
Loughborough University
Loughborough, UK

Nasar Meer
University of Glasgow
Glasgow, UK

Tariq Modood
University of Bristol
Bristol, UK

The politics of identity and citizenship has assumed increasing importance as our polities have become significantly more culturally, ethnically and religiously diverse. Different types of scholars, including philosophers, sociologists, political scientists and historians make contributions to this field and this series showcases a variety of innovative contributions to it. Focusing on a range of different countries, and utilizing the insights of different disciplines, the series helps to illuminate an increasingly controversial area of research and titles in it will be of interest to a number of audiences including scholars, students and other interested individuals.

Sam Taylor Hill

Challenging Alienation in the British Working-Class

Building a Community of Equals

palgrave
macmillan

Sam Taylor Hill
University of Bristol
Bristol, UK

ISSN 2947-6100 ISSN 2947-6119 (electronic)
Palgrave Politics of Identity and Citizenship Series
ISBN 978-3-031-59249-2 ISBN 978-3-031-59250-8 (eBook)
https://doi.org/10.1007/978-3-031-59250-8

Credit line: Peter Zelei Images/ Getty Images

This Palgrave Macmillan imprint is published by the registered company Springer Nature Switzerland AG.
The registered company address is: Gewerbestrasse 11, 6330 Cham, Switzerland

Paper in this product is recyclable.

Contents

CHAPTER 1

Introduction

I began this book initially as a PhD in 2019 at the end of a decade that had been characterised by the fallout from the Great Recession, austerity, and a Brexit vote that left the country increasingly divided. This was a time of upheaval and new attention was being paid to the working-class as the subject of discussions around the rise of populism and the underlying structural changes and experiences which impacted it. Such attention resonated with experiences in my own life. As someone from a working-class background, I was immersed in narratives that the Labour Party had left working-people behind, which was often to be heard from Labour voters themselves, alongside a cynical apathy that saw politics as for everyone but 'us'. I had also seen first-hand how wages had stagnated and left people struggling, how attitudes towards workers were often disrespectful, and how decisions made by elites did little to benefit those at the bottom of the socio-economic hierarchy, even as inequality skyrocketed. This academic trend highlighted some of these experiences and, although a negative way of coming to study politics, has inspired me to pursue research that captures the struggle that working-people go through and, hopefully, offers some kind of remedy to them. To this end, the book asks why working-people are so often 'left behind', and what might we do about it?

These questions are especially relevant when we think about the developments within the working-class that have occurred in the last decade.

S. Taylor Hill, *Challenging Alienation in the British Working-Class*, Palgrave Politics of Identity and Citizenship Series,
https://doi.org/10.1007/978-3-031-59250-8_1

For instance, working-people are cited by Sandel and the right-communitarians as being *the* group that contributed to the growth of the populist-right (Eatwell and Goodwin 2018; Sandel 2020; Sobolewska and Ford 2020). It was touted as being responsible for the election of Donald Trump, whilst in this country we have seen a white working-class unification around an anti-migrant platform in the early years of the 2010s, before coalescing around the issue of Brexit, which fundamentally altered our relationship with the European Union and set in motion some of the key developments in British politics that were to occur over the next seven years. Indeed, in the wake of Brexit, we have seen a steady increase in episodes of social discord, whilst our political stability has been threatened by a corresponding 'crisis of democracy' in which we have witnessed two early elections, the downfall of four governments, a series of votes of no confidence, and the rise of a Boris Johnson-led Conservative Party which subjected Labour to its worst defeat in memory through a combination of its support for Brexit and a cultural-conservatism which declared a 'War on Woke', and which has itself now unravelled to be replaced by a government that has thus far failed to curb the burgeoning cost-of-living crisis.

The legacy of this populism has been disunity, instability, and the sundering of community upon a fractious, culturally charged basis, whilst working-class people have been hit hard by an unprecedented cost-of-living crisis and remain in a position that is likely to decline further. Indeed, even with Keir Starmer's Labour Party set to win the next election, there is no great fanfare or optimism. Bereft of working-class MPs, and with a leader that has already been criticised for his 'broken promises' and whose approval rating sits at -12, Labour's ascendancy is probably best understood as the only realistic alternative to a government that has ultimately overseen a significant reversal in Britain's fortunes over the past 14 years (Stacey and Crerar 2024; YouGov 2024). This is a key moment for British politics, as disenchantment becomes more widespread and citizens feel let down by successive governments; there is a very real danger of yet another populist surge, or a further decade of decline, in which the gap between rich and poor continues to increase exponentially (Hill 2023). Without a reconsideration of our society, and the way that we understand the issues faced by the working-class, there is potential for further degradation in the livelihoods of our citizens and of our very political system (Brown 2024). To arrest this decline there is an urgent need to develop a framework for conceptualising the issues of working-class people, who suffer so visibly at present, and a following theory that can serve as the basis for their renewal within, and for the benefit of, our country.

The idea behind this focus is twofold. First, the working-class continues to suffer in a country that many feel has left them behind. This is well-established in the literature and something which the book focuses on throughout. Second, many of the structures that have ultimately degraded the working-class, and much of what has been lost, including our sense of community, routes to dignification, and a feeling of personal or collective control, or a belief that one matters, have implications across class and for the country as a whole—it is a reflection of what we are as a country, where we are going, and how we treat our citizens. In this sense, in seeking to support and renew the working-class, one sees hope for the development of a position which can address some of the deep and persistent structural problems which have taken root within our society and put us on better footing for the future. It is in this stead that one looks to characterise the working-class experience as one that is consistent with alienation and seeks some remedy for its position with a politics that is ethical, socialist, and nationalist in orientation, seeing a combination of these as crucial to challenging the toxic populist—nationalism of the right-communitarians with a view to restoring to working-people a sense of agency, dignity, and recognition within a wider reciprocal community. This is a position that hopes to remedy the damage caused by right-populism over the past seven years and to restore working-people to a position of regard. It in this stead that one continues, maintaining a focus on the working-class that ultimately leads us towards a Progressive Nationalism that could be the key to a more extensive, deeper, national renewal—the kind necessary to restore our country.

Motivating Questions and Methodology

Following from this, the conceptual framework that one develops can best be described as one of alienation, and the core purpose of this book is to identify:

1. What alienation is and what its core characteristics are.
2. Whether it is an appropriate label for the issues that working-class people face.

Having deliberated upon these questions, and provided an answer which suggests that the working-class are suffering from alienation in the form of community breakdown, agential decline, and the loss of dignity, one subsequently seeks to address the additional question:

3. What can be done to ameliorate its effects?

This latter question takes the book in a more conceptual direction. This may seem a strange step to the reader, both in that one's philosophical foundation is over a century old and that alienation is something which is felt in practice. However, one holds it as a necessary step. The drawing together of these works to address a contemporary issue is justified on the basis that they speak to those things which we currently lack and conceive of only within the bounds of our present. In many respects, we have forgotten what community, for instance, means other than in a far more individualised sense than that of the Idealists, whilst we have erected barriers between the individual and the community which Idealism, or Socialist Pluralism, sees as artificial. In discussing these theories, one comes to engage with contemporary debates—for instance, around notions like the common good which have been seeing a resurgence through Michael Sandel in relation to working-class concerns and which themselves connect with arguments made by right communitarians like David Goodhart. The book also contributes to the resurrection of British Idealism as a framework to explore contemporary issues, synthesising Idealism with the socialism of G.D.H. Cole and Harold Laski. Thus, the works selected maintain a continued relevance for contemporary debates and scholarly pursuits.

One likewise makes use of significant secondary data in detailing the present condition of the working-class. One does not engage in primary fieldwork for two reasons. First, there is already much research that has been done, especially post-Brexit vote, to study the working-class existence, which one makes extensive use of throughout the book. Second, one sees in these literatures that we are lacking theoretical frameworks to understand and address these issues. One therefore settles on using pre-existing work to establish that the working-class is suffering from alienation and subsequently outlines a theoretical framework for its amelioration.

It does this because the right-communitarian account, although useful in highlighting the factors, like community breakdown and the loss of dignity, and of agency, which cause alienation, advocates solutions that leave in place damaging structures and neglect to consider the problem at its most fundamental level as the disassociation between subject and object. These authors neglect to understand alienation as a concept, borne out of a rich philosophical tradition that has historically been a focal point for the left. To understand how to challenge alienation, we must reconsider it conceptually. Indeed, many of the issues raised by the right-communitarians can be best understood within the context of the neglected British Idealist and Socialist traditions. These groups maintain a stronger theoretical connection with alienation as outlined by Hegel and Marx.

From this, one establishes that alienation can be challenged by (1) Idealism because it recognises the importance of human bonds and relationships as key in the development of meaning and a sense of community, (2) Socialist Pluralism because it gives account for our desire to see us influence the world, and (3) Guild and Ethical Socialism because of their moral inclinations and devotion to the problem of human dignity. This is an abridged overview of the contribution of each to the amelioration of alienation, but it serves to demonstrate the view of the book that we must return to the central themes of dignity, agency, and community, which are covered at great length by these neglected scholars. This will be placed within a contemporary context later in the book to demonstrate that it has the capacity to ameliorate alienation on a practical level too.

One returns to these themes momentarily, having first sketched out the shape of the book.

Shape of the Book

It begins with a chapter situating the core ideas of the work so that it is clear to the reader how its various parts come together.

Chapters 3 and 4 then define the working-class and alienation. Within this first chapter one draws upon the works of Bourdieu and Savage to suggest that working-class-ness is built upon an economic, social, and cultural basis that is broadly relational between its members and which is related to certain historical and contemporary tendencies.

Chapter 4 addresses the concept of alienation, making use of Hegelian philosophy, before discussing Marx's 1844 Manuscripts, which emphasise the fetishisation of 'alien' structures under capitalism in opposition to human flourishing. This is brought together with Macintyre's discussion of community and narrative breakdown. Taken together, these works lead one to establish the three core characteristics of alienation as related to the loss or lack of community, dignity, and agency.

One then determines the extent to which the working-class is alienated within Chap. 5. Here we see a sustained consideration of these three characteristics, with input from right-communitarians like Goodhart and Kaufmann, to populist scholars Eatwell and Goodwin, as well as left-leaning accounts by Sandel, Cruddas, McKenzie, and others. This chapter also gives direction to the book, setting out its distinctive components, and introduces the reader to concepts like the common good, as well as defending the identification of alienation as separate from either an anomie or social capital diagnosis of the classes' problems.

Chapters 6 and 7 make a break from the first half of the book and propose an answer to this third question concerning alienation's amelioration. Chapter 6 gives an overview of the British Idealist tradition. Herein one establishes the value of the common good and returns to the idea of flourishing to give an account of it. We also see some discussion of the individual/community debate between liberals and communitarians wherein one suggests that Idealism charts a path between them with a thicker conception of morality than its more liberal counterparts, but a thinner conception than many communitarians.

Following on from the discussion of Idealism, one will say in Chap. 7 that, although many aspects of it are commendable and will play an important role in grounding theory, there is a need to combine it with 'socialist' theoretical perspectives to understand the role of capitalism in inhibiting dignity. This imbues Idealism with a more well-rounded adherence to social justice, as well as an explicit rejection of neoliberal-capitalist, echoing the arguments introduced in Chap. 5. This chapter draws to a close by emphasising the importance of civil society, adherence to the common good, and the compatibility of Idealism with these socialisms, leading to the creation of Idealist-Socialism.

Chapters 8, 9, and 10 are dedicated to the application of this theory to the three characteristics of alienation, tied together here as a three-part theory of Progressive Nationalism which delves into the economy and civil society. Chapter 8 outlines the multicultural aspect of this to renew belonging and dignity across the working-class and its sub-groups, whilst one presents a case for the development of the economy around the common good in Chap. 9, especially keeping the dignity and agency components in mind, before outlining the agential importance of civil society expansion in Chap. 10.

One concludes by reiterating the understanding of alienation as applied to the British working-class, before setting out the core principles, constitutive of an ethos, which one details as part of its suggestion for the amelioration of alienation. This amounts to a reassertion of the need to ground an understanding of the common good within the economic sphere, to adopt a policy of civil society expansion, and to propagate an inclusive Progressive Nationalism. One ends by reflecting on the book's findings and makes recommendations for further research.

Bibliography

Brown, Gordon. "Tables without Food, Bedrooms without Beds. Grinding Child Poverty in Britain Calls for Anger—and a Plan." *The Guardian*, February 8, 2024, sec. Opinion. https://www.theguardian.com/commentisfree/2024/feb/08/child-poverty-britain-anger-gordon-brown.

Eatwell, Roger, and Matthew Goodwin. *National Populism: The Revolt Against Liberal Democracy*. Penguin, 2018.

Hill, Amelia. "UK Spends More Financing Inequality in Favour of Rich than Rest of Europe, Report Finds." *The Guardian*, November 27, 2023, sec. Inequality. https://www.theguardian.com/inequality/2023/nov/27/uk-spends-more-financing-inequality-in-favour-of-rich-than-rest-of-europe-report-finds.

Sandel, Michael J. *The Tyranny of Merit: What's Become of the Common Good?* Penguin UK, 2020.

Sobolewska, Maria, Robert Ford. *Brexitland: Identity, Diversity and the Reshaping of British Politics*. Cambridge University Press, 2020.

Stacey, Kiran, Pippa Crerar. "Starmer to Announce Scaling Back of £28bn Green Investment Plan." *The Guardian*, February 7, 2024, sec. Politics. https://www.theguardian.com/politics/2024/feb/07/keir-starmer-to-announce-scaling-back-of-28bn-green-investment-plan.

YouGov. "How Well Is Keir Starmer Doing as Labour Leader?". https://yougov.co.uk/topics/politics/trackers/keir-starmer-approval-rating. Accessed 6 Feb 2024.

CHAPTER 2

Situating Idealist-Socialism

Given the scope of this book, this chapter outlines how it connects with contemporary debates and subsequently brings those debates together to address working-class alienation. One begins by outlining the book's diagnosis as against the later Marxian notion of exploitation, seeing the latter as neglecting the importance of *spirit*. One then presents the right-communitarian explanation for alienation, including their focus on structural and cultural decline, as well as their populist nationalist answer to this problem, from which one later diverges. This divergence features an emphasis on nationalism within the progressive multicultural politics of the left, which one asserts as playing a core role in the amelioration of alienation through the provision of meaning, as against a cosmopolitan alternative. Having established this position one identifies the central thread of Idealism that connects the ideas within this book, using this to relate with contemporary debates between liberal-individualists and communitarians, as well as in respect to questions concerning the purpose of our economy. One concludes by stressing that though this work engages across several debates, these components form a comprehensive understanding of the problem of alienation, as well as the Idealist-Socialist position offered as a corrective.

S. Taylor Hill, *Challenging Alienation in the British Working-Class*, Palgrave Politics of Identity and Citizenship Series,
https://doi.org/10.1007/978-3-031-59250-8_2

Alienation and Exploitation

The book engages with Marx in outlining a theoretical framework for alienation. One places an emphasis on the ideas of a Young Marx, rather than the later Marxist focus on exploitation. One moves towards this earlier position by following a Hegelian logic which privileges 'spirit' over the later Marxian materialism, though one recognises the importance of materials in contributing to dignity. However, this is not sufficient alone given that material goods do not provide purpose nor affect the bonds that make life something *more*.

The early Marx asserts that without ideas or bonds, we cannot fully flourish. Hegel (2018) and he suggest that we should be able to see ourselves reflected in the world, including our values, understandings, and *Gattungswesen*,[1] which together with others constitute community. The ideal community for this Young Marx is one where we can exert agency over our society equally, seeing to it that we can contribute to something *greater* than ourselves (Marx 2000). This roots an ideal of self-worth and meaning as central tenets of a fulfilled life and asserts that we must be able to conceive of possibilities and enjoy the cultivation of bonds, not to further transactions but to experience shared interests and affections. To this end then, this central focus upon human worth should not be usurped by a materialistic focus, which Marx (2000, 30–33) contends occurs under capitalism with the transformation of the worker into a resource for the cultivation of wealth—devoid of humanity, without agency, and no longer an end in themselves. This notion of alienation, with its reference to equal human worth, capacity for agential action, and the desire for meaning within a receptive community, reflects much of the contemporary desires of working-people across Britain, who face degradation at work and exclusion from politics and feel unable to shape their country. This is a point that Cruddas (2021), Sandel (2020), and the right-communitarians allude to, citing how working-class values, relationships, and their decline since the 1980s have been especially atomising to a previously strong sense of community (Goodhart 2020). This new world with its overt-transactionalism, lack of narrative, or meaningful recognition does nothing to renew purpose nor to inspire our creativeness for common ends. In

[1] 'Species-essence' refers to our desires to be an active natural being, exhibiting emotions, seeking bonds and affections, and a need of people for a breadth of personal development, as well as physical needs for food, water, clothing, shelter, etc.

this respect, alienation accurately characterises the working-class experience, which is one of degraded agency, the sundering of community, and the loss of *meaning*, with a corresponding impact on our capacity to find dignity in what we do.

One rejects the concept of exploitation to capture this condition within capitalism because it does not speak to this meaning element. Instead, Marx adopts a more mechanistic position by explaining that exploitation refers to how the working-class are *forced* by their lack of ownership to accept whatever conditions are offered to them (Screpanti 2019). The desperation that this engenders often leads capitalists to use their privileged position to *exploit* workers, appropriating for themselves the value created by the workers' labour. This concept reflects Marx's view that the working-class do not get the "fruits of their labour", to which they are entitled, but it does not go any further towards spirit or refer to those values that the Young Marx noted as part of our species-essence (Marx 2018, 413). This does not make exploitation a worthless concept, and it certainly has much relevance when used in tandem with moral objections to capitalism, advanced by the socialistic component of this book, but one nevertheless points out that the popular frame of exploitation, referred to in a significant amount of contemporary scholarship, lacks the breadth to entirely characterise the working-class experience. For this reason, one stresses alienation, seeing that exploitation can be part of our discussion, but that it lacks analytical value as a comprehensive explanation for the present struggles of the British working-class.

The Right-Communitarian Position

The book takes seriously the claims made within the right-communitarian literature, which cites alienation as arising out of the transformation of the United Kingdom from a country in which the working-class had their interests represented within parliament by the Labour Party and within wider society by their associations, seeing themselves as active shapers of their nation. These communitarians identify two core 'declines', structural and cultural, and see that much of the contemporary struggles of the working-class can be understood in relation to them. This finds itself expressed in Chap. 5, but let us outline the core of this position.

This first decline can be considered a structural failure brought on by industrial deterioration, the Thatcherite constraint of the unions, and the transformation of the economy into one reliant on cognitive knowledge, itself made subservient to wealth (Goodhart 2020). This echoes the left-communitarian argument (Sandel 2020), sharing a structural diagnosis which one defends as the backdrop against which additional indignities were inflicted on the class. In this sense, one does not critique the right-communitarian position and sees that the decline of working-class associations had a corresponding negative impact on their agential ability to shape the nation, to press claims upon it, or to develop their class dignity. Essentially, where in the post-war era their associations had been afforded a place within the national-corporatist structure of governance and their work recognised as bringing value to the country, since the 1980s those associations have been effectively sidelined by governments, and their work largely dismissed.

Additionally, Kaufmann (2018) contends that structural decline was coupled with a cultural decline/shock. As the world became more globalised, the political shift of the Labour Party towards a pro-immigration, socially liberal platform with a neo-liberal economic policy, was to move the party away from historic working-class values focused on fairness, solidarity, and a rooted ideal of community. Here the right-communitarian argument of commentators like Goodhart finds common ground with Labour MP Jon Cruddas (2021), as well as Liza McKenzie (2018), and Evans and Tilley (2017), who each consider the changing nature of the Labour Party as having a corresponding impact on a working-class ability to root and express itself. Where the right-communitarians differ here is in the way that they stress that social liberalism, termed under the umbrella of 'identity politics', was met with initial disinterest from the white working-class especially and then dismay as conditions failed to improve. This was to exacerbate a *perceived* favouritism of minority groups thanks to the passing of progressive legislation on racial injustice, LGBTQ+ rights, and the like, at the same time as offering other working-class subgroups nothing in the way of secure jobs or frames through which to understand themselves (Goodhart 2017).

Kaufmann (2018) ties to this the increase in migrant numbers and sees migration as having an impact on those last vestiges of rooted community. He asserts that the lack of working-class associations in local areas at the same time as an influx of migrants meant that there was no opportunity for those living in these areas to engage with their new neighbours. This, coupled with anti-migrant rhetoric, was to fracture the community further as the, predominantly white, working-class witnessed their communities or close-by neighbourhoods transformed and feared for the further decline of a way of life and ties that were the last vestiges of their historic frames of self-understanding. The result of this has been distrust and tension between erstwhile working-class sub-groups, which has been to divide communities and increase alienation.

The shift of the Labour Party under Blair towards a 'disproportionate' focus on social liberalism and economic neoliberalism was said to underline these concerns and brought into disregard working-people who continued to struggle unaided or only partially aided by socially liberal legislation. To put this simply, many within the class felt that their political agent had abandoned them for a new electoral coalition of university-educated middle class, minority peoples, and the unemployed (Cruddas 2021). Such thinking was to form the basis of what Eatwell and Goodwin (2018) calls the "Politics of Resentment"—a perspective which holds that events such as the Brexit vote can be justified as a release of working-class frustration and a desire to again be recognised within this country as integral members. This politics, devoid of meaningful economic intervention and with a disproportionate focus on 'identity politics', was then to alienate the working-class from one another and to leave them and their associations largely unable to improve material circumstances, as well as without a means of understanding themselves in reference to those frames which had defined a more dignified existence in the post-war era.

Evaluating This Position

One does not deny the potency of these arguments and would partially agree with these claims. In fact, a section of the working-class was alienated by structural and cultural changes, especially those who took away the jobs and associational connections that had provided them an income and social status. This can be partly understood too in the context of a globalisation, advanced by New Labour, which undermined 'hand' and 'heart' roles—the mainstay of the working-class as defined later in Chap. 3—in favour of a focus on knowledge as the means for the living of the good life. Similarly, it would be difficult to deny evidence of community disunity/distrust between working-class sub-groups, with polarisation around religion, culture, and race/ethnicity. As we see in Chap. 5, there is traction in such arguments, as well as for Kaufmann's (2018) claim that we have witnessed a disproportionate focus on the social realm rather than the provision of security for many working-people through those frames which had once brought them dignity.

However, one takes aim at the right-communitarians' nationalism, seeing their view as founded on a logic which has not sought to quantify the extent of perceived issues nor makes space for the multicultural entity that Britain has become. The plight of minority groups cannot be understated, and many of those groups are working-class. Although the social liberalism of New Labour gave new emphasis to social issues, it would be hard to argue that they benefited from the plight of their fellows. In fact, most minority groups within the working-class suffer those same precarities, feel excluded within our society, and sense the same tension within their communities (Evans and Tilley 2017). In this way, though one agrees that social liberalism became a core component of the New Labour platform at the same time as more traditional focuses on the dignity of labour, material condition of working-people, and their capacity for agential assertion declined, it would not be accurate to suggest that minority peoples profited off this situation. Rather, they still feel those same pressures, yet are now confronted with a politics of resentment which has led to the further fracturing of community.

The right-communitarian answer to this is the reassertion of a populist ethno-cultural nationalism which privileges the white majority in the class. Kaufmann especially sees this as a necessity, suggesting that only a more majoritarian-assimilationist model of belonging will be sufficient to deal with 'identity politics', which he, and Goodhart (2017, 2020), sees as diminishing the working-class within the national community. One will detail this position later in this chapter, but let us assert a fundamental point—that we cannot root the working-class with a majoritarian nationalism that quashes 'identity politics' in favour of an assimilationist stance rooted in ethno-cultural centrism.

This is only likely to open new lines of conflict. Identity politics as the cause of such decline is insufficient in exploring the problem and as an answer is only likely to sow a discord that achieves none of these structural objectives for the class nor provides a means of ameliorating these tensions. This is why one takes the right-communitarian argument towards different ends, seeing such resentment as having been born out of an alienation from community, as well as a political class that genuinely did fail to treat working-class aspirations, values, and desires, in anything but a transactional sense—offering only limited material compensation at a time when structure and culture were shifting further away from their historic way of life, with aforementioned consequences for their rooted sense of purpose, security, and dignity. This can be applied across the working-class and has created tensions that eat away at core values of solidarity, fairness, and community. Thus, where the right-communitarians blame identity politics and social liberalism, one takes a more holistic stance to say that it is true that New Labour shifted its focus away from the working-class, repackaging some interests under the frame of minority rights, but really continued the practice of structural and cultural decline which was to rob working-people of agency, dignity, and a more expansive sense of community. We might define this as the uprooting of the classes' structures without any provision to replace them with frames that connect with them or circumstances which improve their lives.

A Nationalist Framing for Non-Alienation

In advancing this claim that populist-majoritarian nationalism is insufficient in challenging alienation, one can be tempted to err towards a liberal-cosmopolitan alternative, which has been popular with some on the left in recent years (Blond 2010; Timothy 2020). However, where one differs from some of the contemporary left is in its preference for a nationalist frame. This involves the partial rejection of a cosmopolitanism which, although admirable, is in practice likely too unrooted to challenge alienation at present. Broadly, whilst one can acknowledge the main thrust of such an argument which seeks ethical equality in the way that we think across borders, this is not a frame through which the working-class tend to view themselves and is to provide an insufficient, abstract foundation upon which to reconstitute the classes' sense of belonging. One takes two more specific issues with the cosmopolitan alternative, namely that it does not give due regard to the importance of groups, cultures, and specific attachments in themselves, and as important frames for meaning generation, and that, second, it does not appear to fit the way in which most working-people see themselves and consequently, at best, lacks resonance with them and, at worst, can be viewed as itself alienating.

On this first point, although one would not disagree with the cosmopolitan principle that human beings are "the ultimate units of moral concern", the focus tends to be on the individualised human being rather than the group or culture (Pogge 1992, 73). Indeed, Appiah's (2015) account of global citizenship does not emphasise appreciation of specific cultural or other attachments on their own terms. Rather, he emphasises mutual respect considering our differences for the purposes of deliberation on important matters and seems then to deny that membership in a particular cultural community is necessary for an individual to flourish. Instead, they are encouraged to pick and choose their attachments (Pogge 1992, 74). One terms this an individualisation of culture to the point that a culture exists only to be 'chosen' (Yuracko in Calhoun 2008, 433). Such a thought is to deny the legitimacy of specific cultures because it treats them as a product, instrumentalised for our uses rather than playing any inherent role in our shaping. In the view of this book, we need an account of these collectives because it is from those that we establish our norms and our frames of self-understanding. We can never really 'choose' our culture, and so to advance an instrumentalised view of it, in which culture can be eschewed in its entirety as useless to the individual, is to reject it on its own terms as the embodiment and collective work of many selves, with a historical pedigree, values, and even institutions that have been vital in developing meaning (Parekh 2000). If we view culture as something of a choice, then it becomes possible for it to take on a transactional quality in which we adopt it only because it suits us. This is effectively to deny its importance as something of itself, that shapes us through language, place, custom, and tradition, and which can, in turn, be shaped by us and become something more than it had once been (Modood 2018, 2020). In this way, culture is something to be appreciated and, whilst there are certain practices which we might well reject, we can still enjoy our attachments or appreciate its role in shaping our sense of individual self. As such, one rejects a cosmopolitanism that transactionalises culture, individualising it so as to make attachment a choice. This is not to say that one does not see some value in an allegiance to the human community in a broad sense but would argue that such cosmopolitan allegiances are themselves not a choice either. In fact, there may be an ethico-rational obligation to our fellows across the globe owing to our existence as a species,[2] and it is in our best interests to pursue a common commitment to the preservation of our world regarding issues like climate change. On this basis, one asserts that specific cultural attachments are legitimate features of our world and that, further, we might uphold additional allegiances to our fellows across the world on issues to maintain our species and the cultures that shape us.

Indeed, specific attachments maintain significance for many working-people that goes beyond a rational recognition and towards emotive rootedness. For example, nations can be inclusive of 'us', our achievements,

[2] T.H. Green suggests the possibility of ever-extending ethical bonds as we come to feel tangibly that 'global' nature of humanity.

our culture, and our particular history and maintain an element of emotiveness in them whereby we feel attached to it because we live within and are shaped by it in an intimate way, embedding ourselves in those aforementioned specifics, adding to them and contributing to nation in our own capacities. In being part of this process, we become attached to our nation and usually come to feel that it is a home, although this can differ in extent. One calls this existence 'rooted' because we can see aspects of ourselves reflected in the nation and can, in a nation that is *inclusive* in its narratives and self-understanding, find a sense of community, of duty, and of responsibility which itself can bring purpose (Modood 2020). By identifying in this way with the nation as the embodiment of our history and collective creative will, we can somewhat transcend a more mundane reality to assert a narrative understanding of self in which we are an important part of the movement towards something much greater than ourselves and consequently embrace others that are deserving of our mutual concern.[3] By reaching this position, one sees that working-people come to 'root' themselves as they associate their daily lives, including their interactions and their institutions, with the idea of Britain itself. These daily aspects make the idea feel more tangible, and so it becomes something which is relatable to aspire towards and to understand one's life in light of.

There is the potential for this to happen to some extent within cosmopolitanism, and one accepts that we might see aspects of our identity realised in ways that are not reliant on the nation.

However, this does not diminish the issue that, in not appealing to nation, and pressing a different frame like cosmopolitanism, those on the left are often failing to speak or act in accordance with a framing of our lives which has genuine popularity amongst the class, and therefore in the view of this book a serious transformative potential to root principles of equal worth, mutual recognition, and the common good. Indeed, this issue can be pressed further to say that, in focusing on a non-national perspective, the left has, to some extent, contributed to the alienation of the working-class by moving beyond the framing which they mostly view their lives and assert their claims in relation to (see Chap. 5). This is to echo some of the criticisms of the contemporary left which see it as 'distant' from the concerns of working-people and as speaking in a language that simply fails to connect (Sandel 2020; Goodhart 2020; Eatwell and Goodwin 2018). In adopting the nation, however, this presents an opportunity to provide a more immediate link to the class that can provide the basis for claims to be made against it for their betterment, with agential potential, whilst the opening of our institutional arrangement predicated on the recognition of national groupings can foster recognition within and across the class. In adopting this position, one recognises that nation is an enduring frame through which to conceive of oneself, which is why it has been adopted so effectively by groups on the right in an exclusive form. One consequently looks to challenge these right-communitarians on their own terrain, because it is familiar to the working-class and therefore most at risk of becoming dominated by a populist majoritarian nationalism which speaks to some sub-groups of the working-class whilst perpetuating the alienation of others.

Thus, one differs substantially from the liberal cosmopolitans, advancing a position that is firmly entrenched in nation, seeing such an entity as both a popular symbol across the working-class and a vehicle through which to advance tangible policies. To this end, one advances a nationalist theory rooted in a conception of the good life that is more restrictive in one sense than the liberal cosmopolitans would countenance. To situate the book's position then would be to say that it rejects both a populist-majoritarian nationalism, seeing it as rooted in an assimilationist view that will do much to destabilise society, and a cosmopolitanism that is too abstract at present and which finds little resonance amongst the subject of this discussion. In place of this, one advances a multicultural Progressive Nationalism, rooted in the experience and culture of this nation and its peoples, which one sees as being able to rebuild community across groups, to recognise our dignified contributions to the national story, and to set out ethical principles upon which a kinder and more inclusive Britain can be realised. This is to take the rootedness from the right-communitarians and shed its factional disunity, as well as the ethical aspirations of cosmopolitanism, to create an alternative for the left to consider at a time when populist-nationalism seems to be gathering traction, with implications for the worsening of alienation amongst our multicultural communities.

Communitarianism

Although this perspective will be detailed more extensively in Chaps. 5 and 6, this communitarian inclination leads one to assert the adequacy of the right-communitarian position as against atomised individualism, loss of markers for a common good, and the degradation of our human bonds and values in the service of greed (Goodhart 2017, 2020). However, one makes a point of departure from the right-communitarian position after having highlighted these claims, breaking from them largely over their proposed solutions to such problems. Indeed, one asserts that though we at present lack unity, it is unfair to characterise this as the fault of our societal diversity, preferring instead to place the blame on a hostile environment for prospective foreign-born citizens and active members of our national community, overly assimilationist and yet without a narrative that is inclusive of them (Kaufmann 2018). One asserts here that such a closed position will only fuel social discord by denying equal narrative place for foreign-born citizens and members of our society by disabling them from connecting to the nation through the stories they tell to understand their place as part of 'us'. Such a disassociation, and active rejection of our own narrative strands, is only likely to cause further discord whilst failing to recognise minority groups who could otherwise be made to feel 'at home' and portrayed as such in the national imaginary. This is to deny them the opportunity to make claims on our nation as equal citizens and is likely to prevent the wider population from associating minority groups with the rest of 'us'. Thus, one rejects the right-communitarian's central thrust of blame and instead posits that our national unity can only adequately be captured through the formation of an inclusive narrative that can express our unique places within our shared community.

In line with this critique of the right, one goes further to place an emphasis on a multicultural communitarian nationalism and sees that the socialists and Idealists have systems or principles that can be applied to such a position, though they did not do so themselves. Here, one integrates an Idealist emphasis on the reconciliation and integration of difference into the common good, seeing its society of societies as conducive to a pluralistic nationalism rooted in a principle of 'unity in difference'. This itself echoes Modood's (2018) multicultural nationalism, which moves beyond the negative critiques of nationalism as overly monistic towards a position which acknowledges differences, yet seeks to integrate them to promote national belonging and mutual recognition. This reconciles a conservative nationalist position with a liberal one somewhat whilst rejecting both of their assimilationist logics in favour of a position which can be described as rooted and integrative, but also receptive to minority and majority groups who have shared in the betterment of our common home, yet often are left out of the stories we tell about it. In this one privileges culture, seeing our culture as one which is rich and diverse, and yet recognisably of us—referencing our self-deprecating and sarcastic humour, our stubbornness, scepticism, and our historical effort to improve the common position, thanks to the work of those involved in the Bristol Bus Boycotts, the working-people of the Chartist movement, and those of the Suffragettes and the Dagenham strike, to name but a few examples. Each of these groups we often forget and yet they have reaffirmed our commitments to democracy, equality, and justice in a way that reflects the country that we can be and already are to some extent.

In line with this, one outlines a nationalist project, with a firm view that we constitute one people—Britons, but who nevertheless differ in the ways that we expand and enhance the British experience. One, therefore, asserts that we should not shy away from nationalism as one has defined it. It is narrative, and in that seeks to include people, to bridge gaps, and to create a Britishness based on the good that will secure for us and our fellow's purpose, fellowship, and dignity. We should be able to take pride in ourselves and our shared home, to tell stories about it, and to see beyond our issues. This is to reassert a necessary vigour to our politics and challenge us to think beyond—to those values, covenants, relationships, bonds, and principles that should define us—to implore us to strive for them whilst retaining a rooted knowledge of our past to aid and inspire us.

In this, one rejects a weaker left-patriotism by asserting that it is not strong enough, or active enough, to integrate people in respect of difference. This is because it often lacks the capacity to develop comprehensive national narratives that citizens can connect to. This partly arises because of its struggle to link various aspects of our rooted experience together, relying instead on a vagueness of principles detached from our common lives or an ad hoc collection of mentions that do nothing to speak to higher value. Indeed, one posits that, to challenge alienation, we must be able to develop a sense of 'us' that is both inclusive for working-people, including minority groups, and has the capacity to provide tangible examples of their commitments to this nation, weaved into a narrative of collective effort. As a result, one differentiates the book's efforts at inclusion from many on the left by explicitly recognising the legitimacy of the national frame whilst simultaneously rejecting the weaker Progressive Patriotism of Keir Starmer's Labour Party (Craig 2022). This is of special relevance at a time when the narrative populist nationalism of the right is ascendant, with consequences for the health of our national community.

Idealism

The Idealist philosophy, with its Hegelian orientation and central focus on themes of dignity, flourishing, mutual recognition, and the common good, alongside the compatible critical-structural ethics of the Guild Socialist and Socialist Pluralist traditions, runs through this book as a unifying strand for these seemingly divergent positions. Indeed, Idealism is philosophically rooted in, and therefore compatible with, this diagnosis of alienation as popularised by the Young Marx and Hegel. Aside from its Hegelian roots, the core ideals of the Idealists provide added philosophical depth, support, and a partial critique to contemporary communitarians like Sandel.

Indeed, in relation to his own adherence to the common good, the principle of reconciliation in service of the Absolute stresses "the idea of organic unity, and, as implied in that, the idea of development" as channelled to create a vision of the good society as a community of mutually dependent and mutually self-developing persons in which different ideas interact to contribute to it (Mander 2014, n.p.). What this means is that, through our differences, we come to realise something ***more,*** namely a coherent understanding of us as both individuals and necessary, embedded, parts of the human community (Mackenzie 2016). This speaks to a position which seeks to transcend the individualism-communitarianism debate by asserting that both are right to assert the centrality of each yet neglect their potential mutuality in a synthesised position focused on our flourishing. This 'flourishing' refers to the development of our capacities so that we might become the best possible version of ourselves, which is individual on the face of it, but is taken towards more communitarian ends when we consider that our best possible self, owing to our upbringing and reliance on community for countless goods, is one that is in tune with our fellows, not uncritical, but respectful, and empathetic—in other words aware of the need to ensure that those who help to shape our community are best placed to do so for a common benefit (Bosanquet 1996).

In fact, the Idealists understand that we need community to be put in the best possible position to flourish, whilst the bonds that we establish and maintain with others enable learning, development, comfort, purpose, and the expression of both our rational and emotional capacities. In this respect they are not dissimilar to communitarians, like Etzioni (2014), Walzer (2008), or Sandel (2012,2020). However, this communitarian dimension makes up but one half of our flourishing as we also see the claim advanced that as we flourish as individuals, we might all flourish. In fact, if our fellows can pursue their own flourishing, and that does not negatively hinder others, then we might reasonably see to it that our society, what we believe to be possible, and more, can be pushed in multiple directions to provide welcome chances for others (Simhony 2014; Simhony and Weinstein 2001). We, therefore, need to consider the argument as not one of individual versus community but, rather, transcend it to understand that the two are mutually coherent components of our flourishing that can enhance one another.

What follows from this is a moral position regarding 'the good life' that is thicker than most liberalisms, yet thinner than most communitarianisms.[3] Although this is detailed extensively in Chap. 6, note that the book engages with this debate by adopting the Greenian implication that we are essentially bound to one another by the common good and must necessarily concern ourselves with what others within our society are doing (Green 2011). This follows the logic that community is essential for our flourishing, whilst individuals within that community should be able to pursue their development without the degradation of their person or life chances by immoral activity, which is likely to sunder bonds of community in turn. Indeed, Green posits that, if we cannot develop this ethical mindset, then it becomes more difficult to realise ourselves, to enjoy the fruits of common endeavour, or to engage within community. To fail in this act is to destabilise community and not only to deprive our fellows of the fullest chance to flourish but also to condemn ourselves to a loss of our moral character and, with that, the chance of greater fulfilment.

Higher-Self and Moral Character

To express this further, one relies on the dual Idealist concepts of Higher-self and moral character, which understand that "the realisation of any one individual's highest life is impossible without the co-operation of others, but…the realisation of other' lives is an essential element…in the realisation of our own" (Mander 2014, 442). This is to restate this reconciled mutuality and the logic offered to justify it but asserts that we realise a 'higher' sense of self as individuals, which includes a sense of purpose and reason for one's being, through community or as part of it—since our lives are inherently shaped by it and our agency conducted within its bounds. Indeed, an individual can improve their emotional capacity by forging friendships, stimulate their intellectual capacity by joining societies, and

[3] For thin theory of the good, see Rawls (2009), Sec. 60, 396–399.

increase their physical and tactical capabilities on a sports team. Each of these activities stimulates the individual in a way that they cannot stimulate themselves alone, whilst the emotional development which necessarily comes from interacting with others creates the bonds and affinities which are required for the strengthening of our "conscientious judgement" as against "short-sighted self-interest" (Green 2007, np). Here community becomes the basis for individual pursuit towards betterment and the creation of 'higher-selves', whilst our interaction should provide the basis for moral strengthening—of our character and capacity to act within the ethical bounds of the wider community, for our betterment and that of our fellows (Green 2011).

This is to bring into line the development of many Higher-selves with the focus of one Higher-self, expressed as the collective effort of our peoples through the creation of something more than the sum of their individual parts. In fact, in developing ourselves, we can come to build institutions that embody our principles, which bring attachment, pride, and understanding, and which leave a legacy for future generations. Such development is to speak to that part of our psyche which moves beyond the satisfaction of our material and rational capacities and towards our emotional-social ones as well (Bosanquet 2015; Green in Morrow 2007, 80). By opening ourselves up to these stimuli we can better move beyond selfishness towards the realisation of our interconnectedness and our duties and responsibilities as members of this community—capable of shaping something more eternal than ourselves. Such realisation is to bring purpose to many selves and is to reaffirm this basic commitment to the equal consideration and worthiness of others as co-architects of this higher state. The awareness of this state, the consideration of one's impact upon their fellows, and the reasoning in line with the good to not profit by the loss of another provides three central goods (Green 2007), namely:

1. It ensures the stability of a community that rests upon bonds of equal worth.
2. It can provide a sense of 'higher' purpose to individuals (Bosanquet 1889).
3. It stresses that our fate is bound up in that of others—that when we suppress the potential of others, we hamper our own capacity to learn from them and our community's capacity to grow as a result of their action and inflict an indignity upon them that might well destabilise these principles of equal worth, jeopardise their moral character as well as our own, and diminish the bonds of community.

As this book argues, such a degradation has already occurred to some extent, explaining in part the alienation of the working-class as stemming from a reckless pursuit of profit, the privileging of an atomised individualism devoid of other-consideration, and the usurpation of principles of equal worth, which has had a corrosive impact on communities, fostering distrust between peoples and contributing to the breakdown of our capacity to provide grounds for mutual flourishing. This is found in the claims of the "left behind", who identify the diminishing of their community, as well as explicit norms of "duty", fairness, or worth (Kirkwood 2020; Healey 2021). They often express a distinct feeling of lost purpose and decry that the moral basis of community has been diminished (McKenzie 2018, 2019). Although detailed in Chap. 5, these issues of atomisation, lost community, and moral degradation connect with aspects of the Idealist philosophy outlined above and are understood to reorientate community. Such a philosophy contains a commitment to our reconciliation and extension of principles which can enable us to look upon one another as of equal worth, with greater trust, as well as provide the grounds for flourishing, with space reserved for the narrative of communal development in which we all have a part to play.

From Idealism to Socialism

However, there are aspects of Idealism that one rejects. For example, one dismisses the metaphysical attachment to the Absolute, though one sees value in the Idealist ability to connect its notions to form a coherent narrative with regard for a higher purpose. One sees such connection as an important part of Idealist theory that is applicable both to the community disunity detailed in Chap. 5 and in part to the Progressive Nationalism outlined in Chap. 8. On this basis, though one rejects the essentialist and religious connotations of Idealist thought, one sees their fundamental desire for reconciliation as providing a useful grounding for the book and its attempts to alleviate alienation with the provision of community and purposeful dignity. Idealism here then is to restate that sense of spirit and to restore the necessity of moral consideration into our political discourse, with a view to the creation of a rooted narrative of dignity as part of community.

Yet, in rejecting the Absolute one must find a principle that speaks to these other notions. One finds this in the common good, which is shared Idealist and Socialist foci. This principle is central to especially Green's philosophy and is raised to pinnacle importance within the book as the overarching desire to secure for individuals, groups, and our community the basis for their flourishing (Tyler 2019). This reflects a reconciliation with the main socialist focus, which is to create a society which enables the "fullest possible capacity for initiative and self-expression" and makes "easy for the people feats of self-government and communal expression" (Cole 1920, 98). This is understood within a pluralistic frame as both giving individuals options for their own self-realisation and providing others with opportunities for learning and growth—which is referred to as flourishing and which one has already detailed. This underlines the coherency of the Idealist and Socialist traditions as centred on a higher commitment to our dual flourishing as individual members of our community.

Both these traditions provide an account of human flourishing which holds a commitment to equality at its core, seeing that the superficial 'flourishing' of one individual through means of greed, selfishness, or deprivation of one's fellows cannot be adequately described as such because it fails to develop those faculties which speak to community and our fellows, who we so rely upon to derive meaning, who we learn from, and who form a core component of any individual life (Tawney 1931). One expresses this commitment in reference to the synthesis of the Idealist Higher-self and moral character as essential components of human flourishing because we are individuals who live within, exercise agency as part of, and derive bonds and meaning from, community. To act otherwise is to prevent the fullest realisation of our capacities as both individuals and members of a community, with its own purpose, capacities, and potential to be something *more* for its members, not only a place to cultivate mutual flourishing, but also meaning and bonds. For both traditions, we consequently should maintain an interest in enhancing that community since it is here that we find "something to live for" (Bosanquet 2013, np), yet successfully synthesise this with an individual agential purpose.

This finds itself expressed in relation to principles of nonselfishness and nonexploitation in which these two ideas are to be at the forefront of our thinking so as to render dignity to others, through our mutual recognition of their worth, and place within society (Green 2007; Tawney 1931). This is to encourage an empathetic mode of thinking in which we must explicitly deny the legitimacy of those actions which violate such moral principles, seeing that selfishness and exploitation must be limited to ensure mutual flourishing, which is so hampered by the pursuit of atomised ends. Such a consideration is to affirm duty and personal responsibility as part of the good, which can extend to the state, but enshrines this striving for moral character as part of our citizenship (Green 2008, 25). In this we must be agents, capable of shaping our lives and of enhancing that of others, without succumbing to those temptations, for excess wealth, power, or some other thing, which in a Marxian sense are to separate us from our core humanity. In this respect, and through this duty, the Idealist and Socialist foci merge to envisage a good that is centred on this flourishing, but which expects the exercise of responsibility to ensure that our community is not undone in pursuit of reified ends.

Socialism

How to achieve this mutualistic flourishing is, however, developed further by the socialists, therefore necessitating this synthesis. Where the Idealists are content to outline a moralistic vision for our society and commit themselves towards some degree of state action and cooperative pursuit, they fall short in reining in the excesses of capitalism and place strict limits on the state in acting to underline the common good. The socialists maintain no such limits and provide an account that reconsiders the bounds of the state and what its role should be within society.

In entering this debate, the Socialist literature engages with contemporary debates around the nature of the state vis-à-vis the historic managerial socialism of the post-war Labour Party, which themselves jar with Idealist and other socialist commitments to personal responsibility, defined in relation to an agency that is rooted in questions of moral character and our capacity to flourish under conditions of dignity. Herein one outlines the importance of the 'enabling state' and its significance for the alleviation of alienation through the provision of agency. To establish this, one adopts a hybrid Laskian social federalism, itself akin to a society of societies, bonded through cooperation with a government whose legitimacy is more directly linked to the principle of government 'with the people' through the intermediary associations. Thus, whilst there is some overlap here with the post-war national-corporate structure in the privileging of civil society associations, like trade unions, as well as a recognition of the sheer complexities that any great shift towards personal responsibility for democratic governance might bring (signalling the end of this position), the net is cast wider than in the post-war years and is underpinned with a narrative, and real, commitment to a position that is explicitly pluralistic and which reframes the legitimacy of the state itself. Examples of hybridity such as this, in which Idealist principles like the Higher-self and moral character are weaved into an institutional framework centred on agential provision in a modern state, serve to root and make more achievable these Idealist principles whilst taking account of issues around the willingness of the populace to engage in politics in depth and consistently, the capacity of the working-class to practice agential action, and the importance of civil society in enabling democratic participation. Overall, we might understand the socialistic component of Idealist-Socialism as a necessary addition to this earlier Idealism through its focus on practical and institutional questions, which themselves are compatible with such underlying principles. These have further implications for the shape and role of the state in the twenty-first century, as well as what we should expect from citizens regarding participation.

Capitalism and the Dignity of Labour

The socialist position maintains additional distinctions too. We might also note its ethical potency in critiquing capitalism and the corresponding values that it promotes. Indeed, Cole, Laski, Tawney, and others are far more deeply critical of capitalism than their Idealist counterparts and capably apply similar principles to their critiques. This represents a valuable addition to an Idealist position which is too quiet on matters of structural importance and power-relational disparity, neglecting their importance in regard to their own principles. This socialistic thrust thus provides another critical component to the Idealist-Socialist position which can itself be used to justify the left-communitarian critique of these economic structures as fundamentally alienating for working-people. Although going further than even Sandel, Cole, Tawney, and Laski launch a scathing critique of capitalism's ethical basis. Such an argument is perhaps best expressed by Tawney, who claims that capitalism's nature is one that privileges "pecuniary gain at the expense of another" and in turn degrades and treats "the poor as instruments" by transforming "wealth" so that it becomes the "foundation of public esteem". In fact, he holds that capitalism does this to an extent that "the mass of men who labour, but who do not acquire wealth, are thought to be vulgar and meaningless and insignificant compared with the few who ac-quire wealth by good fortune" (Tawney 1961, 141, 34–35). Following on from this earlier claim that values matter for the health of our society, we see in Tawney's quote an accurate summary of the socialist position, namely that the ultra-competitive reification of wealth as above human worth and needs is to place us at odds with one another and to promote an atomised individualism. These values, including disconnection and the praising of selfish self-interest, are merely to push decent people to the bottom of society or to force them to adopt positions which will only serve to bolster disassociated self-interest, greed, and drive financial acquisition at the expense of fulfilling work and the good that it can bring to flourishing. Here we establish capitalism as having a corrosive impact on our society.

To illustrate this, each takes aim at economic relations within most contemporary businesses as an example of where "capitalism succeeds in imparting this servile character to what should be a great agent of spiritual enfranchisement" (Cole 1920, 99). This criticism is expressed in two parts. The first is a critique of the hierarchical nature of inequality which forcibly bonds working-people to those who pay them by virtue of the fundamental need to survive, made worse by the circumstances of the time that enable government to penalise those who reject poor work, and who at the same time provide sub-par welfare payments to those in need (McKenzie 2015). This is to trivialise working-people as 'lesser' and follows a line of critique initially not too dissimilar to Green's in which the nature of one's position, reliant on work, forces them to undertake employment that is not their choice to take, effectively undermining their agency to pursue work that is of value to them. Such a situation in which working-people are forced to accept imposition is decried by Laski in the most emotive terms as he cites how the "separation of management from labour" and the poor conditions forced upon them with "[n]o right to express… ideas…(and) no organised opportunity for suggestion" renders them "in a full sense…a slave" (Laski 2014, 434). One underlines this in reference to pay stagnation, cuts to one's hours and contracts, and union decline, seeing such episodes as fundamentally strengthening servility at the expense of the workers' position and capacity for agential action.

Second is Laski's central thrust against capitalism, which is that it fails to unlock the potential of citizens, forcing them into a non-receptive service in which they serve as "tools" without "consideration for their personality as human beings" (Laski 2014, 476). It is fundamentally alienating in this respect, and the imposition from above and limited security is just to further underline the precarious, inhuman nature of this position. In fact, more than anything, capitalism degrades the worker by rendering them devoid of their humanity, subjecting them to spiritual domination and material deprivation in which they cannot take control of either their work or wider livelihoods owing to factors including undignified pay, poor work/life balance, or a lack of structures conducive to their participation. This is taken to stunt their flourishing in pursuit of profit and to usurp the value that one should derive from work. We see this expressed within contemporary Britain in relation to the gig economy, retail, and the health and social care sector predominantly, in which it is typical to receive minimal contracted hours, for pay at a rate below the living wage, without adequate sick or holiday pay coverage (Bloodworth 2018). There is no dignified, secure provision in such positions, despite the obvious necessity of such jobs during the pandemic.

This latter consideration is one that the book places a significant amount of focus on. Work should evoke dignity and not be subject to the "domination of capitalism and capitalist morality", expressed as those impulses which limit the capacity of working-people to gain not just fair material reward but also recognition (Cole 1920, 97). This is to reiterate an earlier concern of Sandel's about unequal control, in this case in relation to work. Indeed, it is such a central part of our lives, filled with meaning, that has the potential to give us purpose, a sense of solidarity, and an outlet for creativity. In essence, it is something that has the potential to root and ground us as beings of value, and it can only be that when working-people are freer to exercise their agency, in which profit is restrained by virtue and where one can "be himself at his best" (Laski 2021, 476). To this end, the socialists assert that workers should be able to exercise control and be recognised as capable of doing so as valuable members of an enterprise. This is to ensure that the "will of labour has full opportunity to impress itself" with some "transference of certain functions completely from the employer to the workers" so that they might organise themselves without fear of over-discipline or micromanagement, both of which we see cited as diminishing working-people (Laski 2021, 437; Bloodworth 2018). In effect, where work should enable learning, allow us to make decisions, develop skills, and find vocation, we see such benefits limited by the capitalist means of organisation, which is profit-driven and hierarchical, without regard for the ability of its workers or their status as human beings. The socialist critique seeks to transform the position of the worker into one of dignity, based upon a mutual recognition of one's worth as an agent capable of purposeful action and vocation, from which they can derive purpose and solidarity.

This critique can be summarised into a finer point about the purpose of our economy and as human beings, capable of flourishing in creative and other pursuits. Essentially, the socialists reject the capitalist mode of production as a burden on flourishing, especially its ethical component, which is held to be important as the basis for social responsibility and the extension of dignity to oneself and others. The socialists, to quote Laski, seek an economic system that "will have a higher standard of honour than a society, built like ours, upon the motive of profit-making" (Laski 2021, 488) in which "business (is) made the servant of moral principles…(and) depends on co-operation" (Laski 2021, 503). Only in this economy can human beings realise themselves as creative agents. There are, of course, multiple suggestions that the socialists make regarding this position, including the nationalisation of the economy with control rendered to workers, yet one here reiterates a further focus as in opposition to distance between community/workplace members which enhances the breakdown of our bonds and relationships. The socialists are keenly aware of this dimension and consider limits on wealth acquisition as necessary to bring people into closer relation, both to tone down misplaced hubris or feelings of superiority and to maintain the meaning of pay in relation to recognisable factors that influence it, including greater physical risk, skill, or knowledge. This connects with a popular resentment of workplace degradation outlined in Chap. 5 and forms the basis for the development of a position in Chap. 9 which expressly argues in favour of those policies which are to increase interaction between different echelons of a company, bypass strict hierarchy, and improve the structures which enable a sense of mutual recognition of one's worth in a given company. Thus, although the socialists ultimately desire the alteration of the capitalist system to give working-people more control over their economy so that it might serve a higher purpose than profit—namely the fulfilment of our spiritual and material needs—one focuses on that component of their thought which seeks interaction on the basis of respect, the flattening of hierarchies, and the extension of a full complement of agential goods, seeing the dignified interaction that is promoted within this as conducive to the alleviation of alienation.

Conclusion

This chapter has endeavoured to fulfil two primary objectives. Firstly, it has sought to situate the book within relevant contemporary debates. In doing so, one has further attempted to fulfil the second objective, which has been to tie together the Idealist, Socialist, and other theories thus far provided into a coherent position.

One connects with the notion of alienation as it is expressed by Hegel and developed by the Young Marx. One sees how material provisions are of undeniable importance to human beings but that "spirit" can be considered that which makes life fundamentally worthwhile. It does so because, despite our material well-being, a life without emotive bonds, or purpose, can be unfulfilled and without direction. A sense of values, principles, and the ability to live life in accordance with both is a core component of self and communal betterment and must at least be considered at the same level as material need because of this. Indeed, though meaning derivation corresponds somewhat to materials and what they express, to place that at the forefront of our thinking would be to understate the way in which meaning, values, and bonds are essential goods to us as human beings. As both Marx and Hegel work, alienation occurs when we cannot see that which we value relate to our lives, indicating a sense that we desire the world to match what we apply to it, to feel part of it as an active shaper of its bounds. We should, therefore, consider material provision but assess such a provision from a position aware of the way it speaks to something more. This is to underline the relevance of the diagnosis of alienation, which encompasses the later-Marxian concept of exploitation, whilst retaining space for these non-material factors and their importance vis-à-vis the working-class experience.

The right-communitarians outline the nature of alienation in contemporary Britain by highlighting the structural and cultural decline of the working-class. They note how their associations, like the trade unions, have witnessed significant decline, whilst the Labour Party moved away from a predominantly working-class party focused on rooted ideals of solidarity and community towards a more neo-liberal globalised and middle-class-dominated party which placed an emphasis on 'identity politics' as above these previous inclinations. This, coupled with an anti-migrant rhetoric, has contributed to the diminishing of working-class agency, dignity, and sense of community. To this end, they reassert a rooted position focused on a populist majoritarian nationalism which is assimilationist in tone. One rejects this as only likely to alienate the working-class further, whilst one sees the contemporary left's cosmopolitan and patriotic alternatives as both insufficient. The former in not appreciating culture on its own terms, nor the importance of the national framing in speaking to the working-class, and the latter as too narratively weak to provide an alternative to the right-communitarian position.

In line with this, one adopts a nationalist frame by taking inspiration from the 'unity in difference' of the Idealist society of societies, as well as from Modood's multicultural nationalism, to press for a reconciled national identity. Such an emphasis is also a response to debates over the suitability of liberal and populist/conservative nationalism in containing divisions and promoting unity in a way that is compatible with flourishing and which fulfils commitments to equal worth. This is taken as a necessary step given the inadequacy of especially the latter in fostering social harmony, and itself provides the book's significant break from the right-communitarian position, which one holds as too assimilationist, ethnically privileging, and unable to connect with particular minority Britons to (1) make them feel valued and (2) foster recognition within our national community. Without achieving these aims, a nationalist position is only likely to foment social discord, unrest, and disunity, owing to its rigid/narrow sense of what it means to be British.

Such logic further underpins the move towards nationalism. Whilst there is much to be said about patriotism as a positive force capable of providing some degree of meaning within individual lives, in relation to this wider alienation, one sees it as too weak. Indeed, patriotism is not a vehicle through which one can popularise a comprehensive narrative of who we are. Rather, because it tends to lack such a comprehensive narrative frame, we can often struggle to link those examples of national pride together in such a way as to constitute 'us'. In a time where populist nationalism is on the rise, with a somewhat clear narrative notion of what Britain is, a weaker left-patriotism may well fail to tell a captivating story to our citizens. In line with this concern, the book challenges this discordant populist-nationalism with a comprehensive narrative of its own that connects divergent examples of Britishness together explicitly to facilitate recognition and shared progress towards a common end of national betterment whilst simultaneously providing space for working-class and minority sub-groups within our national discourses and those stories we tell of 'us'. National identity is taken here to be a continual process that requires effort and active inclusion to bring seemingly disconnected groups together, to renew community, and to restore a sense of dignity as arising out of those bonds, as well as our contribution to something *more* than ourselves.

The reconciled position of the Idealists and Socialists speaks to this and intertwines itself with the alienation by appealing to the relationships that provide the foundation for a stable and prosperous community. Such a community is taken by the Idealists to be an example of the reconciliation of individual with collective so as to produce a strongly coherent unity between the two, in which they not only mutually benefit from one another, but also provide the basis for the development of a Higher-self and state of many selves by (1) providing the foundation for the enhancement of one's moral character in line with those principles of recognition, nonselfishness, and nonexploitation that respect equal worth and (2) becoming more than the sum of individual parts—as something that is of us, with institutions, principles, and a character of its own that we ourselves do shape, but only in tandem with our fellows. One highlights these points in relation to two core debates. On this first matter, we have seen how Idealism intersects with the tension caused by the liberal individualist versus communitarian debate about the compatibility of individual with collective by arguing that both are important components of one overarching whole. Secondly, one asserts a recognition of community and those 'higher' purposes, singling this out to redress questions around the loss of meaning, purpose, or related forms of dignity within our society. Taken together, one sees in the principles and values propagated by the Idealists, and supported by the Socialists, a means to move beyond such debates and away from a transactional politics towards one that appeals to notions like fairness, recognition, equal worth, and solidarity and which can inspire a renewed sense that the working-class can rebuild that community that we so rely upon to flourish.

In considering this, the socialists maintain a committed opposition to capitalism and an awareness of power relations that resonates with, and supports, much of the left-communitarian critique of contemporary society. Indeed, we see in these critiques an opposition to unequal control, understood in relation to the capitalist economic sphere, which fundamentally alienates working-people and corrupts our morality through the inculcation of atomising norms of selfishness and greed. This realisation is coupled with a recognition of what should be the sanctity of work and the dignity of labour as potentially powerful tools in challenging alienation, as well as its usurpation within a capitalist mode of production that is overly hierarchical and makes no effort to recognise the value of its workers, either materially or spiritually. One settles on this socialist position in seeing that it has relevance not only to debates around the nature of work in contemporary Britain, but also to those left-communitarian critiques of the structures which inherently damage our capacity for flourishing.

Coupled with this latter consideration of structural alienation, Laski and Cole develop the ideal of the enabling state which can take the Idealist notion of the society of societies and develop it in favour of a cooperative system of social federalism, in which government derives its legitimacy from working with the people (through the intermediary associations) to ensure that their needs are met and views are considered. This speaks to the agential component of alienation and itself is seen to resonate with a unified communitarian critique of contemporary governance, which sees the state and government as having left the working-class "behind", without due regard for their concerns or desires. In this way, one connects with contemporary working-class issues as raised within the communitarian literature, developing this in the direction of further agency for working-people, with regard to the development of the 'enabling state' and the means of its legitimation.

Taken together, the book becomes intertwined with several debates across a variety of fields. It does so owing to its theoretical breadth, adopting Hegelian-Marxian, Idealist, Guild, Ethical, and Socialist pluralist concepts alongside more contemporary theories of nationalism and multiculturalism in its attempt to first diagnose and then challenge alienation in the British working-class. However, as this chapter has demonstrated, these debates remain relevant to such a question of alienation and are themselves important considerations for the theory that the book develops. As such, whilst one rejects exploitation alone, the right-communitarian answer to alienation, and asserts the intertwining of community with individual in Idealism, and its subsequent ethical foundation for the socialist critique of capitalism and our state structures, we nevertheless see some common themes emerge around the centrality of agency, dignity, and a healthy respect for community within this chapter. This is developed regarding the need for a unifying narrative and stands as an example of how such potentially disparate positions can come together in a coherent way to address the problem of alienation more comprehensively than through a narrower frame.

Bibliography

Appiah, Kwame Anthony. *Cosmopolitanism: Ethics in a World of Strangers.* Penguin UK, 2015.

Blond, Phillip. *Red Tory: How Left and Right Have Broken Britain and How We Can Fix It.* Faber and Faber, 2010.

Bloodworth, James. *Hired: Six Months undercover in low-wage Britain.* Atlantic Books, 2018.

Bosanquet, Bernard. *Essays and Addresses.* Sonnenschein, 1889.

Bosanquet, Bernard. *Politics and Philosophy.* Routledge/Thoemmes, 1996.

Bosanquet, Bernard. *Science and Philosophy (Routledge Revivals): And Other Essays.* Routledge, 2013.

Bosanquet, Bernard. *The Introduction to Hegel's Philosophy of Fine Art.* Routledge, 2015.

Calhoun, Craig. 'Cosmopolitanism in the Modern Social Imaginary'. *Daedalus* 137, no. 3 (July 2008): 105–14.

Cole, GDH. *Guild Socialism Restated.* Leonard Parsons, 1920.

Craig, John. 'Starmer Puts Patriotism at Heart of Labour Strategy in Ambitious Speech'. *Sky News* 3 January 2022. https://news.sky.com/story/starmer-puts-

patriotism-at-heart-of-labour-strategy-in-ambitious-speech-12508566. Accessed 19 Feb 2022.
Cruddas, Jon. *The Dignity of Labour*. Polity Press, 2021.
Eatwell, Roger, and Matthew Goodwin. *National Populism: The Revolt Against Liberal Democracy*. Penguin, 2018.
Etzioni, Amitai. *The Common Good*. John Wiley & Sons, 2014.
Evans, Geoffrey, and James Tilley. *The New Politics of Class: The Political Exclusion of the British Working Class*. Oxford University Press, 2017.
Goodhart, David. *Head Hand Heart: The Struggle for Dignity and Status in the twenty first Century*. Penguin UK, 2020.
Goodhart, David. *The Road to Somewhere: The Populist Revolt and the Future of Politics*. Penguin, 2017.
Green, T.H. *Prolegomena to Ethics*. Read Books, 2007.
Green, T.H. *Lectures on the Principles of Political Obligation*. Cambridge Scholars Publishing, 2008.
Green, T.H. *Works of Thomas Hill Green*. Cambridge University Press, 2011.
Healey, John. 'Labour's Priority Must Be Britain's Real Middle: The 10m on Ordinary Incomes'. *LabourList*. https://labourlist.org/2021/04/labours-priority-must-be-britains-real-middle-the-10m-on-ordinary-incomes/. Accessed 24 May 2021.
Hegel, Georg Wilhelm Fredrich. *Georg Wilhelm Friedrich Hegel: The Phenomenology of Spirit*. Cambridge University Press, 2018.
Kaufmann, Eric. *Whiteshift: Populism, Immigration and the Future of White Majorities*. Penguin, UK, 2018.
Kirkwood, Diane. 'Why Britain's Values Divide Should Matter to Labour'. *UK in a changing Europe*, 28 January 2020, https://ukandeu.ac.uk/why-britains-values-divide-should-matter-to-labour/. Accessed 10 May 2021.
Laski, Harold. *A Grammar of Politics (Works of Harold J. Laski)*. Routledge, 2014.
Laski, Harold. *The Works of Harold J. Laski*. Routledge, 2021.
Mackenzie, J.S. *Fundamental Problems of Life: An Essay on Citizenship as Pursuit of Values*Routledge 2016.
Mander, W. J. *The Oxford Handbook of British Philosophy in the Nineteenth Century*. OUP, 2014.
Marx, Karl. *Capital Volume 1*. Lulu, 2018.
Marx, Karl. *Economic & Philosophic Manuscripts of 1844*. Marxists.org, 2000.
McKenzie, Lisa. '"We Don't Exist to Them, Do We?": Why Working-Class People Voted for Brexit' LSE Brexit, 15 January 2018. https://blogs.lse.ac.uk/brexit/2018/01/15/we-dont-exist-to-them-do-we-why-working-class-people-voted-for-brexit. Accessed 13 Jan 2020.
McKenzie, Lisa. 'Many Working-Class People Believe in Brexit. Who Can Blame Them?' LSE Brexit, 31 January 2019. https://blogs.lse.ac.uk/brexit/2019/01/31/many-working-class-people-believe-in-brexit-who-can-blame-them/. Accessed 13 Jan 2020.

McKenzie, Lisa. *Getting By: Estates, Class and Culture in Austerity Britain.* Policy Press, 2015.

Modood, Tariq. 'Multicultural Nationalism'. *openDemocracy* 13 August 2018. https://www.opendemocracy.net/en/can-europe-make-it/multicultural-nationalism/. Accessed 23 Sep 2021.

Modood, Tariq. 'Multiculturalism as a New Form of Nationalism?' *Nations and Nationalism* 26, no. 2 (2020): 308–13.

Morrow, John. *T.H. Green.* Ashgate, 2007.

Parekh, Bhikhu. *Rethinking Multiculturalism: Cultural Diversity and Political Theory.* Harvard University Press, 2000.

Pogge, Thomas W. 'Cosmopolitanism and Sovereignty'. *Ethics* 103, no. 1 (1992): 48–75.

Rawls, John. *A Theory of Justice.* Harvard University Press, 2009.

Sandel, Michael J. *The Tyranny of Merit: What's Become of the Common Good?* Penguin UK, 2020.

Sandel, Michael J. *What Money Can't Buy: The Moral Limits of Markets.* Penguin UK, 2012.

Screpanti, Ernesto. *Labour and Value: Rethinking Marx's Theory of Exploitation.* Open Book Publishers, 2019.

Simhony, Avital. 'The Political Thought of the British Idealists'. In Mander, W.J. *The Oxford Handbook of British Philosophy in the Nineteenth Century.* OUP, 2014.

Simhony, Avital, and D. Weinstein. *The New Liberalism: Reconciling Liberty and Community.* Cambridge University Press, 2001.

Tawney, R.H. *Equality.* Unwin Books, 1931

Tawney, R.H. *The Acquisitive Society.* Fontana Library, 1961.

Timothy, Nick. *Remaking One Nation: The Future of Conservatism.* John Wiley and Sons, 2020.

Tyler, Colin. 'Thomas Hill Green'. In *The Stanford Encyclopedia of Philosophy*, edited by Edward N. Zalta, Summer 2019. Metaphysics Research Lab, Stanford University, 2019. https://plato.stanford.edu/archives/sum2019/entries/green/.

Walzer, Michael. *Spheres of Justice: A Defense of Pluralism and Equality.* Basic Books, 2008.

CHAPTER 3

Defining the 'Working-Class'

Before we can go further, there is a need to define the working-class. However, one does not have sufficient space to develop its own position and so makes use of a pre-existing framework developed by Savage (2015), to define it, seeing this as the most appropriate way of characterising a class that is diverse, but which maintains relevant and overlapping historical and normative characteristics which tie it together. This chapter, though brief, defines the working-class so that we might determine subsequently the extent to which it can be considered alienated. One begins by outlining the normative elements of class definition, before highlighting historical class tendencies, which one will refer to at various points within the book.

Bourdieusian Class Theory

The basis for the book's definition of class arises out of Savage et al.'s (2013) development of Bourdieusian class theory. Bourdieu centres his theory of class around the normative idea that different classes can be defined according to the amounts and types of capital that they possess. He defines capital as "accumulated labor that…contains a tendency to persist in its being, is a force inscribed in the objectivity of things so that everything is not equally possible or impossible. And the structure of the distribution of the different types and subtypes of capital at a given

S. Taylor Hill, *Challenging Alienation in the British Working-Class*, Palgrave Politics of Identity and Citizenship Series,
https://doi.org/10.1007/978-3-031-59250-8_3

moment in time represents the immanent structure of the social world" (Bourdieu 1986, 241–242). This means that there are a set of constraints, inscribed in the structures that we create, which govern how we might act and determine our life chances. In relation to these structures, we see the emergence of classes, whose accumulated labour (or the exploitation of other classes' accumulated labour) sets them apart from one another. To be at the top, one must hold a significant amount of capital. Thus, Bourdieu considers the amount and composition of three forms of capital to determine an individual's position in social space, that is, social, economic, and cultural capital. He stresses the interplay between these as they are converted into, and used to acquire, one another (Bourdieu 1986). For example, he suggests that economic capital can be converted into cultural capital because access to financial resources can be used to pay for 'higher' cultural access, including private schooling, which in turn enables the creation of networks that increase one's social capital. These capitals can, therefore, reinforce one another and maintain class distinctions, bringing people of similar circumstances together to solidify class belonging. From the realisation of these often economically rooted similarities, a class culture develops.

This has been developed by Savage et al. (2013) to formulate an understanding of the working-class that acknowledges the existence of numerous branches which embody the capitals in their own ways. A useful example of this development is the *Great British Class Survey*, which considers the working-class as able to be split into three working-classes known as the precariat, the traditional working-class (TWC), and the emergent service workers (ESW), alongside the class-straddling new affluent workers (NAW), who are nevertheless tied to the class as their relatives, through their upbringing, and in relation to class culture (Reay in Calver 2022). In this schema the precariat scores the lowest across all three measures of capital, with an average income of £8253 per year, few social contacts, and little to no qualifications, culminating in extreme insecurity, an inability to find meaningful work, and little hope for social mobility. Above them sit the ESW and TWC, who both score low on economic capital but are subject to different property relations as the ESW tend to rent but earn an average of £21,000 per year and the TWC who are likely to own their own homes but earn an average of £13,000 per year. Culturally, the TWC's highbrow cultural capital score is low, and scores on emerging cultural capital are particularly low, which is placed in contrast to the ESW who score higher in emerging culture and lower in highbrow and maintain a few more social contacts around their class. Above these are the straddling class, known as the NAW, who maintain similar social contacts as the TWC and have similar rates of university attendance but earn more on average at £29,000 and have higher levels of cultural capital (Savage et al. 2013). He gives a breakdown for the sub-groups too, asserting that around 15% of the population belong to a precariat that appears to be growing, whilst 14% belong to the TWC and 19% to the ESW. This places the total figure for the working-class at 48% of the population, with the rest being split between the class-straddling NAW at 15% and the established middle-class at around 25% of the population, with a further 6% defined as technical middle-class and the same number as elites (Savage et al. 2013; Savage 2015).

Factoring Sub-groups into Class

The book makes note of working-class sub-groups, which is typically referring to one of the sub-groups in Savage's framework above or a sub-group based around an identifying pole, such as race, ethnicity, religion, or, in the case of the Scottish, nation. The book highlights these groups in relation to the explicit identification of a white working-class sub-group within much of the literature and wishes here to draw attention to the working-classes' diversity, as well as to underline the critique made that a focus on just the white working-class will undoubtedly leave many working-people no better off and potentially deepen alienation.

In discussing working-class sub-groups, it can be difficult to determine exact figures. Whilst Malik (2019) notes that many ethnic minority citizens from particularly Bangladeshi and Pakistani backgrounds are part of this precariat group and are proportionally more than their white fellows, there is no exact figure. Similarly, the Office for National Statistics (2018) does not use class as a measure, and so any judgements made of its data can be a challenge for interpretation because it measures median income within the ethnic grouping, with no breakdown of differences within those sub-groups. Using a combination of income data from the ONS and Census (2011) data, however, we can estimate that 66.5% of Bangladeshi Britons find themselves in the lowest two income quantiles of a population of 447,201, which would make roughly 297,338 economically working-class. We also see that out of a British-Pakistani population of 1,124,511, 61% earn within the lowest two quantiles. This breakdown can be developed further too to suggest that, of the 1,864,890 black and

Afro-Caribbean Britons, 57.2% earn within the lowest two quartiles. As a percentage, each of these groups has a higher proportion of their ethnic group that is economically working-class, though their numbers are clearly dwarfed by the white working-class in sheer numerical terms. Indeed, the number of white Britons that we find within these quartiles is 48.6% of a population of some 48,209,395 million (ONS 2021; Census 2011).

Taken together, using a mixture of ONS and Census data, and Savage's (2013) framework which puts the working-class at between 48% and 63% of the population, 48% being the three bottom sub-groups, and up to 63% reflecting the inclusion of a class-straddling NAW group, we can suggest that there are approximately 28 million working-class people within Britain at its lowest estimate, of which 23,622,598 are white, 1,062,987 are black, 685,951 are Pakistani, and 297,388 are Bangladeshi, though that leaves 2,331,076 unaccounted for in this analysis. This could include a series of additional ethnic or other sub-groupings, as well as a portion of the NAW sub-group, who may reach into the third income percentile and therefore not be included here. There is scope to update this methodology on the publishing of the next Census and with targeted research into sub-groups. However, note here both the relative proportion of working-people within their societal sub-group and the total number of working-people from those sub-groups who make up the wider working-class whole. We see here a majority that is white, yet with not insignificant numbers of people from other ethnic groups that we must take account of in our considerations on class (Calver 2022).

This notion of sub-groups has subsequently been improved by Savage (2015, 2021) to identify the ways in which the working-class have become 'working classes', in effect echoing the implication made by E.P. Thompson (2002) that the broader working-class could be split into relational sub-groups with their own distinctions.

Working-Class(es)?

Savage (2013) advances this claim in identifying the relationships between the working-class sub-groups. Indeed, he begins by asserting that the precariat and other 'satellite' classes are related to the traditional working-class. In fact, the NAW and ESW tend to be literally related to the TWC as their children and have similar upbringings to their parents, with a focus on what he calls 'working-class values', which we will discuss subsequently. What is most interesting, however, is that whilst the NAW and ESW are situated within a working-class habitus, they are also subject to different structures from their parents, which influences their lives. This is something that he points out as both these groups can:

> Be said to exemplify the stark break in working-class culture which has been evident as a result of de-industrialisation, mass unemployment, immigration and the restructuring of urban space… To this extent, new social formations appear to be emerging out of the tendrils of the traditional working-class. (Savage et al. 2013, 246)

This suggests that working-class culture or, rather, the complex subcultures that exist within it are changing, in part due to structural developments. There is a danger of overplaying this to break the bond between the "tendrils" of the TWC, but this would be a mistake because of the shared culture, circumstance, and habitus that persist among members of the broader working-class (Crozier et al. 2019). Rather, one adopts this understanding to assert as Savage does that the class itself is, in fact, defined in part by its diversity.

Shared Occupational and Economic Characteristics

To continue this definition, we can point to several features which Savage (2015) and others argue are common across the class. In fact, on a basic level he asserts that the working-class can be defined fundamentally according to their economic position, which tends to be financially insecure in comparison to those above them in the class hierarchy. In fact, aside from the class-straddling NAW, who share cultural similarities with the other sub-groups, the precariat, TWC, and ESW earn below average national wages and are far from insulated against sudden price increases in utilities and other goods, which can have a significant impact upon their well-being, though the impact does differ between sub-groups. This amounts to a lack of discretionary income vis-à-vis other classes and is a common element that distinguishes the working-class sub-groups from those above them, who are more insulated from price increases and maintain a discretionary income that is not significantly undermined by basic costs, such as rent and utilities—in fact most of those in the classes above them will own their own home, while the majority of working-people, aside from those that are part of the TWC and who tend to be the oldest members of the class, do not (Savage et al. 2013). We might, therefore, consider the classes' precarious relationship with capital as distinguishing it to some extent.

Further, and partly related to this, we can also define the class according to the forms of work they undertake, despite having shifted with the advent of the Knowledge Economy and the closure of historic working-class professions. Indeed, the Knowledge Economy refers to the transformation of our economy from one with a significant focus on manufacturing and the production of tangible goods to that of providing services in jobs that increasingly require a university-level education to get into. The working-class often does not find themselves in these jobs, aside from its NAW group, typically because they do not have the necessary qualifications (Sandel 2020; Goodhart 2020).

Despite these changes in the shape of our economy, however, the class maintain jobs which can typically be described under the umbrella term 'blue collar'. This encapsulates manual, semi-manual, and non-cognitive forms of work, ranging from traditional industries to retail and the related category of 'pink collar' work in care and nursing, which tend to be structured in similar ways.

These jobs are likely to be paid at an hourly rate, though some forms of work, like public-sector nursing, can differ. They tend not to require a degree to work in too, though the process of 'graduatisation' which one discusses in Chap. 5 has forced a partial shift as the more 'prestigious' working-class roles, namely nursing which is recognised as vital by the public, have moved to require degrees from new applicants. These are also some of the most common roles for those who reach the NAW category. Nevertheless, we can define the working-classes according to a tendency to be in blue- or pink-collar work, which is characterised usually by an hourly wage and which requires below-university education levels. To this one can add those in the gig economy, where workers also earn an hourly rate often below living wage and maintain weak contracts with little to no entitlements, much in the same way that others in the class do. Together, these roles make up the foundations of our economy and revolve around manual and service work (Goodhart 2020; Sandel 2020; Cruddas 2021). For Savage, the working-class is than those that are in 'traditional' working-class jobs, workers in the emerging gig economy, and others in 'pink collar' jobs, who each lack discretionary income, usually earn below average wage, which stands at about £33,000 p.a., and tend to suffer from a degree of precarity or insecurity in their economic arrangements (IFS 2022). This trend is only bucked by the NAW sub-group that tends to be most able to attain average UK income, whilst it should also be noted at the other end of the spectrum that elements within the precariat are reliant on welfare for their income or as part of their income, with in-work claimants increasing (Standing 2016, 2019). This analysis therefore understands similarities between the sub-groups yet makes some room for some differences in their economic positions.[1]

Culture and Class

However, occupational and economic characteristics do not only define the class. Rather, E.P. Thompson (2002) sees class as a relationship in which working-people form communities that are born out of their shared challenges.[2] From this develops a socially structured class culture. This class culture can be understood within the Bourdieusian framework using the notion of habitus. Cultural capital is considered by Bourdieu to become embodied within the habitus, which refers to our lived norms, tastes, and preferences, seeing these as key indicators of one's class (Bourdieu 1977, 94). To identify features of this, let us consider some components of working-class culture historically. Here we see an inclination towards the national frame, the importance of community, and the relevancy of particular values amongst members of the class, which amount to a class culture that has evolved over time, but which has persisted in part throughout the developments of the past 50 or so years. The features identified are by no means definitive but are nevertheless relevant to the issues that will be discussed in subsequent chapters.

Nation

The nation tends to be an important framing for the working-class that express significant regard for Britain and its culture. Indeed, recent research by More In Common (2020) suggests that over 70% of people,

[1] See Evans and Mellon (2016) and Crozier et al. (2019) for data on self-identification and class hybridity. Some 41% of those in higher-income managerial professions consider themselves working-class in identarian and cultural terms, adding another layer to the notion of class habitus and the differences within it.

[2] This has been restated by Johnson (in Calver 2022) as an understanding of working-classness as a collective struggle for recognition, "working day in day out, working hard, doing things right", as in contrast to "those they feel don't have to work as hard, yet get more rewarded".

the majority of whom are from working-class backgrounds, see the nation as important and explicitly value it. This has been a historic feature of the class. Edgerton (2021) traces this development over time, considering at length the development of a Labour Party that had come to effectively represent most of the class in the post-war years as being an avowedly 'nationalist' party, which spoke in the national frame, sought to inspire with its rhetoric, and pursued policies aimed at 'national betterment' with the working-class in mind. Such was the importance of this frame for the class that he even goes so far as to suggest that the decline of the national framing within the Labour Party as part of its rebranding as the global New Labour was to undermine working-class confidence in, and ability to identify with, it. One will return to the discussion of New Labour in Chap. 5, but here let us note some of the specific features of this national framing, which we often see expressed in the rhetoric of the historic Labour Party and members of the working-class today—including minority subgroups that often make claims for recognition on this basis (More in Common 2020; Cruddas 2021).

On this first point, Edgerton (2021) suggests that the Labour Party under Attlee and Wilson especially premised their nationalism on an idea of collective progress bound up with a focus on duty and obligation within the national community. These two values, duty and obligation, are a consistent theme in post-war Labour rhetoric and became themselves a focal point for party ideologues like Tawney (1961, 1964) and Laski (2020), as well as later figures like Tony Benn (2012). They were often presented with a clear narrative intent which was to underpin what these figures labelled as patriotism but which Edgerton (2021) sees as nationalist because of their decisive narrative vision for the future of our country (see Chap. 8). Typically, such values were understood by the party to refer to its commitment to redistribution within community, presented as a duty of those who profit from our social structure towards those who do not for a common national benefit, as well as solidarity, which was seen to oblige citizens to look out for one another within their respective communities because citizens were regarded as a locus of value in their contribution to the nation.

These values appear to have resonated with the working-class too and still have some resonance. In fact, Cruddas (2021) highlights the notion of solidarity in many working-class communities that, having witnessed significant socio-economic distress, nevertheless tend to be considerate to those that they view as belonging within what is left of their community.

Similarly, historically it was common to witness working-class concentration around the core associations of the community, including the working-people's clubs and trade unions, which Bieder (2015) sees as promoting a belonging that tended towards mutuality in a given area. This was often expressed in a subjective sense as a belief that one could rely on their fellows, that they were honest, and that others might face similar challenges to them, alongside a more objective view through the organisation of shared childcare groups, with Virdee (2014) emphasising the cross-ethnicity nature of these, though not without some tensions. Such experience was not wholly nationalist in orientation, but the values inherent in these actions were seen to provide the basis of a working-class nationalism.[3]

Interestingly, Goodhart (2017, 2020), Eatwell and Goodwin (2018), and Kaufmann (2018) each support this tendency towards duty and obligation, as well as that corresponding ideal of solidarity, as being a core component of working-class self-understanding. What flows from this is, however, a position which orientates such values around a socially conservative interpretation of community in which those who are seen to be authentic working-class people are defined increasingly in ethnic terms, seeing white workers as 'traditional' working-class people most deserving of this recognition. This perspective does have some resonance for particularly older and white working-people who Sobolewska and Ford (2020) recognise as being nostalgic for the reintroduction of these values into British society in a form that they largely understood to have occurred before structural decline post-1980 and the subsequent wave of globalisation and immigration which expanded throughout the late 1990s and 2000s. We thus see a continuation of these values amongst a section of the working-class, albeit transformed along more socially conservative lines in response to the changes that have occurred as community has declined (Surridge 2021).[4] This is certainly an exclusive understanding of working-class values but taken here one nevertheless sees their continued resonance

[3] Note here that attachment to nation is not specifically working-class. In fact, the European Social Survey (2020) identifies similar regard for nation across class. However, here we see a working-class nationalism centred on values like solidarity which are understood to be diminished and recognition for working-class people in nation alongside it (Evans and Tilley 2017).

[4] Which they perceive to be linked.

as a characteristic of the class, albeit perhaps limited along ethno-cultural lines somewhat.[5]

Taken together, regard for the importance of nation should be considered a tendency of the class given its continued prevalence in the psyche of its members, as well as its historical roots as a core focus of the Labour Party's vision, and source of pride for working-people. One, therefore, highlights the importance of the national frame in the lives of many working-class people, both historically and within contemporary Britain, citing more specifically this resonance of duty and obligation with the class position, as well as the solidarity which, although diminished, still flows from it. One also makes some space here for the challenging of this socially conservative framing over the course of the book, so that such values of duty and obligation within the national frame can be better understood as characteristic and applicable to the class as a whole, rather than simply its white members.

Community and its Values

Blackshaw (2013) suggests that working-class citizens also tend towards forms of collective action and develop a prestige system that prioritises 'practical' skills. Pyakuryal (1970, 16) builds on this to suggest that the working-class adopt this disposition in order not only to cope with structure, but also to impose their own agency upon it. As such, one historically saw the development of tight-knit communal associations in the concentrated working-class areas of the UK. Here, one usually witnessed develop a sense of community-derived 'prestige' that came through actions that the working-class could control, such as their own 'hard work', which was seen as a means of securing a dignity that one could not gain through other means, like educational achievement, since the realities of life tended to make university attendance structurally difficult because of the cost associated with it, at least until the expansion of higher education in the 2000s (Evans and Tilley 2017, 44–47). Since then, we have seen development of a more nuanced interpretation, in which there is some scope for working-class students to pursue a university education, but Goodhart (2020) and Cruddas (2021) nevertheless identify a strong tradition of 'practicality' within working-class communities, which maintain respect

[5] Since minority working-class sub-groups, as Virdee (2014) highlights, practise their own forms of solidarity and mutual obligation but often struggle to connect across such lines.

for professions and trades that are often discounted in wider society (Taylor 2016). One makes note of this in identifying the tendencies of the working-class because it is this regard for one another's forms of work that is seen to be underrepresented, and disrespected, within the Knowledge Economy. This raises questions over the extent to which working-class values are seen to be part of the national imaginary, with significance for their sense of dignity vis-à-vis other classes in society. In reference to Blackshaw (2013), Cruddas (2021) highlights that the main structural difference between this past working-class privileging of 'practical' work and their current understanding is that, historically, they had been able to impose agency over society by ensuring reasonable pay and fair reward through the Labour Party and trade unions, yet now see themselves as detached from such associations. This reveals a structural component to working-class decline in which there is a disconnect between that which they value and what they can see realised within our society.

This also indicates that values are an important component of working-class life. According to Sandel (2020) and Savage (2015), though explicit class consciousness has declined as inequality has worsened, many working-class people root their identity in notions of class, using the frameworks that it inspires to formulate their objections and concerns regarding contemporary society. We see this expressed by Cruddas, who, in speaking of the working-class, asserts that its members tend to place significant emphasis on values like 'hard work' and 'fair play', seeing the two linked together when working-people demand fair pay for the work that they do, for instance.[6] McKenzie (2015, 2017) supports this, citing that her discussions with working-people were value-laden and revolved around these notions of fairness, hard work, honesty, and integrity, with preference for the binding together of peoples within the frame of community—in which duty and obligation were to go hand in hand. This expresses a perspective which is not wholly individualistic and which maintains a tentative link with a historic working-class culture that privileged a form of life rooted in common endeavour and a corresponding set of norms and values—from which prestige was derived (Savage 2021).

These ideas were also expressed by the Labour Party and trade unions that emphasised the dignity of labour, fair pay for fair work, and similar

[6] Note here that hard work is not being touted as exclusive to the working-class. Rather, it is a value that they support and is often brought to the forefront of their existence because they see it go unrecognised. This will be discussed in Chap. 5.

slogans which express a basic desire for decent treatment within our society, accorded to ethical standards. As Thompson (2002) notes, there was prestige/respect to be found within class by acting within these community-determined boundaries, reflecting in part the structural circumstances of a class that had a history of creating its own interdependent forms of prestige which they could control, done so within a frame of community that they had relied upon for support. These were not values that were expressed *comprehensively*, but rather guiding ideas of right and wrong, decency, and basic respect for others, so far as was possible under their circumstances and other social influences[7] (Hobsbawm 1996, 2020). This, of course, leaves scope for nuance and was by no means practised consistently by each member of the class, yet here we see a more general sense that seeks to see society and its members act in particular ways, often with consequences for those who do not (Smith 2012). What this amounts to is a perspective which desires people to act as part of a 'give and take' relationship, expressing a focus more so on interdependence than independence, which is itself reflective of the historic preference for community. This feeds into an analysis of class in the twenty-first century which asserts that the working-class tend to feel that their claims for prestige, their agency, and their structures of collective action have been undermined. We see in their discussions of these problems a component of class which has a moral tone, expressing concern for the values that our society espouses, as well as for the health of our community—which they had structurally relied upon to navigate their circumstances and to impose a collective agency upon (Thompson 2002; Eley 2013). Taken together, we can therefore assert a working-class preference for community which is matched with a corresponding desire for interdependence and respect for the values that facilitate it, of which 'hard work' and 'fair play' are but two noted in the literature.

Conclusion

One understands the working-class as a group that can be defined according to several normative and historic, or cultural, characteristics. At its most simplistic the working-class is the group which is at the bottom of

[7] Racism and other discriminatory attitudes undermine the breadth of this community and did so historically too, yet this is not a class influence (Virdee 2014; Cruddas 2021).

the economic hierarchy with its members typically earning below average wages in manual, semi-manual, and non-cognitive roles. These are characterised by low pay, insecurity, and limited entitlements. On a more substantive or specific level, Savage takes this economic basis to define the working-class as any of the lower four groups up to and including the 'new affluent workers' within his framework, seeing a broad economic similarity which is delineated against intra-class diversity in terms of cultural and social capital, though this remains relational. Indeed, the working-class embody a limited amount of capital overall with varying degrees of home ownership, for example, whilst also ranging from precarity to a small degree of financial security. There are differences of position within the class, but such differences do not break the bonds between them, especially when we consider class as a relationship which has produced a working-class habitus.

As we have seen, Savage (2015) identifies how people typically recognise themselves as belonging to the working-class and can tangibly be bound to it. This reflects the notion that class is a relationship, rather than just an economic position, in which individuals add to and develop cultural behaviours within a wider collective (Thompson 2002; Savage and Miles 1994). To illustrate this we have identified some contemporary and historic components of class culture. In particular, one identifies the continued relevance of the nation and national frame for working-people. This has been taken to socially conservative ends by the white working-class sub-group, yet one sees commonality between the contents of this conservative position and a historic working-class culture that made space for the performance of duty, obligation, and the extension of solidarity to those who were seen to 'belong' to that class. This belonging has always been somewhat contested and not wholly inclusive, yet working-class sub-groups maintain an internal sub-group solidarity even if this does not always extend across broader class bounds. Similarly and partially tied to these values is the importance of community and the interdependence from which flows a shared culture that places emphasis on that which the working-class can control. Namely, one sees a tendency to value 'practical' work and to extend respect for that work for members of the class which is not prevalent within wider society. This raises the question of values too, namely the way in which the working-class now struggle to exercise their collective agency in our society. Such agential decline, and the way that McKenzie and Cruddas see the working-class as raising their concerns, reveals a preference for moralistic and ethical values within the class related to their claims for betterment and this aforementioned centrality of community. As such, one comes to identify some notable tendencies of the class, which include its privileging of the national frame, the centrality of interdependence and the values that flow from it, and the importance of community rooted in solidarity, duty, and obligation, which are held to be the bedrock of common endeavour. This is by no means a definitive list, and there is some leeway for working-class sub-groups to develop these inclinations in different directions, especially when beset by differing structural circumstances, but these are nevertheless tendencies that are worth noting as broadly characteristic of the class.

Understood together one defines the working-class as:

1. The four lowest groups up to and including the NAW in Savage's framework, though this group has more in common culturally than economically with its fellows.
2. A class of people beset by similar structural and other issues including varying degrees of economic insecurity.
3. Typically involved in physical work.
4. Which is constitutive of a class culture that has historically been premised on interdependence, with a strong emphasis on the values that flow from and facilitate it.

Bibliography

Benn, Tony. *The End Of An Era: Diaries 1980–1990*. Random House, 2012.

Bieder, Harris. *White Working-Class Voices: Multiculturalism, Community-Building, and Change*. Policy Press, 2015.

Blackshaw, Tony. *Working-Class Life in Northern England, 1945–2010: The Pre-History and After-Life of the Inbetweener Generation*. Springer, 2013.

Bourdieu, Pierre. *Outline of a Theory of Practice*. Cambridge University Press, 1977.

Bourdieu, Pierre. The forms of capital. In J. Richardson (ed) *Handbook of Theory and Research for the Sociology of Education*. Greenwood, 1986. pp. 241–258.

Calver, Tom. 'The New Class Rules? It's Not about the Money', *The Times*. https://www.thetimes.co.uk/article/the-new-class-rules-its-not-about-the-money-z9kxjcx3j. Accessed 13 Dec 2022.

Crozier, Gill, Diane Reay, and John Clayton. 'Working the Borderlands: Working-Class Students Constructing Hybrid Identities and Asserting Their Place in Higher Education'. *British Journal of Sociology of Education* 40, no. 7 (3 October 2019): 922–937.

Cruddas, Jon. *The Dignity of Labour*. Polity Press, 2021.

Eatwell, Roger, and Matthew Goodwin. *National Populism: The Revolt Against Liberal Democracy*. Penguin, 2018.
Edgerton, David. *The Rise and Fall of the British Nation*. Penguin Books, 2021.
Eley, Geoff. *Working-Class Agency, Past and Present. Labor Studies in Working-Class History of the Americas*. 10, no. 3 2013: 35–39.
Evans, Geoffrey, and James Tilley. *The New Politics of Class: The Political Exclusion of the British Working Class*. Oxford University Press, 2017.
Evans, Geoffrey, and Jonathan Mellon. 'Social Class: Identity, Awareness and Political Attitudes: Why are we still working-class? *British Social Attitudes* 33, 2016.
Goodhart, David. *Head Hand Heart: The Struggle for Dignity and Status in the twenty first Century*. Penguin UK, 2020.
Goodhart, David. *The Road to Somewhere: The Populist Revolt and the Future of Politics*. Penguin, 2017.
Hobsbawm, Eric. *The Age Of Extremes: 1914–1991*. Hachette, UK, 2020.
Hobsbawm, Eric. *The Age of Revolution: 1749–1848*. Knopf Doubleday Publishing Group, 1996.
Institute for Fiscal Studies. 'Living Standards, Poverty and Inequality in the UK: 2022'. 14 July 2022.
Kaufmann, Eric. *Whiteshift: Populism, Immigration and the Future of White Majorities*. Penguin, UK, 2018.
Laski, Harold. *The Works of Harold J. Laski*. Routledge, 2020.
Malik, Kenan. 'Working class versus minorities? That's looking at it the wrong way', *Guardian* 14 July 2019. https://www.theguardian.com/commentisfree/2019/jul/14/divided-britain-ethnic-pay-gap. Accessed 14 Jan 2024.
May 2023. https://www.britainschoice.uk/.
McKenzie, Lisa. 'The Class Politics of Prejudice: Brexit and the Land of No-Hope and Glory'. *The British Journal of Sociology* 68, no. S1 (2017): 265–80.
McKenzie, Lisa. *Getting By: Estates, Class and Culture in Austerity Britain*. Policy Press, 2015.
More In Common. 'Britain's Choice, More in Common's New Report on the UK'. 2020. https://ifs.org.uk/publications/living-standards-poverty-and-inequality-uk-2022. Accessed 24 Nov 2022.
Office for National Statistics. 'Employment by Occupation'. https://www.ethnicity-facts-figures.service.gov.uk/work-pay-and-benefits/employment/employment-by-occupation/latest. Accessed 21 May 2021.
Office for National Statistics. 'Population of England and Wales'. https://www.ethnicity-facts-figures.service.gov.uk/uk-population-by-ethnicity/national-and-regional-populations/population-of-england-and-wales/latest#by-ethnicity. Accessed 1 Dec 2022c.
Office for National Statistics. '2011 census'. https://www.ons.gov.uk/census/2011census

Pyakuryal, Kailash. 'Weberian Model of Social Stratification—a Viewpoint'. *Occasional Papers in Sociology and Anthropology* no. 7 (1 January 1970): 14–25.
Sandel, Michael. The Tyranny of Merit: What's become of the Common Good? Penguin, 2020.
Savage, Michael, and Andrew Miles. *The Remaking of the British Working Class, 1840–1940.* Routledge, 1994.
Savage, Mike, Fiona Devine, Niall Cunningham, Mark Taylor, Yaojun Li, Johs Hjellbrekke, Brigitte Le Roux, Sam Friedman, and Andrew Miles. 'A New Model of Social Class? Findings from the BBC's Great British Class Survey Experiment'. *Sociology* 47, no. 2 (1 April 2013): 219–250.
Savage, Mike. *Social Class in the Twenty First Century.* Penguin, 2015.
Savage, Mike. *The Return of Inequality.* Harvard University Press, 2021.
Smith, K. *Fairness, Class and Belonging in Contemporary England.* Springer, 2012.
Sobolewska, Maria, and Robert Ford. *Brexitland: Identity, Diversity and the Reshaping of British Politics.* Cambridge University Press, 2020.
Standing, Guy. *Plunder of the Commons: A Manifesto for Sharing Public Wealth.* Penguin UK, 2019.
Standing, Guy. *The Precariat: The New Dangerous Class.* Bloomsburg, 2016.
Surridge, Paula. 'Beyond Binaries: Understanding the Fragmentation of British Politics'. *Political Insight* 12, no. 4 (1 December 2021): 32–35.
Tawney, R.H. *Equality.* Unwin Books, 1964.
Tawney, R.H. *The Acquisitive Society.* Fontana Library, 1961.
Taylor, Yvette. *Classed Intersections: Spaces, Selves, Knowledges.* Routledge, 2016.
Thompson, E.P. *The Making of the English Working Class.* Penguin, 2002.
Virdee, Satnam. *Racism, Class and the Racialized Outsider.* Bloomsbury Publishing, 2014.

CHAPTER 4

Defining Alienation

This chapter will explore the development of alienation to produce a clearer definition of the term. It will begin by analysing the concept of alienation within the work of Hegel. This will form the basis for the critique and expansion of the concept which occurs within the works of Karl Marx, notably the 1844 Manuscripts, which can be understood as the key texts elucidating the ideas of a 'Young Marx' dedicated to philosophical humanism rather than 'scientific' socialism. At this stage, having established in some depth the key tenets and developments of alienation, the chapter will move to determine how it has been used within Alasdair Macintyre's works, primarily his 1981 work *After Virtue*, to critique a capitalist-derived individualism as fundamentally alienating through its inability to promote a rooted ethical ideal. The issues raised within this text will, in turn, underpin a critique of a contemporary neoliberalism, labelled as liberal-individualism by Macintyre, which continues to produce alienation. The key components of alienation will then be summarised to suggest that it is made up of three interlocking parts, these being a lack of agency and meaning and the separation of oneself from the community.

S. Taylor Hill, *Challenging Alienation in the British Working-Class*, Palgrave Politics of Identity and Citizenship Series,
https://doi.org/10.1007/978-3-031-59250-8_4

Hegel

Hegel suggests that alienation occurs when an individual becomes estranged from their species-essence (Marx later termed this *Gattungswesen*) and is unable to re-connect the two. A key component of this essence is *Geist* (Hegel 2018, xviii). This term, according to Hegelian scholars such as Dupre, can be roughly interpreted to mean 'spirit' or 'consciousness'. For Hegel, this *Geist* is essentially something which can consciously recognise itself as a world and of the world as itself.

What one is suggesting here is that the world and the spirit are fundamentally related and, to some extent, form a single interconnected entity (Hegel 2018, 117–118). This connectivity defines feelings of non-alienation because for something to be considered alien, it must, by definition, be an other, unfamiliar, and/or somehow distant. In relation to an individual human being then, to be non-alienated one must be able to see themselves reflected within the world and the world around reflected inside of them. This demonstrates the connectivity between the two in which the individual becomes able to almost implicitly understand and, crucially, relate to the world around them as if it were an extension or expression of their being. To some extent, Hegel seems to understand this exactly as a product of being or the expression of that being. He establishes this with the notion of objectification, which he sees as the driver of historical development.

Objectification refers to the process of realising our ideas as tangible products within the world (Hegel 2018, 199). For example, one might objectify the idea of shelter by building houses.

However, issues arise when the mind objectifies itself to innumerable different material products and institutions because it can fail to see that these things are its creations, instead seeing them to be 'alien'. For Hegel, human history is the process of overcoming this alienation through a step-by-step recognition of the world, by the human mind, as its product.

This is a complex idea, but it can be clarified further when we consider that the main 'symptoms' or indicators of alienation are feelings such as a lack of self-worth, or of dignity, and an inability to recognise or develop meaning. These feelings each represent alienation by virtue of the fact that they encourage someone to see themselves as 'coerced', leading a life that they do not have control over. In this case, their lives could well be characterised as unfree in a Hegelian sense because they are unable to use their cognitive faculties to comprehend how the forces around them have influence over the decisions that they do or do not make. For Hegel, this individual has become estranged/alienated because they are not able to act freely, when free(dom) is defined as being aware of the forces that might encourage an individual to act in a given way but can come to a rational decision that is in line with their mind nonetheless (Hegel 2018, 16). Having defined freedom primarily as an outcome of the sufficient development of one's cognitive faculties, and alienation as an inability to control one's own life regardless of outside forces, we might now come to Hegel's 'solution' to the problem. Indeed, as alienation here is defined primarily as a feeling which is subjective and related to the individual, Hegel moves to suggest that one can 'overcome' alienation by jettisoning our mental reservations about the world around us. This encourages us to recognise that we have plenty of opportunities for self-realisation because the world is 'a home' that we are intrinsically tied to and can shape towards our needs (Hardimon 1994, 121). For example, if a person feels alienated by politics then Hegel might see this as evidence of them having not yet found a way of identifying that the political structures of the modern social world do constitute such a home because they enable individuals to realise themselves as members of a family, as economic agents, and as citizens (Hegel 2018, 23, 311, 396). To become non-alienated they must, therefore, re-connect with 'reality', which requires an attitudinal change in which we attempt to reconcile ourselves with the world around us and pinpoint how things might be moulded to better reflect us.

This search for the re-connection of mind and object, and that object's further utilisation and subjugation in service of the mind's quest for freedom, defines the historical process within the works of Hegel. For example, he sees human life, its objects, and its institutions as in a constant state of change in which they are renewed, reformed, and replaced through the interaction of ideas.

These changes occur naturally in the dialectical process (Maybee 2020). This refers to when one mode of living (the thesis) enters a logical, often conflicting, 'discussion' with another (the antithesis) until such a time as the two can be remedied (the synthesis). This occurs repeatedly throughout history, with the synthesis becoming the new thesis, driving its development forward until such a time as the mind and its products can be brought back into relation, though this final goal remains somewhat elusive (Singh and Mohapatra 2008, 15). Under this process, Hegel to some extent assumes a level of alienation within society that is to be met and remedied over time as our institutions and norms change. This offers some significance in the processes' definition as it establishes that alienation should diminish over time as citizens come to shape their community in a way that is reflective of themselves as a collective and an individual, identifying the necessity of mutuality in these relationships as a foundational element of non-alienation. In other words, agency is tied not only to the individual, but to the way in which the individual has a hand in the collective shaping of the future of their society through engagement with the dialectical process. Here then one must be able to feel influential in the collective development of something greater than themselves, which we shall return to in our subsequent discussion of Macintyre. Agency then refers to mastery of oneself and an ability to see oneself reflected in community, but it additionally refers to agential action for a collective purpose.[1]

Thus, Hegel views alienation in an agential-communal sense, suggesting that one is not alienated if they are able to contribute to change in the world around them and to see themselves reflected in it. Here, one must be able to both exercise control over their life and recognise their place within the frameworks of the wider community. Though this provides a useful understanding of the importance of agency in challenging alienation, one turns to Marx to further underline this second component given that Hegel does little to recognise the potential relationship between agency and structure in a wholly negative sense. Indeed, as Marx suggests, structure, and in particular the capitalist structure, places severe constraints on the agency of working-people and provides a challenge to their dignity and sense of commonality. Thus, where Hegel identifies the underlying agential dimension of alienation and recognises the importance of bringing into relation individual with community, we must turn to Marx to develop a greater understanding of what we might label as the 'dignity' component.

Marx

Hegel's conception of history was influential for Karl Marx, who adopted his dialectic perspective. Perhaps one of the most interesting results of Marx's interpretation of this process was in the way that he used it to show that alienation is not a wholly negative phenomenon (Marx 2000). To explore this idea further, we must first say that Hegel defined alienation on the most fundamental level as a disconnection between two things that

[1] A contemporary example of this might be collective action as part of a trade union.

should otherwise be related. As we have seen, the mind and the object are related naturally because the mind has produced that object. However, according to Marx (2000), in the social world we might permit some level of alienation so long as it produces a positive outcome. One such example of this might be to permit a degree of alienation between the individual and the collective whereby the two maintain a great number of links to one another, but wherein that individual is given sufficient space to establish their own identity which is distinct from those around them (Fareld and Kuch 2021). Within this example, the ties between the two are not wholly cut but, rather, altered. For Marx, this has played out within the dialectic of history in three stages. The first stage of history was, for want of a better term, a totalitarian one in which the community defines the individual and every aspect of their being in "undifferentiated unity" (Cohen 1974, 237). This contrasts with the second stage, defined as one of "differentiated disunity" in which individuals care only for themselves, scarcely thinking of the identity and interests of the wider community (Cohen 1974, 237–238). However, neither of these stages finds an adequate balance between the community and individuals, to the detriment of both. This realisation leads to the third stage of history, which Marx deems to be the communist phase, which embodies the stage of differentiated unity (Marx 2000; Inwood 1992, 36). Here desirable versions of community and individuality flourish together. Indeed, in their new forms, communal and individual identities, and communal and individual interests, presuppose and reinforce one another, but remain partly separate so that they can also flourish in and of themselves. This is a useful distinction for Marx to make because it recognises that the individual is shaped by the community in which they live and are intrinsically connected to it, but that they remain an individual with specific interests, goals, or characteristics which make them unique.[2] Crucially, it establishes that the community, regardless of individual identity, will always continue to define them in some way and that, therefore, they should be an active part of it, using their individual expertise to ensure that it continues to progress and that others within it also have sufficient space to flourish (Gould 1980). Such a fundamentally positive understanding of the interconnectedness of the individual with the collective is supportive of a more mutualistic bond between the two which recognises that one does not have to supersede the other in every sense, whilst we might also permit some separation between

[2] An idea we will return to in subsequent chapters.

them in cases conducive to the development of freedom. Thus, Marx demonstrates that alienation, when it occurs in a negative way to sever the ties between the individual and the collective, can cause serious harm because it robs that person of part of their identity and the community of something that could contribute to its maintenance and development.

This represents a serious problem for a given society to contend with and one which is in the best interests of both citizen and community to remedy. However, such a situation requires more than a Hegelian prescription for the remedy of alienation. In fact, this is something that Marx realised and subsequently tied to his critique of the capitalist system. Indeed, although he takes inspiration from Hegel for many of his ideas, he sees his understanding of alienation as a purely subjective phenomenon as naïve. For Marx, there is no doubt that alienation can be about mental reservations and the inability of an individual to see oneself within the objects of the world around them, but to say that it is only about individual mindset is to ignore the forces which actively prevent one from connecting with that world or self-actualising. This is perhaps best evidenced by the Marxian understanding of the alienation of labour, which is to be primarily understood as the result of objective structural problems. Within the 1844 Manuscripts, Marx depicts this in relation to four examples, which are constitutive of alienation in themselves but may not be applied comprehensively to every worker in the same manner (Marx 2000, 29–31). First, he identifies alienation from the object that the worker produces when it is immediately taken away from them to be sold by their employer. Second, he suggests that work can become a torment through the monotony which is engendered by the extreme division of labour to the point that one worker is relegated to the position of a cog in a large machine. Third is that the worker can become alienated if they have no say in what they produce or to what ends they produce it. Finally, Marx sees how it might dawn on the worker that their lack of power to decide what they produce or why leads them to realise that such work does nothing to fulfil mutual, definitively human, needs but, rather, to service the mode of exchange and the accumulation of capital by their employer as is the express aim of the capitalist system. Within each of these circumstances, the worker is ultimately reduced to a mechanism designed to produce profit in service of capitalism and in each case loses some part of themselves (Marx 2000, 30–33). They have lost their species-essence because their minds are restricted from producing objects for others that satisfy their needs. In this example, the structure of the capitalist system consequently provides real obstacles for the working-class individuals to overcome and ensures that they remain in an alienated position whereby they cannot be agents of their own destiny. This is a development of Hegel's relationship between object and subject to say that alienation is far more than a mental reservation, it is a physical one as well defined in part by domination and active agential degradation.[3]

Marx terms this subordination as fetishism. In this case, the fetishism of capital limits the minds of every group within society by making them subservient to the objects which they created, imbuing in them the sense that they must produce capital to survive lest society would collapse (Marx 2000, 53). The worker must find work or die of starvation, and in finding this work, they must subject themselves to alienation, suffering, and emasculation to maintain their lives and to give tribute to the deity of capital through their labour. The worker and capitalist are separated by structure and can no longer see each other as human having found themselves in roles that garner mutual loathing for one another. The capitalist thus sees the worker as an annoyance that eats into their profits, and the worker sees the capitalist as their exploiter, but both are locked together by the system that they serve (Marx 2000, 4–6). The underlying point that Marx is attempting to make in explaining this situation is that the structures that we have created have become so alienated from the way that the mind imagined them, as something which was to be used in service of our human needs and has become its own independent entity which has in turn distorted the relationship between individuals, leading to the development of damaging norms which destroy our humanity and ability to relate to one another (Marx 2000, 39). Under these systems we are objectively alienated because there is genuinely no way of developing meaning or dignity in what we do when our only aim is to generate capital, which in no way promotes the community togetherness from which we can foster mutually beneficial, unique, and positive facets of our identity (Marx 2000, 22). In this way alienation is underlined by adherence to a structure which undermines the bonds necessary for community and which extends norms that clash with erstwhile notions of worth as derived from it.

Marx, of course, provides a solution to this issue, which is the overthrow of the capitalist system through revolution (Marx and Engels 2019).

[3] It is worthwhile noting too that a worker does not need to experience all four examples of alienation to be considered as such. Rather, experiencing any one of these can have a significant impact on a worker's well-being and sense of connection.

This aspect of his theory has become somewhat convoluted, not only because Marx wrote little on what would occur during and after this revolution, but also because of the varied means by which it has been interpreted by his 'disciples', from Marxist-Leninists and Maoists to Left Communists and other forms of more 'libertarian' Marxism. The point that one wishes to make here is more nuanced than simply a discussion of communism. Instead, one seeks to understand the underlying 'remedy' that Marx provides for alienation, past the tearing down of those structures which oppress and subjugate us. Indeed, Marx, especially in his 1844 Manuscripts, develops a deeply humanistic understanding of life. He sees that we, as human beings, have a distinct 'species-essence' which makes us want to live in community with others. He believes that community gives us a sense of purpose wherein we can look to take up tasks that mutually benefit each of us. The feelings which we develop out of doing this are fundamentally fulfilling ones, like dignity and love (Marx 2000, 46). For this humanist Marx, these genuine human feelings and the connections with others within our community constitute something so real that we will happily do anything for it once we have experienced it (Marx 2000, 53–54). The sense that he is describing is somewhat elusive to definition, but it may broadly be understood as the recognition of a purposeful life, from which we can draw contentedness. The precursor to this is human connectivity and the development of meaningful relationships, which is why he proposes a communal form of living that is intersected with individuality so that we can learn from one another, have interesting discussions, design new objects, and institutions, and act to service the spontaneity of human desires. As such, alienation refers to a process that separates us from this capacity for relational connectivity and which severs the link between community and meaning generation. Put simply, Marx emphasises alienation as detachment from community and its ability to generate social goods such as recognition, meaning, and dignified respect.

This is not to gloss over the problems which are associated with Marx's works, however. The greatest problem with Marx, acknowledged by supporters and critics alike, is that his turn to scientific socialism, which predicted the downfall of the capitalist system, thanks to its inherent contradictions, has failed to occur (Liedman 2018). In fact, capitalism has become more entrenched than Marx imagined. It has brought greater material prosperity and, if we are to believe scholars like Marcuse, it has made the workers even more subservient to it by transforming them into consumers (Marcuse 2002). The workers here remain alienated, but they are also rendered passive, with no alternative to look towards. This is, however, to underline the degradation that Marx felt would occur under capitalism and point towards an alienation which detaches us from our ability to generate meaningful attachments (Bernstein 1994). Essentially, what we witness within the Marxian interpretation is the development of a form which rids the working-class of their agency by making them passive tools in the creation of wealth, building on Hegel to assert that working-people have little chance to see themselves reflected in a socio-economic structure that dominates them and which has now persisted longer than Marx thought likely. This rendered/structural passivity and subservience to the capitalist mode of production has a significant and corresponding impact on their ability to generate meaning, which is a prerequisite for dignity, since their relations have become 'poisoned' by these processes of reification and fetishisation (Hilton 2003). Such distortions are taken here to cloud one's ability to form relationships that are not transactional, promote a competitive and ultimately destructive individualism, and prevent human needs from being recognised within society in a way that corresponds to working-class values. To put this complex web of alienation perhaps more simply, Marx builds on Hegel's agential-communal definition of alienation, in which one has a sense of self that is not realised within community, to suggest that the working-class under capitalism see their values not only unrecognised but stripped away and replaced by a morality that does little to generate meaning. In this way, one not only is unrecognised within community and unable to shape it, but also has their dignity actively eroded within a society that privileges reified ends and struggles to treat particularly those in low-income jobs as ends in themselves.

Macintyre

In the search for meaning we turn to Macintyre, who draws on Marx to critique an individualist-capitalist hybrid that has no ability to promote virtue, defined as ethical action in accordance with the recognition of our fellows in community. Macintyre sees capitalism in a 'Marxist' sense as unduly prioritising non-human needs through the reification of capital. This, he argues, forces society to adapt its norms, goals, and aims to reflect those things that capitalism requires for its continuation, namely monetary wealth and the systems that underpin it. This corrupts our humanity and the notion of value. Indeed, for Macintyre, capitalism has rendered value a term that is often associated with wealth (Macintyre 2007, 148). Therefore, for something to have value, it must either be worth a significant amount of money or be able to produce a significant amount in turn. Such an understanding of the concept renders discussion about value amoral and disconnected from genuine human needs or relationships because we are defining it in financial terms, not in human ones.[4] This merely serves to strengthen the grip of capitalism because we cannot imagine so easily a world in which things in themselves are valued not for money, but for something more 'human', like the happiness that they produce or the meaning that they bring to people's lives. In this case, we simply become more alienated from what it means to be a human and fall into a survival mentality whereby we work to consume, lacking social identity or a sense of anything greater than ourselves. Thus, Macintyre uses Marx's theory of alienation and fetishism implicitly, if not explicitly, to explain how capitalism has grown beyond the control of humanity (Macintyre 2007, 107). From this position it has been able to change culture and understanding, in turn further subordinating humanity to its needs to produce capital and all that comes with that, namely, poverty, inequality, and greed. In this world we have become separated from our species-essence and are no longer working towards something meaningful, like the realisation of the common good or the good life. Consequently, Macintyre understands capitalism as having corrupted humanity to the extent that we now struggle to realise or fulfil our genuine human goods, perhaps even going beyond Marx here to directly link alienation and fetishism to moral degeneration and an inability to reflect what many working-people hold dear.

Macintyre goes further too, taking aim at liberal-individualism for its subservience to capitalism and failure to actively promote the good, taking a far more ethics-oriented perspective in comparison to Marx's economistic focus. He says that we have not been able to overcome capitalism because it has become so embedded within our culture, as well as because we have no way of determining what we 'ought' to be as human beings. For Macintyre, liberal-individualism offers no vision for the future, common values, or 'good' to strive towards, and leaves an ethical void. In fact, in his view, its laws even do away with justice by prioritising instead fundamental capitalistic necessities such as private property at the expense of things like the communal need for, say, land upon which to grow crops to

[4] Human needs are referred to as emotional needs for attachment, love, or meaning.

sustain life. In this example, we have prioritised the needs of the capitalist mode of production because we have fetishised it over the genuine human need for sustenance, which is a pre-requisite for the development of our faculties. This is compounded by the fact that his liberal-individualist state could not do anything about this because it is emotivist[5] and too committed to neutrality to make any radical commitment to the combatting of injustice (Macintyre 2007). Taking this idea of emotivism, Macintyre suggests that liberal-individualism privatises morality, rendering it unto the realm of the individual for them to decide what is right or wrong. By making individuals the sole arbiter of right and wrong, as well as virtue and non-virtue, we allow society to degenerate into moral chaos whereby many individuals merely take a means-ends view of the world in which any means is justified so long as they are able to satisfy their own preferences, which is itself a product of a capitalist-derived individualism. Although sometimes unfair in his critique of liberalism owing to his overgeneralisation, the underlying point which Macintyre (2007, 2016) is making here is one about community and the fracturing of its moral bedrock under the weight of a selfish individualism, partly developed out of capitalist morality. On this point, and within this frame, he has something important to note about the nature of alienation as arising out of what he might call an unvirtuous society, which the Idealists and Socialists would call an unethical one, defined as such because we have lost or are losing our ability to value one another in our considerations.

Macintyre (2007) sees such consideration as vital to the sustenance of a just society as thought for others is achieved not only through the practice of duties and responsibilities, which can themselves be drawn upon as a source of meaning for citizens, but also because the practice of reciprocity and shared commitment to principle provides a foundation of equal worth whereby we can recognise others as valuable members of the community. He sees that, by having an ethical frame for community that makes it expressly clear that we must commit ourselves to others, we are better placed to extend a dignity to our citizens, as well as to create a community that one can find recognition and meaning within. The prognosis for a society that fails in this is particularly bleak and de-humanising. By losing something as crucial as our ethical foundation, we are robbed of the ability to enjoy these common goods which otherwise arise out of mutuality and

[5] An ethical theory which regards value judgements as expressions of feeling or attitude and prescriptions of action rather than assertions or reports of anything tangible.

deprive citizens of the fullest ability to realise meaning within their lives (Macintyre 2016). He even extends this to our structures, suggesting that a lack of an ethical basis for society is only likely to hamper our ability to realise social change and can, in the context of the working-class, harm their capacity for meaningful agency and mutual recognition. Indeed, take for example the decline of the trade unions. As we become more selfish in our interests, not desiring to pay into unions because they are not seen as providing immediate gratification, we lose the ability to gain things that can only come through collective action, in this case the use of collective bargaining to improve working conditions, not to mention the social and educational aspects of unionism which are related to the promotion of solidarity, community, and dignity in work.

Taken together, the loss of an ethical basis for community because of selfish individualisation atomises us and robs us of the ability to generate meaningful relationships, as well as denying us those goods, both material and 'spiritual', which we can only gain in common (Macintyre 2007, 156). In essence, by embracing an individualism that is devoid of express moral sentiment, the desire for duty and responsibility to be extended to others, we deprive ourselves of the capacity to share bonds of equal worth. This has resulted in lost community amongst the working-class as these ethical principles provided a bedrock of dignity whereby working-people could be recognised, at least within their class, for their decency and not by the hierarchical standards of wealth which pervade individualised society. This contributes to alienation as we become distanced from our community and find our capacity for meaning generation and, in the case of the unions, agential action, severely stunted.

Rootedness

Macintyre (2007, 2016) asserts in relation to this individualisation an additional element of alienation which we might identify as 'rootlessness'. This speaks to the idea that, in individualising society, people tend to lose attachment to their communities and, with that, the potential for a sense of purpose. Indeed, he sees such people as 'listless' and less able to connect with those aspects of our shared existence which provide us with a sense of value that is much more than merely 'of ourselves' and as belonging to something that is more 'eternal'. For Macintyre this is conceived in both a local and a national frame, as belonging to one's locality and as being part of the shared work that, in this case, is Britain. This is juxtaposed within his thought by cosmopolitanism, which he criticises as essentially listless due to its tendencies to proffer a vision of a global community that simply struggles to resonate with many, including working, people and which does not necessarily seek to privilege culture as of inherent value as rooting people to place and their fellows (Kleingeld and Brown 2019). In contemporary society, he therefore asserts a drift towards such rootlessness, perpetuated by globalisation and the dominance of a neoliberal-capitalist order, which comes to fundamentally undermine the capacity for people to feel 'at home', rooted and able to commit themselves to a narrative understanding of self and of people—their fellows. In relation to alienation, Macintyre highlights an underlying need for us to place meaning at the forefront of our lives and to live within a community which upholds standards, duties, and responsibilities to one another in a way that promotes equal worth and capacity for virtue (Davenport 2012). He argues that this lack at present and suggests that without our moral tether or consideration for virtue, we will only allow society to degenerate further, away from any position which can uphold common respect and the sense of equal worth which is necessary to generate dignity. Whilst we might again see his critique of cosmopolitan rootlessness as a little too harsh, one notes here how loss of rooted purpose, or a sense of belonging, alienates us from the ability to fully develop a sense of self, whilst acting to potentially undermine the national framing upon which ideals of duty and responsibility have tended to flourish.

Macintyre's Narrative

In response, Macintyre asserts that a narrative understanding of oneself, of one's capacity as an independent reasoner, one's dependence on others and on the social practices and traditions in which one participates, all tend towards the alleviation of alienation (Macintyre 2007, 121–125). This is primarily because it gives our temporary existence on this Earth a deeper level of meaning as we are seen to be 'standing on the shoulders of giants', living our lives virtuously so that those that come after us can live better lives in which values of equal worth, dignity, and respect are enshrined. It is worthwhile entertaining the narrative idea because it enables one to create a vision for the future and act upon or in accordance with it. It begs us to think of what we want to be and how we would like our point in history to be defined, how we should engage with others, and what our purpose might be. This is quite a romantic perspective but is seen by Macintyre as necessary to transcend the current struggles of the present to construct a clearer vision for the society that we would like to become (Davenport 2012). Although Macintyre (2016) can be unclear in how his narrative might work, he says to look to the past root and anchor a narrative of ourselves that connects with people and promotes an idea of virtue, or a common good, that we can see ourselves collectively as part of. Thus, he asserts a narrative idea of historical progress, visualising the society that we would like to aim for, whilst simultaneously serving to reconnect us with the past, though it is pertinent to stress that we must also remain aware of the complexities of historical reality (Schneewind 1982). This finds its expression in the final chapter of the book with respect to Progressive Nationalism and helps to underpin a form of alienation here that has occurred within the working-class. In fact, as we have moved towards a system of globalised neoliberal-capitalism, the working-class have lost many of those foundational structures within their communities and are no longer able to view themselves within the same rooted frame which they had been able to in the post-war years. This unrooting, coupled with the structural and cultural changes unleashed by the globalised 'Knowledge Economy', has been to usurp working-class values and to leave many within the class without sufficient means to situate themselves, to recognise their value, or to engage in that same level of community that they had previously. One will develop this further in the subsequent chapter.

Defining Alienation

Bringing these ideas together, it becomes possible to assert that there exist three fundamental characteristics which define and contribute to alienation within contemporary society. Each of these revolves around that most basic notion of alienation as described by Hegel, which asserts it as arising fundamentally out of our inability to see ourselves and that which we value reflected in the world. This finds itself expressed here in relation to:

1. *Community*: The first of these problems is that of the separation of the individual from the community. Community is the primary means for the realisation of human need because it is necessarily collaborative, encouraging us to engage with one another so that we might better understand others and ourselves. For Hegel, community helps us to find our place in the world by interacting with family

members, economic agents, and the political apparatus, as a member, citizen, friend, and other identity-defining roles. The same can be said for Marx, who considers that sometimes the individual must be distinct from the community, namely when it gives them their own personal identity, but that the common brings its own identity to that person, as well as social benefits, like purpose, and the ability to engage in mutually beneficial relationships on social, economic, and political grounds. The community in Marx is, therefore, the means to greater human ends in which we develop our faculties in ways that an atomised individual could not. Macintyre's whole critique of individualism is based on the premise that it atomises us and 'privatises' morality. Without community we are robbed of a sense of identity or purpose, just as in Marx. However, it is more than that. We lose a sense of right and wrong, how to treat one another, and what it means to be human beings. For each of these thinkers, loss of community is alienating primarily because the collective gives us a purpose, forms a key part of our identity, and provides us with a route to a better future that is more attainable if we work in common, whilst it is also premised on a principle of equal worth necessary for the extension of mutual dignity.

2. *Agency*: The loss of agency is the second component of alienation. For Hegel (2018), this occurs when one cannot recognise themselves within the world around them and, consequently, feels powerless because they perceive their life as being decided by forces outside of their control. Marx (2000) elaborates upon this to say that one feels this way, not only because they are disconnected from the world around them psychologically, but also because, physically, there are structures in place that prevent the individual from exercising agency. Macintyre (2007) takes these ideas as the basis for his own critique, seeing the economic structure of capitalism, and the allied political structure of liberal-individualism, as creating a culture and institutions that distort and undermine human need. The feeling of powerlessness which occurs as part of the loss of agency, therefore, alienates individuals who feel, and recognise, that the contemporary structures of society do not enable them to engage in the processes that can improve their lives. One is thus alienated because they are actively excluded from holding decision-making power or from being part of associations that hold it. One, therefore, lacks control or the feeling of being in control of their lives

whilst simultaneously finding themselves unable to adequately shape community in tandem with others.

3. *Dignity*: The loss of dignity, defined by each of the intellectuals as related to the loss of an individual's ability to recognise their value, represents the third component of alienation. Hegel (2018) suggests that dignity is lost when individuals cannot gain a sense of meaning in what they do nor develop a strong identity based on their relationships. Marx (2000) sees dignity as intrinsically related to the recognition of human needs and the ability of an individual to objectify that need using their creative impulses. Dignity, however, is taken away from individuals when they are forced to follow orders and is trumped by the fetishisation of capital. This subservience alienates people from the relationships and actions which give meaning to life and, instead, replaces these feelings with ones primarily centred on survival through work. This theme is also present within Macintyre (2007), who relates dignity to the ability of a person to see oneself as part of a narrative, created in tandem with others. To lose meaning alienates individuals because it leaves them without direction and enables reified values of wealth to deny working-people their equal worth and dignity. It is psychologically damaging and detrimental to the development of the human species because, without it, we cannot understand the world around us and are further rendered separate from our fellow human beings, categorised into hierarchies which do nothing to express our integrity. Just like the other characteristics outlined above, dignity is necessary to make life worthwhile.

Having outlined the three main components of alienation we are now equipped with an understanding of it that is sufficiently able to describe the problems faced by the working-class within Britain.

Bibliography

Bernstein, J. M. *Frankfurt School: Vol. 1*. Taylor & Francis, 1994.

Cohen, Gerald Allan. "Marx's Dialectic of Labour", *Philosophy & Public Affairs*. 1974, 3(3): 235–261.

Davenport, John J. *Narrative Identity, Autonomy, and Mortality: From Frankfurt and MacIntyre to Kierkegaard*. Routledge, 2012.

Fareld, Victoria, and Hannes Kuch. *From Marx to Hegel and Back: Capitalism, Critique, and Utopia*. Bloomsbury Publishing, 2021.

Gould, Carol C. *Marx's Social Ontology: Individuality and Community in Marx's Theory of Social Reality*. MIT Press, 1980.

Hardimon, Michael. *Hegel's Social Philosophy. The Project of Reconciliation*. Cambridge University Press, 1994.

Hegel, Georg Wilhelm Fredrich. *Georg Wilhelm Friedrich Hegel: The Phenomenology of Spirit*. Cambridge University Press, 2018.

Hilton, Matthew. *Consumerism in Twentieth-Century Britain: The Search for a Historical Movement*. Cambridge University Press, 2003.

Inwood, Michael. *A Hegel Dictionary*. Blackwell, 1992.

Kleingeld, Pauline, and Eric Brown. 'Cosmopolitanism'. In *The Stanford Encyclopedia of Philosophy*, edited by Edward N. Zalta, Winter 2019. Metaphysics Research Lab, Stanford University, 2019. https://plato.stanford.edu/archives/win2019/entries/cosmopolitanism/.

Liedman, Sven-Eric. *A World to Win: The Life and Works of Karl Marx*. Verso Books, 2018.

MacIntyre, Alasdair. *After Virtue: A Study in Moral Theory*. 3rd ed. Notre Dame, IN: University of Notre Dame Press, 2007.

Macintyre, Alasdair. *Ethics in the Conflicts of Modernity: An Essay on Desire, Practical Reasoning, and Narrative*. Cambridge University Press, 2016.

Marcuse, Herbert. *One-Dimensional Man. Studies in the Ideology of Advanced Industrial Society*. Routledge, 2002.

Marx, Karl and Friedrich Engels. *The Communist Manifesto*. General Press, 2019.

Marx, Karl. *Economic & Philosophic Manuscripts of 1844*. Marxists.org, 2000.

Maybee, Julie E. 'Hegel's Dialectics'. In *The Stanford Encyclopedia of Philosophy*, edited by Edward N. Zalta, Winter 2020. Metaphysics Research Lab, Stanford University, 2020. https://plato.stanford.edu/archives/win2020/entries/hegel-dialectics/.

Schneewind, J. B. 'Virtue, Narrative, and Community: MacIntyre and Morality'. *The Journal of Philosophy* 79, no. 11 (1982): 653–63.

Singh, Aakash, Rimina Mohapatra. *Reading Hegel: The Introductions*. re.press, 2008.

CHAPTER 5

Is the Working-Class Alienated?

This chapter assesses the experience of the working-class in reference to alienation to determine if they can be considered as such. It will contend that, if the working-class suffer a loss of these three characteristics, it can be considered as alienated. To highlight these three key areas, one will focus upon the effect that the Knowledge Economy has had on working-class dignity and agency, how our narratives and bonds have been eroded by neoliberalism, and, finally, the way in which structural decline and the changing face of the Labour Party have limited agency and a sense of working-class identity. One includes within these discussions reference to two theories, namely social capital and anomie, and demonstrates how these notions do not fully explain the working-class experience within Britain.

Dignity: Is Working-Class Dignity in Decline?

Meritocracy and the Knowledge Economy

For both Goodhart (2020) and Sandel (2020), a loss of dignity within the working-class can be explained in reference to three interconnected parts, namely the limitation of routes for social mobility, the inflation of credentials, and the de-valuing of non-cognitive roles within society. Taking this first point, both highlight how, in the past, working-class people had more

S. Taylor Hill, *Challenging Alienation in the British Working-Class*, Palgrave Politics of Identity and Citizenship Series,
https://doi.org/10.1007/978-3-031-59250-8_5

opportunity to better themselves whilst remaining rooted within their communities. Indeed, as university education remained uncommon, most working-class people, including the most intelligent workers, remained close to home and took up positions which either were rooted in the trades sector, in shop-floor or administrative work, or within key public services and associations. Most of these roles did not require a university education and were generally seen as 'good jobs' that gave people a decent living and community-derived prestige (Goodhart 2020, 195). The outlook towards these jobs, which are now being de-valued, was one which was not centred on value as derived from how much money one earned but, instead, based upon contribution to the community. What one saw in the past was multiple routes to not only social mobility but dignity, which was built into many jobs and was tied to a stronger sense of community. With the breakdown of community, the closure of workplaces, the cuts to public services, and the destruction of associations, one has seen the decline in prestige associated with those positions (Sandel 2020). Many in the working-class then did lose not only their jobs but also what was attached to them—their community and, with that, their dignity. In their place they saw arise a new 'value' based upon the narrow pursuit of wealth.

Tyranny of Merit

These changes have been accompanied by a cultural shift towards merit and the attainment of credentials, which had been part of society in the past but found itself less pronounced since most people did not go into higher education and were able to live dignified lives, perhaps most within the post-war years (Sandel 2020; Edgerton 2021). However, in the twenty-first century where poorer regions have few suitable jobs, people must almost leave those communities to find employment, usually in large cities such as London, in which well-paying jobs require a bachelor's degree or more (Goodhart 2020, 16). This has narrowed the possibility of social mobility for many people who do not either have the time, resources, or ability to go through university (Sandel 2020). The result of this narrowing has been to create a situation in which a majority do not go to university, whilst a sizeable minority leave their communities for good upon graduating. In both cases there are issues as, within the university group, many must stay on to acquire a Master's degree or higher so that they can 'get ahead', whilst others become under-employed in non-degree work because there is an oversupply of graduates and an undersupply of well-paid middle-class jobs. For those without a degree, these people are immediately labelled as "losers" and have many jobs closed off to them (Goodhart 2020, 93–95).

For Sandel especially, this demonstrates what he calls the "tyranny of merit", which is to make working-class people out to be "failures" deserving of their reduced status if they do not go to university. They deserve this status because they are not seen to possess sufficient knowledge, skill, ambition, nor perhaps work ethic. Having not gone to university, there is also a distinct lack of educational opportunities as the university has, to some extent, become synonymous with education, to the detriment of vocational courses. A degree now confers greater respect than what is an equivalent vocational qualification, whilst qualifications like the City and Guilds carry much less weight than say, a Russell Group University (Goodhart 2020, 242). To make matters worse, not even universities are equal, and one finds that those considered 'lesser' have a higher number of working-class students and alumni (English and Bolton 2015). We thus see a situation where working-class people tend to become even more alienated as, not only are they less likely to attend university in the first instance, but those that 'make it' often find themselves in universities that lack prestige, and consequently suffer in their prospects for social mobility (Reay 2021). This underlines Goodhart's claim that by making university and, more than that, a top 20 university the single route to social mobility, we de-value others and limit their opportunities to acquire prestigious jobs. In this one sees how even a job that is skilled and pays relatively well, like a plumber or electrician, nevertheless lacks the prestige associated with roles which require a degree. What we see here then is not only a situation in which most workers do not have 'trades' and receive poor pay, but that even those who do are not adequately recognised for their skills, in spite of what pay they can obtain for them.

This has a corresponding impact upon the working-class psyche, which Sandel picks up on to suggest that having seen a particular kind of university-derived knowledge pushed to the forefront, those that miss out are made to feel they are worthless than their fellow citizens. Such a sense is borne out by the statistical evidence, as those without a degree are likely to be stuck in so-called unskilled jobs, which offer low pay, poor security, and variable but often poor conditions, with median wages at least £10,000 lower than those with a degree (IFS 2020). This represents, for Sandel (2020), Cruddas (2021), and Goodhart (2020), a clear example of indignity as employers fail to treat their staff with the respect that they deserve, neglect to provide them with security, and are consequently seen to be exploitative and, in Marxian terms, alienating. The failure to ensure 'good work' and the degradation of one's role to that of an 'unskilled' worker underlines such demeaning treatment, whilst a lack of recognition for skilled non-university workers undermines their more sustainable economic position (Bloodworth 2018, 36).

De-Valuation

Related to this is the de-valuation of non-cognitive and lower-cognitive work that has occurred as we have shifted towards the "Knowledge Economy" which has been promoted consistently in the era of globalisation (Blair 2000). It follows from this that there is a premium placed on knowledge and a sense that knowledge is the only factor which can drive progress. However, this is only part of the problem as not even knowledge is a guarantor of dignified status. To some extent, it has become itself trumped by money and material assets (Kromydas 2017). In fact, the measure of success within our community is not the academic, who one would assume to be the ultimate arbiter of knowledge, but the CEO, who is 'successful' because they are rich and have obtained significant power as a result of their topping the 'meritocratic hierarchy', assuming the prestige associated with that (Peters 2020). In this way, knowledge is treated as a means to acquire the levels of wealth and power which define 'success' and therefore finds itself important but instrumentalised as a part of the way that we interpret our social standing and opportunities. Here we see the de-valuation of those who do not have a university degree, alongside a recognition that wealth and power come to usurp knowledge towards the top of the meritocratic hierarchy as markers for success. The result of this is to create a system that is only loosely meritocratic, and knowledge-based, and instead revolves around the acquisition of a combination of wealth and power which is unobtainable for most working-people (Unger 2022). Here, knowledge is a means to rise, but not an end in itself.

Goodhart (2020) questions the value of this perspective. He cites our emotional intelligence and our physical ability, as well as the skills that find themselves most at home within what he calls 'hand' and 'heart' roles. In his view, these skills, and the jobs that they find themselves associated with, are diminished because they do not carry cognitive prestige, do not require university education, and are not associated with wealth. Attempts to improve these jobs too have tended to come in the form of "graduatisation", which refers to the process of turning a job that did not require a degree, such as a nurse, into one that does, with the result being that yet another profession is closed off to non-graduates and prestige further associated with a university education (Goodhart 2020, 214). Again, the working-class suffer most in this instance as their jobs are the least likely to be classed as 'cognitive', whilst many of the old-dignified jobs in our public services become "graduatised" and increasingly inaccessible. In consequence, the range of jobs that confer dignity is becoming narrower, whilst access to these jobs is being increasingly limited by "graduatisation", something that inevitably leaves many people structurally locked out of those roles which could have brought them dignity. In other words, we concentrate prestige at the top and make this contingent on financial gain, locking it behind a wall of credentials whilst leaving little for others to find dignity in. Not only then are many jobs becoming "alienating" but the opportunities to escape those jobs are disappearing. Such a phenomenon lays bare the hardships that the working-class face and exemplifies the daily indignities that many suffer. In fact, Goodhart details declining autonomy and responsibility in many of these now lower-status occupations. Not only is the worker faced with poor wages, but their work is increasingly micromanaged and the individual worker's voice lost, especially in non-unionised workplaces. This contributes to alienation in the classical Marxian sense as workers are increasingly likely to hold jobs in which they have no say in how their work is organised, up from 42% of jobs to 57% between 2005 and 2015 (Goodhart 2020; Bloodworth 2018). The result of this is to limit self-expression, motivation, and self-determination as workers become replaceable since all they bring to a job is their routinised labour. According to Goodhart (2020, 194–196) and Evans and Tilley (2017) such workers are literally de-valued and made to think that their work is merely a 'job'. For many, work has lost its emotional impetus and the purpose that we derive from it. As routinisation and de-valuation occur, we see a shift in the mental well-being of non-cognitive workers, whereby they are unlikely to believe that their work helps others or is of use to society.

Capitalist Culture

The relationship between values, dignity, and the neoliberal Knowledge Economy is significant. It is worth noting that many of these issues, alienation in the Marxian sense, loss of dignity, and a social mobility rooted in wealth, arguably stem from the internalisation of a capitalistic-neoliberal culture which places value upon those things that bring the greatest financial and material rewards rather than what they do for society (Tawney 1931; Cruddas 2021). In fact, this would explain why care and other work is so de-valued, since it does not translate into a measurable profit/loss and is therefore difficult to value when placed within a wealth-orientated framework. The search for profit in care also has significant implications for the lives of workers in the sector, who are increasingly pushed harder, with fewer resources, to care for more patients, which inevitably results in declining standards, de-sensitivity, and other negative effects that are associated with transforming care into an enterprise rather than a social good. Sandel (2012) stresses that we have become too focused upon market value as defining wider social value. We lose clarity in doing this and forget that these issues are ones that we have created for ourselves by fetishising structures that do not promote flourishing, disseminating morally damaging ideals whilst clouding our ability to identify human needs (Tawney 1931; Sandel 2020). This view is supported by Cruddas, who tracks the decline of the "dignity of labour" as marketisation occurs and reveals a corresponding breakdown in social goods, solidarity, and security within the working-class (Cruddas 2021). Subsequently, dignity is undermined by our economic system, which has a corrosive impact on our values, our sense of self-worth, as well as the value of 'good work'. This will find its expression through the British Idealists[1] and Socialists later within the book and will lead one to question the value of an economy which demoralises us and makes those who have 'succeeded' feel justified in their privilege. Against this, one will establish a common good rooted in purposeful dignity supported by communal bonds and responsibilities that help to promote flourishing between and across class.

Why Does This Constitute Alienation?

There are those that may identify that some working-people do not define themselves as being alienated and may dismiss the diagnosis on this basis. However, one sees no alternative when we consider the lives that many working-class people are forced to live and the lack of recognition that

[1] British Idealism is a broad category so note that when the book refers to the Idealists it is in reference to those focused upon here and makes no claims that are universal across all those within the tradition.

they receive. This is as much a social condition for the working-class as it is an individual condition. Indeed, there is little doubt that dignity has been degraded for working-people and the unemployed working-class for that matter, and, given their treatment, we should be surprised that more people do not recognise their existence as alienating. We can explore this situation further in relation to unemployment and working-class attitudes to it.

There is a growing sense, identified by Bloodworth (2018), that some people no longer tend to seek employment because the jobs available to them are degrading. In fact, even if one is proud of their work, it is nevertheless deeply frustrating to realise that others within our society do not value the good that one does. This, coupled with the implication in many companies that one is a resource, afforded minimum wage, and few contracted hours per week to minimise entitlements, leads one to consider that it should really come as no surprise that some people are unwilling to put themselves through this (TUC 2020). As Bloodworth and Cruddas (2021) suggest, some of these unemployed people recognise their alienation explicitly and the lack of 'good work' as a key contributor to it.

They would rather live on the breadline with their dignity than engage in work that degrades them (Bloodworth 2018; McKenzie 2015). However, this represents a minority of people. For the majority, work is better than being unemployed. Whilst this stance certainly has some resonance and can be understood in the context of the class habitus and the limited income which the welfare state currently offers, the bar is set so low to consider that having work makes up for the indignity that one must suffer within it (Wilson 2021). It is a way of justifying the world that is borne from some degree of alienation—to think oneself as privileged to have work that can be degrading and to resonate with it to give meaning to one's life. This is a meaning born out of powerlessness to control one's circumstances—taking solace in those small things that we can cling on to despite one's exploitation (Umney 2018). The work itself may be important, but the structures within the workplace, the status that it confers, and the sense of having been wronged, present even when one takes pride in their role, can take a considerable toll on the psyche of the worker to the point that, when pay stagnates, when hours are cut, or when higher-ups impose themselves, one sees that as part of work (Bloodworth 2018). This is *perhaps* the most widespread example of alienation as many working-class people experience it and yet have suffered these circumstances for so long that it has become normalised (McKenzie 2015). This reflects an awareness that one can be alienated and yet misrecognise it as 'normal' (Leopold 2022). It is not then that the working-class do not suffer alienation; it is that their outlooks can be shaped by it. We shall come back to this later within the chapter, but we see here how a lack of agency interplays with the problem of dignity to create a nexus of alienation, which in turn becomes a social condition for the class.

Community: Is a Working-Class Sense of Community in Decline?

Structural Decline and Isolation

Goodhart (2020), Eatwell and Goodwin (2018), and Kaufmann (2018) highlight how the working-class sense of community has been diminished in recent years. They point, like McKenzie (2017) and Cruddas (2021), to the structural decline, loss of jobs, and social upheaval felt by the class from the 1980s onwards as one of the underlying causes for the breakdown of community. Cruddas details how the closure of the Ford plant in Dagenham, which had provided many of the jobs available within the local area, had a clear impact on the working-class community in recent years. Indeed, Ford had been a common structure in the lives of many working-people and had, to some extent, bonded people from Dagenham together. They could understand one-another, were likely to be able to relate to each other's issues, and had common points of reference. The unions often kept the company in check and ensured that working-people were, as far as was possible, able to engage in community. Life was certainly not easy, and many working-people did struggle, but a combination of strong unions and communal solidarity ensured that people could interact with one-another, engage in activities, and enjoy considerable participation (Bloodworth 2018). If they could not, then they could at least imagine that others faced the same struggles as them and could attempt change together. They had a community both real and imagined and could rely upon it in their struggles.

However, as this work declined, many people either moved elsewhere or were forced to find new work. The changing face of Dagenham over these years, and the wider structural decline of the industrial sector, the trade union movement, and the closure of many working-people's associations and meeting places, as well as the increase in admission to 'working-class sports' like football, shattered this ideal of community (Cruddas 2021; Bloodworth 2018). For many, now facing increased hardship, and without the structures that had once been available as a source of association and common reference, workers now began to become increasingly separated from their communities. This was a common occurrence across the country. In the North of England, where industry had all but vanished, working-people saw a decline in their motivation and became increasingly likely to suffer from poor mental health, whilst, according to these scholars, they lost a sense of deeper purpose too. Without those key cornerstones of community, and without one-another, working-people therefore became demoralised and were unable to fully navigate their changing circumstances. This is particularly hard to deny, and Evans and Tilley (2017), as well as Eatwell and Goodwin (2018, 40), reveal that the working-class recognise their bonds as having declined significantly, to the point where their communities are considered "unrecognisable". Thus, the working-class have been left comparatively isolated from community, both structurally due to the decline of their associations and in narrative terms.

Culture Crisis

This decline is further exacerbated by cultural tensions. A number of these working-class respondents, mostly white and older, cite the changing demographics of their localities as a key source of crisis. This is a point to which Kaufmann speaks, although not unproblematically. Indeed, he notes how community has declined as diversity has increased. There are various reasons for this that are cited by scholars from across the political spectrum. For the purposes of this chapter, we shall consider the problem of (1) intra-class hostility and the role of (2) structural and narrative decline in facilitating community loss.

Intra-Class Hostility

Kaufmann (2018) and Goodhart (2020) point to an influx of migrants into traditionally working-class areas accompanied by a sense of 'loss'. It has been accompanied by this as minority groups have, according to Goodhart, tended to begin re-shaping communities to better reflect their new-found diversity. For the working-class people already there, having suffered the decline of their communities because of structural loss, now feel such loss compounded by cultural and ethnodemographic changes. The fears that arise out of this is said by Kaufmann (2018) to reinforce negative stereotyping and to exacerbate the feeling of community loss because relations degenerate either into segregation or into resentfulness. The means to ameliorate such hostility between the existing working-class population and the new population, which is likely to be working-class in economic terms, is virtually non-existent too, again owing to structural decline. This lends weight to the notion of being left behind, connecting with narratives already present within our society that resonate with many, typically white working-class people who feel that 'their' leaders prioritise so-called minority concerns and identity politics, to the detriment of their issues, which find expression through a racial-class lens (Goodhart 2020; Virdee 2014). In this way, the white working-class struggle to navigate the landscape of cultural change and find it especially difficult to re-integrate themselves into a narrative of progress since their daily experience of life is alienating. They believe genuinely that they are ignored by government and left without a community to rely upon.

It is worth noting briefly too the media's role in perpetuating these divisions. Indeed, Stocker (2017,75) highlights how the tabloid press, notably popular newspapers like the *Daily Express* and *The Sun*, popularised a narrative in which Britain's white working-class were losing out to, particularly, migrants, minorities, and their families. Between January 2000 and January 2006, *The Sun*, *Daily Mail*, and *Daily Express* had published some 8163 articles supporting such claims, whilst simultaneously urging the government to adopt a series of hardline policies to "Stop the Asylum Madness" and prevent "Asylum Seekers spreading AIDS around Britain", erstwhile framed in such a way as to suggest that it was normal working-people who were suffering from this "epidemic". The impact of such persistent rhetoric cannot be understated. In fact, by 2006 the British public believed that the country took in 23% of the world's asylum seekers and that minorities made up some 26% of the population. The actual figures were under 2% and 7%, respectively, whilst the claims made by these newspapers were consistently found to be false, according to a later UN report (Stocker 2017, 75–76). However, they perpetuated a misinformed narrative in which the government was seen to be prioritising minority groups and foreign nationals at the expense of, in particular, the white working-class, who are most likely to suffer from structural and other degradations. According to Stocker (2017), the popularisation of such divisive narratives contributed significantly to community decline by fostering mistrust between majority white and minority citizens and, on occasion, precipitated violence, whilst immigration policy became yet another area in which the government were 'betraying' the white working-class—a whole sub-group in the wider class that had repeatedly been told that their livelihoods were declining because of said migration and who continued to believe so in the lead up to Brexit (Kaufmann 2018).

Alienation is, therefore, related to community loss here as the white working-class felt that they could not assert their claims for recognition, whilst the circumstances and old forms of association have been left to crumble and have been replaced by 'foreign' ones that they cannot engage with, and people who they struggle to form communities with (Kaufmann 2018, 410). For Kaufmann then, the loss of community encourages a belief that, as a white working-class individual, one is being ignored by government in favour of people who are perceived not to be citizens, whilst influxes of new groups into an area exacerbate feelings of loss and fill people with a fear that they will suffer further damage to their dignity through community-cultural breakdown. Although many of the underlying causes and explanations for such feelings can be understood as misinformed, as Stocker (2017) details, the anger and hostility that they bred cannot be understated. Indeed, although misdirected, such anger reflects a reality in which the working-class have lost the communities that had sustained them and face circumstances and situations which are undignifying. Here we see an intersection between two characteristics of alienation.

Culture, Structure, and Identity Politics

Thus, culture is seen as an issue by many, typically white working-class people, who, having already suffered one structural loss, now perceive themselves to be suffering another cultural one. However, this problem is perhaps misunderstood and is a continued outcome of structural loss which Cruddas (2021) recognises as being exacerbated by the Labour Party during its time in government. He cites how the changing priority of identity politics is important within this story. In fact, the search for equality is something that has long been part of the Labour and working-class tradition in some form, and despite some tension (Virdee 2014). Historically, it has been the party which has passed the Race Relations Acts, created the Commission for Racial Equality, decriminalised homosexuality, and, through groups like the Labour Black Sections and LGBT+ Labour Group, created space for the consideration of minority working-class concerns, carrying out these actions whilst maintaining a commitment to other working-class issues (Sivanandan 2019). However, Cruddas highlights how the Labour Party, after its defeats in the 1980s, lost sight of these wider concerns and its mission to uphold the dignity of work and became more focused on ensuring minority rights were extended and upheld. This turn found support from the young, socially progressive, and minority groups, but it lost the support of other working-class subgroups because it appeared that 'universal' working-people's issues were being ignored in favour of minorities. This was to breed support for groups like the BNP, and later the UKIP and Brexit parties, and drove a wedge between those who might otherwise have been recognised as fellow workers with overlapping concerns (Eatwell and Goodwin 2018; Cruddas 2021; Kaufmann 2018).[2] The growth of identity politics at the same time as a structural decline of working-class communities thus created a *perception* of favouritism. The consequences of this have been considerable. It has contributed to the rise of right-wing populism, as well as serving as 'evidence' for those who seek to fight social progress through the 'war on woke', with some socially conservative and disgruntled working-class voters throwing their lot in with these groups (Sobolewska and Ford 2020). The rise of this discourse has been to diminish class-solidarity and to further tear apart communities, dividing them increasingly based on race/ethnicity, whilst serving to alienate from one-another all involved (McKenzie 2017). The left has, therefore, inadvertently contributed to what Eatwell and Goodwin call a "politics of resentment" which now exacerbates social division and community breakdown, threatens hard-won rights, and leaves working-class suffering left unanswered and distorted by racialisation (Eatwell and Goodwin 2018).

The class here becomes alienated from itself and loses its corresponding ability to shape British society or address issues which harm its members.

One sees in this analysis a significant decline in the old structures which enabled people to develop a sense of community, as well as the fallout from this. Such structural decline has now been matched with a growing hostility, caused by a sense of deep loss on behalf of many white working-class people, which further exacerbates the problem of community

[2] Further to this, Eatwell and Goodwin (2018) suggest that this trend took place across the West as social democratic parties moved towards a social liberalism which was to be matched by economic neoliberalism. In this sense, the actions of the Labour Party during this time were matched by their fellows on the continent with similar results.

breakdown. The working-class suffer most in this as minority and majority peoples struggle to see each other as equals, grow distrustful of one-another, and consequently find it difficult to build community anew. These challenges worsen alienation and undermine a cohesive sense of working-class-ness, which in turn makes it harder to exert collective agency.

Disconnection from a National Narrative

This disconnection is also prevalent within our national politics and the stories that we tell to make sense of our lives. Cruddas (2021) and Sandel (2012, 2020) highlight the importance of a cohesive narrative that includes and enables people to see themselves as living in-common. This has traditionally been achieved among the working-class in reference to patriotism, which resonates with working-people to the extent that most of the ~70% of people who describe themselves as such also consider themselves to be working-class, including most minority peoples within Britain (More in Common 2020). However, at present there is a distinct lack of vision for working-people to buy into. For example, Cruddas (2021) and McKenzie (2017) point to their conversations with working-people and the moral issues that are included when they air their concerns. They cite discussions surrounding concepts such as "fairness", "justice", "equality", and "solidarity" and complain that they do not see this reflected within our politics, which they suggest has lost its ability to inspire. Sandel (2020) speaks to this. He tracks how our moral discourse has changed over time and demonstrates how the "big questions" of morality, injustice, and inequality, essentially those challenges which people face on a daily basis and which used to galvanise people into action, have been replaced by a sterile "rhetoric of rising" in which politicians now speak of encouraging "opportunity" which, in itself, lacks any meaning and is reflective of the societal shift towards the individualised Knowledge Economy (Sandel 2020). Indeed, he cites how, in the United States, Obama shifted from a moral rhetoric, which had been popular and had inspired a great deal of "hope", to one of improving "opportunity". In fact, over the course of his Presidency he uttered the phrase "[Y]ou can make it if you try" over 140 times, despite the fact that many people, just as in this country, could not "make it" (Sandel 2020). In a society dominated by market norms, and success associated with wealth, it should perhaps come as no surprise that working-people do not believe this narrative and decry the loss of a common struggle. Obama, on reflection, recognises this, saying, "I'd failed to tell the American people a story they could believe in", with Sandel adding that "people are hungry for a public discourse that addresses big questions about … what makes for a just society. What we owe one another as citizens" (Obama 2020; Sandel 2020). This has significance for Britain too. Many working-class people are dissatisfied with the lack of direction for our country. We often see vague platitudes about making Britain "great" or "world beating" but nothing sustained and no clear vision for the future that makes sense to people or that they can identify with (Rutter 2020). The working-class are alienated here because they are unable to imagine themselves to belong to something *more*. Where, in previous decades, the working-class had means of meaning-creation owing to the structures of the associations, the unions, and a Labour Party with some links to an ethical socialist core or, at least, a clear enough vision for a future Britain, they now lack each of these things, without which it becomes significantly harder to find one's place or to see themselves in common.

Populist-Nationalism

This is partly why we have seen a surge in support for populist groups, and causes like Brexit, because they have offered something that appears different to politics as usual. There has been talk of greatness in which Britain was to reach new heights free of the shackles of Europe. One understands why some might buy into this as it looks beyond the market norms that degrade them. Unfortunately, this narrative, which one labels as populist-nationalist, is likely to enhance alienation. Indeed, the national narrative popularised by government is exclusive and divisive. It actively promotes "culture wars". For example, in advocating for the protection of statues celebrating, for the most part, people that most Britons had probably never heard of, nor would have likely agreed with (Beckett 2020). However, the reaction has been significant. The statues debate elicited these same feelings of cultural loss, as well as a heated reaction from many minority peoples, and others who do not want statues of slave traders glorified in their country (Policy Exchange 2023). Such examples underline the narrative issue. The vitriolic rhetoric of government, as well as the inability of the left to offer some alternative, is likely to tear at the working-class and widen already-deep divisions. The present national narrative, whilst appealing to some, is therefore alienating for many working-people, because it either contributes to social discord or leaves them unrecognised.

In fact, one sees minority working-class people pushed to the margins of society and denied a place within such a narrative. They are robbed of the prestige associated with belonging and hindered from obtaining a wider purpose. One highlights this because the literature tends to revolve around the white working-class, or a generalised working-class, rather than minority peoples. In fact, minority workers have long suffered from a lack of recognition as constituent members of the British nation, whilst the working-class nature of many of these peoples has been highlighted by Stuart Hall to often worsen their situation, leading to ostracism or, alternatively, where good has been done by minority groups, either their non-recognition or a recognition which takes no account of race. As Akala (2019) argues in relation to the 'Black' community, when one does something worthy of praise, they are no longer 'black' or 'black-British', they are just British. For Hall and Akala, this is a case of misrecognition because being, in this case, black working-class and being British are fundamentally interlinked parts of one's identity that define their existence. Indeed, Hall notes that race and class are both concepts which involved the erection of "those systems of meaning, concepts, categories and representations which make sense of the world, and through which individuals come to 'live' … in an imaginary way, their relation to the real, material conditions of their existence" (Hall 1980, 334). It is, therefore, important to consider them as they provide a narrative framing for one's life, much like community, which makes sense of the context in which we live. Our narratives should connect and resonate with different aspects of people's identities, either by referencing them deliberately or by giving space for people to bring their identities into the context of community—to recognise every reasonable citizen.

This is not the case for the working-class today, perhaps especially for those who are minorities. In many respects they have not been recognised or been given sufficient space to be so. Although efforts have been made to facilitate equal rights, and to undermine discrimination in law, minority peoples do not see those aspects of their identity recognised on an institutional or narrative level. Indeed, we do not see, for example, the contribution of British-Caribbeans to the re-building of Britain after the Second World War, nor their disproportionate role in ensuring the success of our NHS, praised (Kramer 2006). There are numerous historical examples of minority groups contributing to the development of the British nation, and yet they are often left out of our narratives.[3] One cannot build community by denying groups a place within it, and this becomes a class issue when we consider that many of these people are working-class and have experienced their class through their race. Most British-Caribbean citizens are employed in working-class jobs, face the same problems as their counterparts, and are often not fully appreciated as members of their class, nor within wider British society (ONS 2020). We see here evidence of exclusion from community as minority groups are unable to see their histories, and their contributions, reflected in the stories that we tell about Britain. This represents alienation from community if one cannot begin to see themselves as belonging within something more eternal than themselves, see their struggles and their contributions go unnoticed, nor be appreciated by the national community. In this instance, a lack of recognition for one's role in shaping our community is demonstrative of alienation from it.

Why Does Community Decline Mean Alienation?

Questions of community breakdown have recently been understood in relation to Social Capital Theory. This theory, developed by Robert Putnam (2001), claims to measure interactions between people and develop structures to promote communication. It analyses tangible resources like private property, alongside intangibles like human capital, and assumes that community breakdown can be reversed primarily by encouraging interaction (Häuberer 2010). One accepts this premise to some extent and sees value in addressing structural issues which hamper community. However, this is insufficient because the theory does not understand 'community' in a deeper sense. The point is to measure forms of capital with the assumption that more capital for more people will create a 'better' community. It is then unclear what it means by community other than it being a physical entity and a network of interactions in which people exchange resources. For this reason, it often appears overly individualistic, rational, and reductionist in the sense that *community* becomes but the sum of its parts. Indeed, social capital is reflective of the detached marketisation that is now prevalent throughout our society. Many of its scholars, Putnam included, focus upon a transaction of resources, and hold that it is desirable, and community is desirable, because it enables

[3] In a poll conducted by ICM (2021), when asked to name a person who had contributed much to British history, only 1% named a non-white person.

individuals to use those resources for their own gain (Castiglione 2008). It does recognise the community's role in establishing norms, and encouraging interaction, but the way that scholars of social capital portray this is without some sense of the ends which it looks towards. Community is taken to exist, and is beneficial for individuals, but it is not much more than that. It becomes a hollow term that refers to a stable network of transactional relationships built upon shared norms. There is a lack of appreciation for anything more than that. Here, community is instrumentalised.

This logic fails to appreciate community's value on a deeper level. It does not give due to *the community* as anything *more*, nor appreciates its potential as the spiritual embodiment of 'us'. What one is suggesting is more Marxian and Hegelian, a sense that we must be respectful of community because it is something that creates meaning, and which we should be able to connect to give our lives purpose. Community in-itself is not about getting ahead; it is about meaning-creation and connectivity in the realisation of flourishing (Hegel 2018). It is born out of moral questions and grand narratives of the good, or the nation. This is important because many working-class people, although practical, are also idealistic and desire a community predicated on notions of fairness, justice, or solidarity, amongst other things. Indeed, in the 2021 Hartlepool by-election, many working-class people complained that the Labour Party "don't have a vision" and offered nothing to the restoration of community (Armstrong 2021). Working-people want this and to be able to find a place within it. They want a way of understanding their daily lives in the context of something *more*.

We have noted how Boris Johnson's Conservatives did this around Brexit to some extent, but this neglects the building of community in terms of its infrastructure, whilst its narrative is one that has increased division thanks to its "culture wars" rhetoric. This is not a healthy basis for the reconstitution of community, and one in which the narrative, whilst appealing to some, is likely to spread further dissent and damage that sense of community that many so desire. This reflects an issue that structure alone cannot solve, and which social capital is ill-equipped to handle. To re-connect people with community, we must be able to appreciate its value and the associated value of narrative. In many respects, it has the potential to enable us to transcend our mundane realities, inspiring a sense of something greater than ourselves. It is this spiritual nature of community that bonds people as much as our relationships.

This has a structural component, and one accepts that social capital has value in this regard, but it is not enough alone because it lacks an understanding of community and the emotive connectedness that can be so powerful in challenging alienation. We may borrow from it practically, yet there is a need to create narratives that connect with people, enable them to make sense of their experiences, and imagine themselves to be part of something greater. The problems facing the working-class can, therefore, be understood as a case of alienation from community. Social Capital Theory might partially acknowledge this, but it cannot explain how important community itself and narratives which are tied to it are and is therefore insufficient in diagnosing the issues faced by the working-class. This book therefore errs from social capital by recognising a Marxian-Hegelian notion of community which is inherent in many working-class discussions and cannot be built upon a structural basis alone.

Agency: Is Working-Class Agency in Decline?

To answer this, one understands agency in two ways, as Representative and Personal. The first of these can be defined in relation to the question of *who shapes X*? Representative agency would be a case in which one sees someone else shape something that is reflective of them. It can take account of the person's views, but it is also somewhat distant, like a political party. The second form can be regarded as the direct impact that an individual can have on a particular process or 'thing'. Personal agency has a structural component to it, like a vote, inclusion in a process, as well as an ability to act. The distinction between these two forms of agency is not necessarily hard, but one uses it to outline the case for agential decline.

Using this, one will note how the Labour Party's ability to communicate with and represent the views of many working-class people has decayed in recent years, alongside a similar decline in the structures which gave working-class people agency and security. One will also reference how the Conservative Party has provided a degree of representative agency for the socially conservative working-class but has done little for them in personal-agential terms, at the same time as limiting both agencies for other working-class sub-groups. The reader should also keep in mind how the Conservative Party has achieved this through methods which harm community. Thus, although many working-people have bought-in to the populism of the Conservative Party, one does not see it as a positive development in the amelioration of alienation.

Structural Change

Before we consider working-class agency at present, it is worth noting the structural changes that have affected it over time. One highlights three phases which are as follows:

1. The post-war social democratic state and effective social mobility.
2. The breakdown of the post-war consensus and the rise of neoliberal globalisation.
3. Neoliberalism and the age of austerity.

Phase 1

The post-war era, up to the 1980s, was characterised by a situation in which the working-class shrank as a result of rising social mobility, but which was matched with improvement in their livelihoods nonetheless (Evans and Tilley 2017). The 1960s saw expanded access to university education, as well as vocational courses, which paved the way for entry into the middle class. At the same time, working conditions, pay, and prestige were enhanced in the factories and other 'working-class' sectors of the economy. This, matched with a relatively new National Health Service, a massive expansion of Council Housing, and the wider strengthening of the welfare state, created a situation in which many working-class people found themselves increasingly better off, because of successful social mobility, tangible improvements within one's work, or the successes of the post-war social democratic consensus. As one has said, this caused the working-class to shrink as more routes opened into those better-paid jobs, and yet one continued to see signs of their betterment, a sense of community, and a dignified place within the nation. Social mobility can, in the post-war era, be regarded as a success. People moved from the working-class into a series of jobs which were more likely to fulfil their interests or goals (Cruddas 2021). The negative consequences of this were blunted by improving working conditions, and working-class jobs brought dignity to those who were in them. They felt the double edge of social mobility less so, felt valued, and had the means to effect further change through their associations. This does not mean that life was easy, but they had a greater sense of dignity, agency, and community needed to live a fulfilling life, and which this book sees as lacking in contemporary society.

However, it is worth noting that this period of increased mobility also set in motion the structural change of the working-class, in which its numerical decline would eventually mean that the Labour Party would have to shift its focus towards the capture of the growing middle-class vote (Sobolweska and Ford 2020).

Phase 2

The election of Margaret Thatcher in 1979 ushered in a new era of neoliberalism with her adherence to minimal-state market fundamentalism, the privatisation of government assets, globalisation, and anti-unionism. The results of this are familiar. Working-class improvements halted as they lost their livelihoods in industry, because of either globalisation's outsourcing to cheaper markets or government's sale of assets, whilst their associations were defeated electorally and physically through the passing of restrictive legislation (Bloodworth 2018; Goodhart 2020). The class entered a period of decline, witnessing the degradation of their work and communities, the rampant growth of inequality, as well as the further shrinkage of their class into a new emerging precariat—apathetic and unstable (Standing 2019). This, coupled with the Labour Party's struggles throughout the 1980s, led to the emergence of New Labour and a further courting of the middle-class vote. The significance of this phase was the rolling back of working-class improvements and institutions, the victory of neoliberal market norms, and the demographic shrinkage of the traditional working-class.

Phase 3

The adoption and further entrenchment of Thatcherite market norms under Tony Blair's New Labour contributed somewhat to the 2007/2008 Banking Crisis and the subsequent period of austerity that followed. This caused social mobility and wages to stagnate for the longest period on record and has seen the narrowing of routes to mobility and the further concentration of 'good work' at the top of this hierarchy (Bloodworth 2018: Sandel 2020). This has a knock-on effect lower down the economic hierarchy as 'good work' has declined to a point in which the younger middle-class find themselves increasingly struggling, as working-people slip into the burgeoning gig economy, thus losing more prestige and security. This is further underlined by the breakdown of the welfare state, thanks in part to government cuts, which now does little to assist in any meaningful way (Evans and Tilley 2017). We now see a reverse of the situation which existed some 50 years ago, and the development of economic and structural degradation. This is matched by the loss of organised workers and members of the class, who no longer appear to be numerous enough to mount a collective-class defence. Such a decline highlights the negative consequences of social mobility, as well as the interplay between class shrinkage, increased precarity, and the defunding of the welfare state. This is the backdrop against which the working-class must express themselves.

The Party of the Middle Class and the Problem of Structural Exclusion

Cruddas (2021) speaks of a value-gap between what has become a middle-class-dominated parliamentary Labour Party and the working-class, and its impact on representative agency. Although perhaps exaggerative in some respects, it is nevertheless worth outlining an otherwise plausible account. He highlights how three successive New Labour governments championed "Education, Education, Education" and social mobility within this new neoliberal Knowledge Economy, which we have already criticised for its tendency to de-value non-cognitive work, to insert market-based value in place of social good, and to create clear winners and losers within our society (Blair 2001). He notes this as being where working-people increasingly lost faith in the party which had long been considered a guardian of their dignity, and a conduit for the shaping of society in their image (Embery 2021; Cruddas 2021; Bloodworth 2018). By turning towards this Knowledge Economy, endorsing university-specific education, and accepting uncritically globalisation and the inequality that came with it, the Labour Party forgot that it was just that: the party of labour born out of the trade union movements and the search for dignity within work. Cruddas points to the growth of working-class alienation as arising out of this shift towards the capture of the middle-class vote and the creation of a society in which there was no clear place for the working-class. They now witnessed 'their' party turn its back on them and fail to stand up for the values which it had once fought to ingrain within the British society.

This is dramatically stated but one must recognise the trauma and change that the working-class, already weakened by the shock of Thatcherism, suffered because of New Labour's policy shift.

Indeed, what Cruddas is arguing is that a key guarantor of working-class dignity, with historical and powerful roots in their communities, ties to the trade unions, and other bodies which had once sought to give voice to, and protect, working-people, had now been seen to shun them. There was no compromise here. New Labour was to embrace neoliberal globalisation and would now actively court the middle-class vote, which would transform the party to the extent that it is now only around 8% working-class in its PLP composition (O'Grady, 2018). Embery (2021) speaks to this in stating that, during the Blair years, blue collar and white collar united in the struggle for social and economic justice—started to fall apart as Labour began to be dominated by the latter, transforming itself into a party of the managerial and professional classes, graduates, and urban liberals.

The party of dignified work became that of technocracy and social mobility. It still sought to help the working-class but not by *listening* to them. Instead, what one saw was a politics emerge in which votes were to be won with 'transactions'. This is reflected in Cruddas' assertion that "votes are the form of exchange, policies the commodities, and elected office the derived profit" (Cruddas 2021, 32). Such a transactional model of politics sought to 'buy' working-class votes which, for many working-people, felt disingenuous. They did not want to be marketised and longed instead to have their voices heard. This was to literally alienate them in Marxian terms, dehumanising them as a commodity. For all the promise of opportunity that came with this marketisation too, the working-class saw little of it. They continued to suffer the effects of globalisation, made worse by a post-New Labour austerity. There seemed to be nothing for them and no one was willing to treat them as constituent members of British society. The impact of this was to further limit the agency of the working-class who, having already lost agency from the restraining of the unions and the breakdown of their communities, now lost its connection to the force which it had viewed as most capable of protecting them. According to Goodwin, this rejection led to a deep-seated political apathy and resentment that would later be unleashed by Brexit (Goodwin 2021; Evans and Tilley 2017, 186).

Assessing the Narrative of Structural Exclusion

Although this argument is made by Cruddas with the addition of examples from his own Dagenham constituency, it is worth considering empirical evidence to underline this narrative. Evans and Tilley (2017) confirm a working-class dissatisfaction with Labour by pointing to the dramatic rise in working-class voter apathy or, to state it in stronger terms, disaffection during New Labour's period in government, as workers lost faith in the party, and politics more generally. According to Evans and Tilley (2017) 23% of those voters who had voted for Labour in 1997 did not vote in the 2001 General Election at all, which is a trend that they see as broadly continuing over time. Heath (2018) too identifies 2001 as a turning point in working-class voter apathy as, previous to this election, it was typical to witness a working-class voter turnout rate which was within 5 percentage points of their middle-class counterparts. However, by 2010, this had become a near 20% gap in turnout between the working- and middle classes, with Heath (2018, 1997) drawing a correlation between the number of Labour candidates from a working-class background and turnout, seeing that the decreasing number of candidates from such backgrounds has increased the likelihood of non-voting, to a point that many working-people do not vote, whilst others no longer vote Labour. In fact, from 1997 to 2010, the percentage of the working-class that voted for Labour fell from 55% to 34%, declining further in 2015 before a small rebound in 2017, which was later wiped out with the decisive Conservative victory in 2019 (IPSOS MORI 1997, 2023a, 2023b, 2023c, 2023d).

This is the context in which we see the decline of the Labour Party's ability to connect with the working-class to the point where only 15% of working-people feel that the party is "close" to them, a considerable decline from even 2010 where 64% of people would have suggested that Labour predominantly stood for working-people (YouGov 2023; Ford and Sobolewska 2020). This part of Cruddas', as well as Kaufmann and Goodhart's, analysis is effectively self-evident. However, this does not necessarily demonstrate wider alienation, and although an argument could be made for increasing levels of apathy being indicative of such, these statistics largely suggest a dissatisfaction with the Labour Party alone. What is needed is a further exploration of the *why* question.

Social mobility statistics indicate dissatisfaction with the direction of society both under New Labour and under successive Conservative governments and reveal a working-class that does, as Cruddas (2021) points out, feel left behind within society. About 86% of working-people see class as the fundamental determiner of opportunity, rather than factors like merit, and see that the 'opportunity' of social mobility has largely meant nothing for them. Their belief that they are left out, and that social mobility has failed, is underlined by deepening structural inequalities as working-class people now earn 17% less on average than those in the middle-class and are significantly less likely to be able to access quality education, nor jobs with any serious chance of progression. Furthermore, since the 1980s, children who grew up in poverty are four times more likely to be stuck in poverty as an adult than children in the 1970s. In fact, child poverty, which fell somewhat under New Labour but still hovered at around 3.5m, is predicted to hit 5.2m by late 2022—meaning that one in three British children are likely to be in poverty and over half of all working-class children, with this being particularly harmful for its British-Pakistani and Bangladeshi sub-groups. This, like many working-class issues, has not sufficiently been addressed by any government. Indeed, the 3% increase in the pay of the poorest workers in the past two decades under both parties' governments has not been enough to reverse the dramatic fall in living standards.

The reality of this for working-class people is significant (Social Mobility Commission 2020). In contemporary Britain many now suffer not only the effects of precarity but there is also a sense that they are being exploited in those jobs which are accessible to them. One such example is a recent study into workers for Amazon, one of the UK's larger employers, which found that over 80% felt that their conditions constituted exploitation. This research by the TUC also detailed complaints against the employer for abuse of contract, safety violations, surveillance, and other actions detrimental to well-being (TUC 2020). Under these circumstances, it is no wonder that only 29% of working-people feel that their job provides them with security (Cruddas 2021). These poor conditions show the increasing precarity of the working-class across its sub-groups in this globalised world and indicate that they really have found themselves unable to alter their new-found position. Their concerns are under-represented, whilst their personal agency is hampered by structural insecurity and exclusion.

The psychological and physical impact of this can be summarised through personal accounts. McKenzie (2017, 274) recounts how these effects have led to the same conclusions from working-people across Britain, from London to small mining villages in Nottinghamshire. Namely, she notes how many of her working-class respondents were convinced that government wanted to "get rid of" them. They were perceived not to be listening to them, looked down upon them, and did not appear to have any "grasp or awareness in acknowledging the working-class experience" (McKenzie 2017, 268). There is a sense in McKenzie's work that working-class people genuinely believe that government, and the Labour Party, has ignored them and has pursued policies that do not take account of their experiences. This is an issue which is raised by numerous working-class people, with one saying that Labour "are for public servants, the middle class, people on benefits. But if you are a working-class person, in a normal job, they just don't seem to care" (Armstrong 2021).[4] It is then accurate for Cruddas to highlight the growth in distance between the Labour Party, the government, and the working-class. McKenzie (2017, 270) supports Cruddas' additional claim that this distance has created trauma within working-class communities. She notes that many of her respondents have concluded that "the Labour Party, that they thought once was supposed to represent working-class people had failed".[5] This is echoed by Labour MP for Rotherham, John Healey, who states that they "feel Labour left them before they left Labour" and suggests that "those who feel let down by Labour describe at best an unwillingness to listen, with no respect for their experience, and at worst a rejection of their views" (Healey 2021).[6] For them, the failure of "their" party and their abandonment simply underlined their new reality. In McKenzie's words this loss has become "the ultimate source of anguish for the people in these communities that had long histories of being part of the Labour movement" (McKenzie 2017, 277).

These works demonstrate the structural inequalities and psychological impacts that pervade the working-class experience. They indicate that the class is not only feeling left behind but is left behind in objective terms too. These structures persisted under New Labour, which did nothing to change the fundamental circumstances of the working-class, give them a voice, nor repeal the Thatcher-era union laws which had severely limited working-class personal and representative agency. This failure and an acceptance of what had gone before was masked by increased public

[4] As noted in Chap. 4, Standing (2016) considers welfare claimants as part of the precariat, yet it is relevant to point to an element of sub-group conflict here and the potential for misdirected anger towards ones' fellows within class.

[5] Sobolewska and Ford (2020, 129) note this as being a historic reason for the party's formation and note the party's origins as a working-class movement as contributing to the 'shock' of this loss.

[6] Though one does recognise that Labour was forced to develop an electoral strategy which was capable of winning control of Parliament, so it is reasonable to have seen some compromises being made in its policy direction, though perhaps not to the extent we have seen.

spending, but the failure to create structures for the expression of agency, coupled with the distancing of the Labour Party from the working-class, was just as significant. This changing position has a deep psychological impact upon the class, and the policies which the party pursued were to further underline the loss experienced within working-class communities. It demonstrated to many that the party, which had long been a vehicle for change, was now a distant group of elites that appeared to care little for the working-class' experience. Consequently, the empirical data confirms Cruddas' argument. Whilst transactional politics delivered some benefits to the working-class, it did little to change the structures which limited their agency. The New Labour government became considerably unpopular over the course of its 13 years in government and alienated further the working-class by taking society in a direction that they did not desire, and which did not afford them a place within it, nor any means to voice their dissent. The examples given of the past two decades lay bare the loss of agency which had occurred within the class, the role that the Labour Party—'their party'—has played in that, and the debilitating disassociation between the subject (the worker) and the object (the shape of our society) which has occurred as Britain has transformed into a globalised Knowledge Economy.

Why Alienation?

Agency is significant here and demonstrates the importance of viewing this cause of working-class degradation as an example of alienation, rather than anomie. Whilst one accepts that anomie can well be part of alienation, and that some working-people experience it on an individual level, to cite anomie as the main explanation for working-class degradation is to neglect the importance of structure in fostering realities of powerlessness.

Anomie suggests that people become listless when the dominant norms within a society breakdown and that people are no longer able to find purpose or understand what is expected of them (Charlesworth 2000, 5). One would suggest that this does not apply to the working-class because their norms have never been wholly dominant throughout society, though they did jostle for control in those post-war years (Edgerton 2021). Wider societal expectations and norms may well have changed as we move into a globalised Knowledge Economy, but it is not accurate to suggest that the norms of the working-class have changed. Rather, a more accurate explanation might be that the working-class have largely maintained their norms and are conscious of what they seek to see society value, and yet are now in a situation which they had not been in within living memory (Kirkwood 2020). Namely, they now have few means to articulate themselves, and few structures which can give them a voice (1) because the unions are in decay (Bloodworth 2018; Cruddas 2021) and (2) because many see the Labour Party as having betrayed them, either in reference to its New Labour re-branding or, in recent years, over issues such as Brexit (McKenzie 2017; Goodwin 2021). The working-class are painfully aware of what is expected of them, and what the dominant norms are, in our society. This is reflected in much of their personal accounts. They can track these changes, and the shape of their expectations, and yet they often disagree with the state of Britain as it is. The working-class does not fully accept these new norms, and yet for the most part has abided by 'the rules' and does its best to find meaning within this new structure. They are not delinquents, and the class maintains some sense of what it had been. In other words, it has not fully individualised, and individuals within it have not resorted to those activities which Durkheim (2018) suggests is characteristic of anomie. The class has, in the past 20 years or so, tended to be dragged along with society, without a means to challenge it. This represents a structural issue, and one which alienation is more appropriate in describing. In many respects, the working-class are angry and, though they accept a great deal of harm, they do this because they have lost an objective ability to change things. They are conscious of the gap between what they would like to do and what they are made capable of doing, and consequently become alienated because they are often aware that something is wrong and yet feel forced to accept it.

Conclusion: The Case for Working-Class Alienation

This chapter has sought to demonstrate that, when measured against the three characteristics of alienation, namely dignity, community, and agency, we have seen a significant decline in the working-class' ability to relate to each in a positive sense.

Dignity

The rise of the Knowledge Economy has brought about a significant shift in our values, and what we consider to be reflective of the good. Sandel, Goodhart, and Bloodworth note that the transformation of our economy has left the working-class degraded as they see value and success associated increasingly with wealth and cognitive ability, rather than that which they had understood their work in relation to, namely a sense of the good. This has limited the prestige associated with traditionally working-class jobs and, coupled with what Sandel calls the "Tyranny of Merit", has left them firmly at the bottom of our society in terms of their security, wealth, and dignity. The psychological and structural impact of this is significant and should not be understated. The working-class, through their treatment and conditions, are made to feel as if they are "losers" and internalise some sense of this. They suffer the negative consequences of the graduatisation and the routinisation of their work. The result of this is that many can no longer find prestigious work, no matter how hard they work or how good they are at their work; it lacks prestige and is not respected, whilst many of the jobs that are available to them cannot be described as examples of 'good work'. These jobs are, in plain Marxian terms, alienating. The treatment of the worker is often demeaning, with their creativity and independence increasingly limited, overseen, and micromanaged by supervisors. The prevalence of minimum hours' contracts pervades the working-class experience and offers little security. In consequence, many working-class people see their work as exploitative and no longer feel secure or attached to their work. It is difficult to find dignity in their workplace existence, which is then to further undermine their sense of dignity in one's contribution to community, as work no longer reflects social good, and one's position is firmly at the bottom of a wealth-based hierarchy which does not take note of that good in the first instance.

This raises a wider concern that there is something fundamentally wrong with that economy and, by extension, the society that gave rise to it. If we cannot see one-another as of equal worth and as contributors to our shared community and are willing only to speak of opportunity when confronted with the hardships of the working-class, then there is an ethical disconnect between us. This has negative consequences for community if we cannot recognise the social value inherent in what we do, but it also has significance for the question of dignity as, if we continue to solely focus on improving social mobility, we may not realise that not everyone is likely to 'get on' in this new economy. To this end, one subsequently explores our ability to shift away from this neoliberal economic model focused on wealth towards a kind rooted in the common good.

Community

Community has long been a characteristic of working-class-ness and served historically to generate attachment and meaning, aided in part in reference to concepts like nation, as well as structures conducive to community building like the associations. However, as this chapter has suggested, these associations and the corresponding sense of living in-common have declined, giving way to increased isolation and political and cultural tension. Indeed, one has noted how the structures associated with class unity and community have been in significant decline post-Thatcher, with union membership dwindling, pubs and working-people's clubs closing, and people moving out of their areas due to hardship. This has led to social dislocation and provides the backdrop against which greater divisions in the working-class have appeared. What one means by this is the opening of distance between the white/majority and minority working-class, who now occupy increasingly segregated spaces, wary of the potential loss of their remaining traditions—for many the last vestiges of a life that made sense.

This disconnection has been born out of misdirected hostility, continued structural decline, and the failures of the left to provide a narrative vision which is inclusive of the working-class in its constitutive parts. As a result of these failures, many white working-class people have become further marginalised having attempted to shape their community with appeals to a kind of identity politics—perhaps labelled white identity politics—that has been rejected in the mainstream. This pushed resentment underground and has remained a key feature, and motivator, or intra-class hostility in our communities, which struggle to work together for common endeavours, including the alleviation of their shared material and structural deprivation. This sense, and the real and perceived failures of the Labour Party under first Blair, and then every leader subsequently to address alienation, as well as the structural inequalities which pervade and encourage misrecognition, has been to degrade working-class communities, dividing them upon ethnic or other lines. We now see a working-class largely without the benefits of community, which is increasingly defensive and which must face the consequences of its disunity in structural and material terms. One places the blame for this at the feet of the Labour Party to some extent for its inability to construct a vision for a common land, as well as the Conservative and other populist-right parties for seizing upon misdiagnosis and misunderstanding to radicalise a section of the working-class which has genuine issues that must be addressed. Such radicalisation is taken to grow the gap between the working-class sub-groups and to worsen community-related alienation as people no longer see one-another as sharing a common destiny.

This initially appears to lend itself to a social capital diagnosis of the problem in which structures alone must be re-built to renew community. However, this would be a mistake because it fails to appreciate the importance of narrative, as detailed earlier within the book by Macintyre, which should be able to bring people together and to inspire them. We have said how the lack of narrative is critical in worsening alienation, and how effectively a populist-national narrative has been in winning over the socially conservative working-class. Yet this is only likely to alienate the entire class by preaching a story that excludes minorities, progressives, and which is no friend to the community longed for by socially conservative workers themselves. It does this because it leaves in place the misrecognitions and now-rooted distrust that pervade the class experience. We do not see in this community any reference to values or of the societal vision that we wish to see realised and to become part of. Sandel speaks to this, noting how our civil discourse is poisoned by marketisation and technocratic norms. This demoralises the working-class and fails to provide something to make sense of their daily lives, nor provides them with hope for a better future.

Where, in previous decades, they could create meaning or see themselves in light of their community, the nation, or the vision of the Labour Party, they now have little to inspire them. One connects this with the failure of recognition in what is left of our communities, as well as within the national narrative, that had erstwhile been created by the populist-nationalism of, especially Boris Johnson's, Conservative Party. This means alienation for minority peoples whose contribution to the nation is not realised nor made part of their portion of our shared story. The outcome of this is further resentment. To address this issue, one explores the potential of a Progressive Nationalist narrative to appeal across the working-class sub-groups, using the British Idealists and English Pluralists as its guide.

Agency

Finally, we have seen how the agency of the working-class has been diminished in recent decades. The chapter has demonstrated this through reference to two forms of agency: representative and personal. We have seen how an inability to craft inclusive narratives which address their concerns over poverty, insecurity, and community loss at the same time as remaining committed to the search for social justice has resulted in a breakdown of representative agency for the working-class. The resentment that this creates ensures that there remains a disconnect between the politics and people.

There are also structural barriers to the exercise of personal agency for the working-class. We have seen how their work has declined towards a state of precarity and/or exploitation, which has a corresponding impact on the life that one can live and the opportunities they can take up. The decline of the trade unions has only worsened these problems of insecurity and inequality at the same time as robbing the working-class of representative agency in the form of an intermediary association which would fight for concessions and personal agency in the sense that working-people could have direct influence within these associations. The Labour Party, as well as successive Conservative governments, is partly to blame for this loss of agency, albeit in somewhat different ways. Indeed, the expansion of the Knowledge Economy and meritocracy because of Tony Blair's transformation of the party into New Labour opened a gap between their traditional supporter base and the kind of future that the party was to pursue. This gap, although initially small, was to widen over the course of the party's 13 years in government as it began to move further away from the values of the working-class in pursuit of a world that did not fully recognise them. This has left many feeling 'left behind', and although the Conservative Party have attempted to woo working-class voters with promises of levelling-up, the underlying structural conditions have not changed nor are likely to change under a government that has refused to pass legislation addressing these issues and will not consider union empowerment. In reference to both forms of agency then, the working-class and their concerns are not adequately represented within society and have not been for some time, whilst the personal agency of working-people is precarious and beset by structural difficulties related to their position and relation to the associations which had once been vehicles of their collective power.

This structural component of agency also is indicative of alienation, rather than anomie, as the working-class are left without a means to challenge changing social norms and, as a class, fail to display the actions characteristic of anomie. To challenge this position, one explores how civil society could be expanded towards agentially beneficial ends.

Across the three characteristics of alienation provided, the working-class have experienced a decline in their standards to a point in which they can be considered as alienated. This is not to say that, in the past, they had not already been alienated, but it is to suggest that the state in which the working-class find themselves in within contemporary Britain is increasingly concerning. Having established that the working-class suffers from alienation, the book will now turn to its amelioration by considering, first, the thought of the British Idealists in setting out some of the principles upon which a less-alienating existence can be built.

Bibliography

YouGov. 'How close is the Labour Party to the working class? YouGov'. https://yougov.co.uk/topics/politics/trackers/how-close-is-the-labour-party-to-the-working-class?crossBreak=c2de. Accessed 19 Sep 2023.

Akala. *Natives: Race and Class in the Ruins of Empire*. John Murray Press, 2019.

Armstrong, Jeremy. 'People of Hartlepool Say Starmer Neglected Working Class Voter in Stark Message'. *Mirror*, 7 May 2021. https://www.mirror.co.uk/news/politics/people-hartlepool-say-keir-starmer-24064097.

Beckett, Andy. 'The Tories' Culture War Is a Reminder That the Right Isn't as Fearless as It Seems.' *The Guardian*, 9 October 2020. http://www.theguardian.com/commentisfree/2020/oct/09/tories-culture-war-right-fearless-boris-johnson-war-on-woke. Accessed 15 May 2023.

Blair, Tony. 'Full Text of Tony Blair's Speech on Education'. *The Guardian*, 23 May 2001. http://www.theguardian.com/politics/2001/may/23/labour.tonyblair.

Bloodworth, James. *Hired: Six Months undercover in low-wage Britain*. Atlantic Books, 2018.

Castiglione, Dario, Jan W. van Deth, and Guglielmo Wolleb. *The Handbook of Social Capital*. OUP, 2008.

Charlesworth, Simon J. *A Phenomenology of Working-Class Experience*. Cambridge University Press, 2000.

Cruddas, Jon. *The Dignity of Labour*. Polity Press, 2021.

Durkheim, Emile. *Suicide, a Study in Sociology*. FTC Press, 2018.

Eatwell, Roger, and Matthew Goodwin. *National Populism: The Revolt Against Liberal Democracy*. Penguin, 2018.

Edgerton, David. *The Rise and Fall of the British Nation*. Penguin Books, 2021.

English, Fenwick W., and Cheryl L. Bolton. *Bourdieu for Educators: Policy and Practice*. SAGE Publications, 2015.

Evans, Geoffrey, and James Tilley. *The New Politics of Class: The Political Exclusion of the British Working Class*. Oxford University Press, 2017.

Goodhart, David. *Head Hand Heart: The Struggle for Dignity and Status in the Twenty First Century*. Penguin, UK, 2020.

Goodwin, Matthew. 'The Blue Wall Won't Save Labour'. *UnHerd*, 19 April 2021. https://unherd.com/2021/04/the-blue-wall-wont-save-labour/. Accessed 19 May 2023.

Hall, Stuart. 'Race, articulation and societies structured in dominance', in: UNESCO (ed.) *Sociological Theories: Race and Colonialism*. UNESCO, 1980: 305–345.

Häuberer, Julia. *Social Capital Theory: Towards a Methodological Foundation*. Springer Science & Business Media, 2010.

Healey, John. 'Labour's Priority Must Be Britain's Real Middle: The 10m on Ordinary Incomes'. *LabourList*. https://labourlist.org/2021/04/labours-priority-must-be-britains-real-middle-the-10m-on-ordinary-incomes/. Accessed 24 May 2021.

Heath, Oliver. 'Policy Alienation, Social Alienation and Working-Class Abstention in Britain, 1964– 2010'. *British Journal of Political Science* 48, no. 4 (October 2018): 1053–1073.

Hegel, Georg Wilhelm Fredrich. *Georg Wilhelm Friedrich Hegel: The Phenomenology of Spirit*. Cambridge University Press, 2018.

ICM. 'Black History Month: How Important Are BAME People in British History?'. https://www.icmunlimited.com/our-work/black-history-month-how-important-are-bame-people-in-british-history/. Accessed 20 May 2023.

Kaufmann, Eric. *Whiteshift: Populism, Immigration and the Future of White Majorities*. Penguin, UK, 2018.

Kirkwood, Diane. 'Why Britain's Values Divide Should Matter to Labour'. UK in a changing Europe, 28 January 2020. https://ukandeu.ac.uk/why-britains-values-divide-should-matter-to-labour/. Accessed 10 May 2021.

Kramer, Ann. *Many Rivers to Cross: Caribbean People in the NHS 1948–1969*. The Stationery Office, 2006.

Kromydas, Theocharis. 'Rethinking Higher Education and Its Relationship with Social Inequalities: Past Knowledge, Present State and Future Potential'. *Palgrave Communications* 3, no. 1 (13 October 2017): 1–12.

Leopold, David. 'Alienation'. In *The Stanford Encyclopedia of Philosophy*, edited by Edward N. Zalta and Uri Nodelman, Winter 2022. Metaphysics Research Lab, Stanford University, 2022. https://plato.stanford.edu/archives/win2022/entries/alienation/.

McKenzie, Lisa. 'The Class Politics of Prejudice: Brexit and the Land of No-Hope and Glory'. *The British Journal of Sociology* 68, no. S1 (2017): 265–280.

McKenzie, Lisa. *Getting By: Estates, Class and Culture in Austerity Britain.* Policy Press, 2015.

More In Common. 'Britain's Choice, More in Common's New Report on the UK'. 2020. https://www.britainschoice.uk/. Accessed 24 May 2023.

O'Grady, Tom. 'Decline in Working Class Politicians, Shifted Labour towards Right Wing Policy'. UCL News, 30 July 2018. https://www.ucl.ac.uk/news/2018/jul/decline-working-class-politicians-shifted-labour-towards-right-wing-policy.

Obama, Barack. *A Promised Land.* Penguin Books, 2020.

Office for National Statistics. 'Average Household Income, UK—Office for National Statistics'. https://www.ons.gov.uk/peoplepopulationandcommunity/personalandhouseholdfinances/incomeandwealth/bulletins/householddisposableincomeandinequality/financialyear2020. Accessed 24 Feb 2022.

Peters, Rebecca Warne. *Implementing Inequality: The Invisible Labor of International Development.* Rutgers University Press, 2020.

Putnam, Robert D. *Bowling Alone.* Simon and Schuster, 2001.

Reay, Diane. 'The Working Classes and Higher Education: Meritocratic Fallacies of Upward Mobility in the United Kingdom'. *European Journal of Education* 56, no. 1 (2021): 53–64.

Rutter, Jill. '"World Beating": The Phrase of 2020?'. UK in a changing Europe, 16 June 2020. https://ukandeu.ac.uk/world-beating-the-phrase-of-2020/. Accessed 10 May 2023.

Sandel, Michael J. *The Tyranny of Merit: What's Become of the Common Good?.* Penguin, UK, 2020.

Sandel, Michael J. *What Money Can't Buy: The Moral Limits of Markets.* Penguin, UK, 2012.

Sivanandan, A. *Communities of Resistance: Writings on Black Struggles for Socialism.* Verso Books, 2019.

Sobolewska, Maria, and Robert Ford. *Brexitland: Identity, Diversity and the Reshaping of British Politics.* Cambridge University Press, 2020.

Standing, Guy. *Plunder of the Commons: A Manifesto for Sharing Public Wealth.* Penguin, UK, 2019.

Standing, Guy. *The Precariat: The New Dangerous Class.* Bloomsburg, 2016.

Stocker, Paul. *English Uprising: Brexit and the Mainstreaming of the Far-Right.* Melville House, UK, 2017.

Tawney, R.H. *Equality.* Unwin Books, 1931

Trades Union Congress. 'Challenging Amazon Report'. 2020. https://www.tuc.org.uk/research-analysis/reports/challenging-amazon-report. Accessed 24 May 2023.

Umney, Charles. *Class Matters: Inequality and Exploitation in Twenty First Century Britain*. Pluto Press, 2018.
Unger, Roberto Mangabeira. *The Knowledge Economy*. Verso Books, 2022.
Virdee, Satnam. *Racism, Class and the Racialized Outsider*. Bloomsbury Publishing, 2014.
Wilson, Shaun. *Living Wages and the Welfare State: The Anglo-American Social Model in Transition*. Policy Press, 2021.
Embery, Paul. 'Labour Isn't Working'. *UnHerd*, 7 May 2021. https://unherd.com/2021/05/labour-isnt-working/. Accessed 19 May 2023.
Policy Exchange. 'Polling—Deltapoll'. https://policyexchange.org.uk/history-matterspolling/. Accessed 18 May 2023.
Ipsos MORI. 'How Britain Voted in 1997'. https://www.ipsos.com/ipsos-mori/en-uk/how-britain-voted-1997. Accessed 24 May 2023a.
Ipsos MORI. 'How Britain Voted In 2001'. https://www.ipsos.com/ipsos-mori/en-uk/how-britain-voted-2001. Accessed 24 May 2023b.
Ipsos MORI. 'How Britain Voted in 2010'. https://www.ipsos.com/ipsos-mori/en-uk/how-britain-voted-2010. Accessed 24 May 2023c.
Ipsos MORI. 'How Britain Voted in 2015'. https://www.ipsos.com/ipsos-mori/en-uk/how-britain-voted-2015. Accessed 24 May 2023d.

CHAPTER 6

The Ethics of British Idealism

This chapter focuses on the thought of the British Idealists, notably T.H. Green and Bosanquet, and identifies, inspired by their thought, a vision for the creation of a society based upon human flourishing within the context of the common good. In doing so it will discuss the principles of the Higher-self and moral character, the "society of societies" which, in the view of the Idealists, renders the individual-collective dichotomy largely void, and the Greenian conception of the common good (Green 2008, 141). Taken together, these notions amount to a philosophy, centred on flourishing, which is pluralistic, stresses compassion, and successfully intertwines groups and individuals in service of a mutually recognisable good. In many respects, and as this chapter suggests, Idealism offers a principled foundation from which to challenge alienation. This chapter forms the ethical core of the book's proposed response.

The Higher-Self

A key component of Idealist thought is the concept of a Higher-self. This refers to the realisation of interconnectivity and the mutualistic bond between individuals within the community, and their importance in ensuring flourishing. Bosanquet (2015) argues that it is within community that we are best able to develop ourselves because here we have access not only

S. Taylor Hill, *Challenging Alienation in the British Working-Class*, Palgrave Politics of Identity and Citizenship Series,
https://doi.org/10.1007/978-3-031-59250-8_6

to services, spaces, and institutions for the interaction of individuals and the cultivation of our talents, but in living in common we are also subjected to a range of stimuli that develop our emotional-social capacities in a way that would be difficult to achieve without others. He posits here that the stronger our interconnectivity, the more likely we are to move towards this state of Higher-selves. Such a state is considered by Bosanquet to be expressed in two ways, namely as the movement towards a higher individual self in which we are better able to realise our capacities through our interactions within community and, second, in the creation of these higher individual selves, the movement towards a society that can better rely on the talents of its members to ensure flourishing in turn.

This relationship provides the basis for his assertion of mutuality between community members. Indeed, he sees that the development of the Higher-self requires community and so orientates a theory of flourishing around this central axis of community by suggesting that we, as citizens, have both an interest and a duty in recognising our fellows as equal Higher-selves. This is encapsulated within the quote "the realisation of any one individual's highest life is impossible without the co-operation of others, but…the realisation of other' lives is an essential element…in the realisation of our own" because, through relating to others, we exercise our fundamental human equality and "universal human worth", which helps to underpin dignity (Mackenzie 2017, 235; Bosanquet 2015). The way that we should act in realising this will be expressed subsequently in reference to moral character, but let us recognise here that Bosanquet's theory asserts a fundamental position of equal worth between human beings within a community and makes the additional claim that, as citizens, we are responsible for the flourishing of our fellows, as well as of our community, to ensure that development in turn. This establishes mutualism at the heart of the Idealist position and asserts the desirability of interaction within the communal frame.

Interestingly, Bosanquet expands on the notion of the collective Higher-self to explicitly detail a component of it which relates to the communal-narrative element of alienation. Indeed, he suggests that though we might view the relationship between individual and individual, and individual and community, as essentially mutual, we should recognise that collectives can create their own goods that we are otherwise incapable of creating alone. For instance, Bosanquet asserts that an individual finds themselves elevated and emotionally contended when they are included in a community that relates to them because it is here that "man finds something to live for"

(Bosanquet 2013, n.p.). In suggesting this, Bosanquet draws from the Aristotelian tradition, reasoning that the individual becomes a higher being when they are involved within the 'polis', which can be translated to refer to either the city or the community. He stresses how such a frame provides the basis for social interaction and the participation of the individual within common institutions, for common ends. In contrast, if an individual were to live in relative seclusion, then they will likely identify themselves in ways that perhaps do not fully reflect who they are, nor are they able to share that identity with others. In comparison, the collective promises several ways to better develop oneself. An individual can improve their emotional capacity by forging friendships, stimulate their intellectual capacity by joining associations, seek spiritual or other guidance in places of worship or educational centres, and increase their physical and tactical capabilities on a sports team. Each of these activities stimulates the individual in a way that they cannot stimulate themselves alone, whilst the emotional development which necessarily comes from interacting with others creates the bonds which are required for the strengthening of moral character. In belonging to community, we also create institutions that embody our collective values, participate in socio-cultural activities that bring us closer to one another, and more generally find a sense of higher purpose by playing our part within the development of community.

In reference to the working-class, we see in this collective element of the Higher-self two important features. First, Bosanquet suggests that our belonging within associations and interactions within community, done so upon a basis consistent with equal worth, enhance our capacities for flourishing, which itself speaks to the necessity of those associations which one discussed in Chap. 5 as having formed an integral part of working-class life historically. Second, it is in community that we have a better chance of generating meaning within our lives, whether that be as part of an association or in respect to a narrative element within community that speaks to our mutual movement towards the improvement of the commons. This latter point resonates with the orientation towards nation in much of the working-class and presents here an opportunity to create a narrative framework premised on equal worth and collective effort which can enable working-people to see themselves, and their lives, as part of something *more*—namely in the expansion of community through its institutions, associations, and interconnectivity between peoples, as well as its capacity to enable flourishing.

Taken together, such a multidimensional means of realising one's Higher-self demonstrates the Idealist belief that social practices are a condition of the meaningful development of persons. Indeed, without participating in the social, forming bonds with others, and learning from them, we would never be able to achieve a more rounded sense of self or recognise our own identity as both an individual and a member of the community. It consequently holds that society should not be framed as individual against collective in which one must necessarily sacrifice some part of itself to the other but, rather, that the two form one entity. The implication here is that community should be considered integral to the realisation of human flourishing, and individual and collective seen as two parts of an interrelated whole. This relationship serves to enhance individual capabilities, ground their identities, and give meaning and praxis to the formation of both a higher individual self and a higher level of community that is capable of better serving its citizens and acting as an icon of their collective effort which one can find purpose within. Drawing from Chap. 5, there is some appetite within the working-class to return to a form of community which, if not explicitly then implicitly, aligns itself with Idealism in maintaining a preference for it as a means of giving meaning and a sense of prestige to their lives (Evans and Tilley 2017; Goodhart 2020). In addition, the mutuality and premise of equal worth established as vital to the continual strengthening of the individual and collective Higher-self leads one to advocate for a position which stresses the necessity of reciprocal social interaction and the reorientation of our focus towards the enhancement of peoples. This aligns with working-class concerns around their treatment in society whilst providing space for the expansion of those civil society associations which had once been vital to their way of life, justified here as necessary for the flourishing of Higher-selves. Subsequently, the Idealist commitment to a Higher-self is pro-social and community focused whilst simultaneously grounding the individual in such a way as to give them purpose, identity, and the means for flourishing.

Moral Character

Green and Bosanquet primarily focus on the development of an ideal moral character, and how one might achieve it, seeing this as the basis for movement towards a state of Higher-selves. In fact, such is the key role that character plays within the philosophy of T.H. Green that Nicholson argues, "Green … centres his moral philosophy not on a system of all-encompassing substantive principles from which one can deduce the acts which ought to be done, but on a type of character in moral agents" (Nicholson 1990, 78). To explore this idea of moral character further, we must refer to the state and society of societies. As we have seen, the Idealists hold that the individual must integrate within the complex institutions which make up society to develop the 'ideal capacities', namely faculties of reason and emotion. Part of this development includes the formation of a strong moral character which, according to Green, is founded centrally on the ability of an individual to undertake "conscientious judgement which has not been perverted by short-sighted self-interest" (Green 2007, n.p.).

Green writes in favour of "conscientious judgement" and, with that, the importance of reason because, in his mind, a sufficiently developed faculty for reason, when matched with a corresponding emotional understanding of the world, will imbue individuals with the capacity for morally informed action. This action becomes central to Green's philosophy as he sees that only when we seek to understand one another on each other's terms can we reach a position of mutual respect. One might interpret this in a purely rational sense as the recognition and digestion of one's defence of their own position, or description of the importance of a certain aspect of their way of life, yet Green sees a purely rational recognition as lacking a core component of our humanity in its absence of emotive understanding. Rather, he sees that we must not only understand one another on a rational basis because human beings are not wholly rational creatures. In fact, we have emotive attachments to one another, to objects in our world, and to notions. These things are not tangible in a rational sense but can come to be understood through the development of our sympathetic and empathetic capabilities. Regarding the development of our moral character then, Green suggests that we must be able to think and act in accordance with these faculties and in favour of the development of our mutual understanding of one another as equal beings worthy of recognition. If we are to live in a community that is successful in ensuring the creation of Higher-selves, and which is the embodiment of the collective effort of those selves, then we must, therefore, practise reasoning which is more deeply 'of us' in the way that it asks us to think of others.

This moral character demands that people act in good faith and consider the implications of their actions on others. When applied to the contemporary society, this has some implications, namely that it may be used to critique it for having, rightly in the view of Green, expanded personal freedom of choice and yet at the same time wrongly having forgotten or ignored those societies and institutions which are necessary to encourage individuals to develop a compassionate moral character.[1] Green especially sees that moral character can do much, even within everyday interactions, to develop kinship and solidarity between people. There is an interplay with the notion of Higher-self here as, only by participating in social networks can people realise this interconnectedness and enrich their lives through the realisation of others as their equal, deserving of love, compassion, and respect. This underlines again that a truly moral person is not one that subscribes to a list of values. They are, in fact, the person that feels connected to those around them and treats them with due consideration. Such an appeal to morality as effectively arising out of solidarity based on human dignity seems of great use to an otherwise diverse society which may hold significantly different views. It colours the ways one interacts with others and may encourage them to adopt a predisposition towards reconciliation or, if taken to more radical ends, the breaking down of those views which tend to undermine respect for dignity, which is a noble end for Green and his fellow Idealists, and which connects especially with commentators like Cruddas and Sandel in Chap. 5.

Maintaining an interconnected society which involves the recognition of each individual or group as capable of conscientious judgement seems to offer a means of improving respect for our fundamental worth and provides space for an erstwhile appreciation of our diversity whilst simultaneously challenging alienation as people find themselves thought about by others and included within the community. Thus, an emphasis on moral character and the prioritisation of conscience and reason, alongside the active encouragement of social interaction between peoples would tend towards the creation of a more inclusive, cohesive community. In respect of the working-class, it holds that our society should seek to include emotional and moral concerns in its reasoning and therefore diminish the transactional and technocratic language which dominates our public discourse. Significantly too, it maintains that everyone deserves to be regarded, whilst it implores different groups within community and class, such as white or conservative workers, to seriously engage in dialogue with minority groups for the purpose of re-forging communal ties based on common respect. With significance for Chap. 8, we might also consider

[1] Sandel's critique in Chap. 5 pertains to this point.

the propagation of moral character as part of a Progressive Nationalism as a foundational element of a healthy community that bestows meaning and dignity upon its members.

Moral Character and Human Flourishing

It is also worth considering the differences between this Idealism-inspired ethical position and that of contemporary liberals and communitarians around the notion of human flourishing and the related question of perfectionism to demonstrate the continued relevance of Idealist ethics regarding questions of the good life.

In sketching out the Liberal Perfectionist preference for autonomy, one highlights the work of Raz (1986), whose privileging of autonomy alongside pluralism forms the moral basis of his conception of the good life. For the purposes of this analysis, one defines this perfectionism using a Rawlsian phrase, seeing it as an example of a comparatively thin conception of the good to the communitarians—though not as thin as a Rawls' (2009) Political Liberalism which stresses fundamental neutrality as the role of the state. Within Raz's view, we see a state that is perfectionist in the sense that it acknowledges a preference for rules and lifestyles which enable individual autonomy. In this, the state encourages a reasonable pluralism, seeing a variety of views, lifestyles, and forms of interaction as enabling suitable choices for rational individuals. This comes together as a perfectionist view of the state which will "create and preserve an environment which respects the independence of agents and furnishes them with an adequate range of options" (Raz 1986, 391).

Raz adds to this a communally sensitive variant of Mill's harm principle, whereby he understands some limits to be placed on individuals by "seeing that they all conform to appropriate standards of behavior" (1986, 5) which will promote autonomy as the fundamental component of said good life.

This is a variant of the harm principle because, unlike Mill, it is indicative of state action as "[s]ometimes failing to improve the situation of another is harming him" (1986, 416). As such, the state will carry out the promotion of what it considers to be morally good options, defined so as those which enhance valuable autonomous action, though it will not prevent individuals from taking 'bad' options unless they harm others without consent. He sees this as non-coercive as the state assumes "that people should lead autonomous lives" but "cannot force them to be moral. All it can do is to provide the conditions..." (1986, 420) by supporting some conceptions of the good actively, and other not at all, with a few instances where it must intervene. Together this amounts to commitment to perfectionist flourishing in which the state acts to promote a pluralistic freedom of choice for individuals, seeing that choice as fundamental to the autonomous good of individuals. As noted in Chap. 2, such an understanding respects to some degree groups, but really instrumentalises them as only providers of choices—which might well be meaningful but are only recognised for what they do to enhance individuals alone, whilst one maintains some concerns around the strength of the Razian harm principle comparative to an Idealist-inspired ethical alternative.

This is distinctive too from the communitarian position of Walzer (1984), Etzioni (2014), and Macintyre (2007), who maintain a more collective sense of perfectionism, defined in reference to community. These communitarians outline a 'thick' conception of the good in which a particular 'moral culture' is promoted outwardly by the state, thereby neglecting liberal notions of neutrality. This relates to perfectionism in the sense that some conceptions of the good are not regarded by communitarians when they conflict with the moral culture pursued by the state. The restrictiveness of this culture, and its 'thickness', can of course vary greatly, and none of these communitarians quite understand nor define moral culture in the same way, but for the purposes of this exposition, let us settle on the fundamental communitarian ideal that the state must promote a somewhat monistic moral culture, oftentimes justified as a means to unify its people. Flourishing, and therefore perfection, is consequently defined by the collective more so in communitarian traditions, arguing that our embeddedness within a society creates the framework within which we realise ourselves, what matters to us, or who we wish to become. We cannot escape community, and our sense of what is perfect is likely to have some relation with the dominant moral culture pursued by the state, whilst our options for the good life will also be influenced by this. The importance of community, for communitarians, thus leads many of them, including Macintyre (2007), to suggest that the good *is* the community. It becomes more than the sum of its parts and is the carrier of traditions, fellowship, and the grounds upon which friendships are built. These provide goods in themselves and are seen to make community intrinsically worthwhile. On a basic level, one must prioritise the security of this community because, if it were to fracture, then all other goods would subsequently crumble. To create a stable community, Etzioni branches into what liberals call the 'private sphere' in decrying what he sees as harmful trends within society, such as divorce. He views this as essential and supports this with legislation that "represent(s)...a proper method of expressing social and moral values" (Etzioni 2014, 47). Etzioni here endeavours to create a thick conception of the good that 'polices' activity within the private sphere in a way that liberals would reject to strengthen the bonds of community in line with a monistic, 'unifying' moral culture. This is not a position shared by the Idealists who, like liberals, reject such a thick conception of the good, though they do provide a thicker conception than most through their ethics.

Idealism, like liberal perfectionism, and unlike certainly Etzioni's (2014) communitarianism, sees individual autonomy as valuable for personal growth. However, we might interpret an Idealist ethics as derived from Green (2003) as being in some ways stronger than Raz's harm principle, whilst they too have a 'deeper' understanding of groups which captures the essence of the communitarian's thicker conception of the good. On this first point, although sceptical of state action as potentially limiting personal growth, Green maintains a position related to his ideals of Higher-self and moral character which seeks the eradication of "social evils" and places limits on those conceptions of the good life which are unethical, namely in the way that they "gain from the loss of another" (Green 2003, 248–251). He applies this clearly to contract, in which he sees that the capitalist acts unethically when they offer sub-standard contracts to a worker who is in no position to refuse (Green, 2023). Such a scenario shows an inability to recognise the human worth of others and belies the necessity of mutual recognition and respect. The state is justified to act here to right this activity on such an ethical basis, which here places greed above the recognition of our fellows as of fundamental worth—taking that away from them in a way that would see the capitalist "gain from the loss of another(s)" dignity (Green 2003, 248). This amounts to a commitment to perfectionist state action in the sense that the state can place some restraints on conceptions of the good life and actions which flow from it if they violate the foundational principles of mutual recognition and respect upon which our flourishing is premised (Brink 2007).[2] The mutualistic component of this ethical foundation, alongside the

[2] Though in a strict Greenian (2008) sense such restraints must be well considered lest "clumsy state intervention" interfere with valid opportunities for personal growth.

overarching commitment to human flourishing of individuals, highlights here such action as dedicated to the protection of persons and an autonomy that is bolstered by the restraint of those who would see others deprived of their dignity.

The Idealists also understand autonomy to be found in the presence of groups and as something which can be practised by them. As we have seen, Bosanquet (2015) and Green (2008) maintain a clear place for the cultivation of talents within collectives and see that belonging and association within the groups of civil society enable that which cannot be enabled through individual effort alone. These Idealists explicitly outline a notion of perfectionism which promotes civil society and the strengthening of groups within it, by the state or by ethically minded individuals, as a fundamental necessity of human flourishing, seeing the creation of a "society of societies" as expanding our capacities and sense of purpose by enabling us to find "something to live for" (Bosanquet 2013, na). The group is seen here to be *more* than a choice. It is a place where we forge bonds and find belonging. This group takes on a collective identity and takes its place within the society of societies as a carrier of ideas, a shaper of knowledge, and a reflection of many selves which can bring together our aspirations for a better society in a fundamental way.

Here one recognises an Idealist-inspired position which sees the value of ethical restraint, which can empower the state to act lest one violate a common good centred on the creation of Higher-selves and the extension of moral character, and which has a more developed understanding of collectives as conducive to the goal of human flourishing. Regarding state action, this results in a perfectionist pursuit of flourishing but goes further than Raz to underline the necessity of ethical action, with evidence of the need to restrain conceptions of the good life which inflict deprivation on others or which fail to uphold mutual recognition and respect. The focus is still on individual flourishing, but it is placed in a context that is aware of the collective and which recognises both the value of them to individuals and the group's role in the shaping of our community, with subsequent consequences for our capacity to flourish as mutually coherent parts of a greater whole. Regard is given here to groups on their own terms, as in the communitarian tradition, yet the limits which are placed on individuals are bound to an ethical compact which enables a greater degree of plurality than in the strict monism of Etzioni's or Macintyre's communitarianism, but which nevertheless places limits on those conceptions of the good life which undermine the flourishing of our fellows or which fail to treat them with mutual respect. This perspective understands flourishing for individuals as related to, and mutually coherent with, the collective, but does not seek to deny autonomy to them unless they violate the moral values of mutual respect and recognition.

Human Flourishing

This has significance for alienation because it orients our flourishing around the development of moral character and the desire to move towards a state of Higher-selves. In consequence, human flourishing requires the support of community and extends rights to people so that they may make claims for materials, education, and other goods, as well as a whole host of other things, because they expand that which one can use to realise themselves. Moral character as an element within this ensures that flourishing also maintains an ethical dimension which is determined partly in reference to one's own ideals, but also to those ideals expressed within community. As such, one sees a flourishing which is related to duty towards others with the express goal of enhancing one's moral character. The Idealists see these duties as conferring rights and virtue as a means of securing those rights. Human flourishing, therefore, requires some collective sense of perfectionism regarding virtue, as we must necessarily be able to treat people with respect, to recognise them, and to value them, if we are to flourish. Idealism is more dutiful here than many liberalisms and ventures into the realm of the 'good life' by defining some aspects of a perfectionist morality, but it does so to create the ethical foundation for the expansion of rights, recognition, and the personal perfection of many selves, and goods, within the community. On this basis, it will critique and limit selfishness and greed, because they violate ethical norms, and therefore rights, but leave alone many other lifestyles. Idealism thus promotes a thicker conception of the good because it explicitly rejects selfish conceptions of it as greatly limiting our fellows within community. Yet, many goods are permitted by this Idealism, including most liberal ones, thus offering a thinner conception, open to greater plurality, than that which communitarians often advance—which is inclusive of the right communitarian position that one takes issue with in Chap. 5. We see here how Idealism is inclined towards communitarianism in a sense that it does promote a good, but that such a good is permissive of, and compatible with, a plurality of them, justifying this on the basis that nonselfishness will inherently better enable them to develop. One goes beyond the liberal-communitarian debate here to ground a conception of the good life which is broadly amicable to both inclinations and which will ground the ethos of Chaps. 9 and 10 and become the basis of a multicultural Progressive Nationalism in Chap. 8.

The State and the Society of Societies

McTaggert states that "harmony between unity and diversity can be established only on the basis of an all-encompassing relation of love between all the characteristic elements of reality, which in turn presupposes thinking of ultimate reality as a community" (McTaggert in Guyer and Horstmann 2023). This quote emphasises the Idealist view that an emotional connection between human beings, which recognises and dignifies them, is essential for establishing a community which is shaped by the knowledge of its members and shapes them in turn. In a community we 'unify' our individual, diverse knowledge of the world, including our experiences, cultures, desires, and emotions, into one entity which appreciates what we as individuals have done to contribute to our reality, and at the same time benefit from being exposed to the reality of others, which offers us the chance for further personal and cooperative development. Here, the community becomes the guardian of our shared knowledge and the embodiment of 'us' through its institutions. By institutions we do not, however, merely refer to the narrow definition of the state apparatus. This is because the Idealists view the state as encompassing government and its institutions, but emphasise too the associations of civil society. In their view, the state is diffused and complex—encompassing each of those collectives that enable flourishing in their own respects, as arbiters of knowledge, learning, and bond-forming.

In this conception of state, where the governmental state is just one group among many, we see emerge what Green calls the "society of societies" (Green 2008, 141). This refers to the numerous groups that exist within the 'state', ranging from religious institutions, books clubs, or sports teams to trade unions, cooperative societies, and a variety of other associations. These exist in a society of societies because, although they are diverse in character and organisation, they each hold and shape knowledge which, in turn, contributes to our potential as a common. In this, a diverse range of societies, or associations, is understood to enhance the capacity of citizens to flourish, whilst it also offers opportunity to cultivate belonging.

There are two core benefits to the amelioration of alienation that stem from this. First, the society of societies lends itself to the creation of an inclusive framework which individuals and groups can subscribe to and take dignity in by considering that they are contributing to a greater 'whole'. For instance, if we adopt a position which places a greater emphasis on civil society associations as cultivating our talents, knowledge, and capacity for social interaction, then we are more likely to be able to appreciate both these associations and belonging within them. In reference to the working-class, this is to privilege in part those associations which had provided them with a dignified sense of belonging previously, including the trade unions, whilst it maintains the importance of a strong civil society in extending bonds of fellowship and solidarity between peoples. Taken in a narrative sense, one therefore sees that membership within these associations can provide its own dignity since it offers individuals a place to belong, and to practise their agency in the development of those things which are important to them, and finally offers a place for the development of collective skills, including in cooperation with others. Second, as we have developed in Chap. 5, we presently lack strong associations that can bring citizens together. The society of societies' privileging of association, and the interlinking of those associations in reference to themes of human flourishing and the common good, is to encourage interaction both within and across associations. Here one sees some potential to cultivate bonds between citizens that have hitherto struggled to interact on a positive basis. This maintains relevance as a practical iteration of one's Progressive Nationalism whilst also forming the basis of Chap. 10's considerations on the expansion of civil society.

Taken together, by looking at our society as one of societies, each with its own traits and differences, we see that we should respect diversity of role, person, culture, or place, to name but a few frames, for their contribution to the common. This idea is important in challenging alienation since it also implores us to consider how we might expand civil society so that working-class people can become more constituent members of it, whether that be as part of the resurrecting of those old associations, like the trade unions, which gave them a sense of collective agency in the past, or in other associations organised around, say, hobbies. What is key here is the realisation that the working-class need associations which they can buy in to as a means of not only exercising collective power, but also creating meaning within their lives through the development of their faculties, skills, and interactions with others. The added narrative element ties this to dignity by expressing the value of belonging in those associations which ultimately enhance flourishing in line with the common good by expanding the bounds of society in different directions.

Common Good

Thus far, we have alluded to, yet not discussed nor defined, the Idealist conception of the common good, which overlaps to some extent with that outlined by Sandel but maintains its own distinctiveness. This section focuses on the good within the thought of T.H. Green, whose understanding of the term, according to Simhony (2014, 452), focuses upon a central "concern for justice; that is, a concern for promoting the good of everyone". In this way, from the outset Green seeks a good which is conducive to flourishing and which has a desire to ensure that a community and its members can develop in common—where the good of one citizen is not to outweigh/deprive that of another.

Pluralism and Equal Worth

This has a pluralistic component to it as the notions of moral character and the movement towards the Higher-self seek to ensure that the bounds of our society can be developed in multiple directions to facilitate diverse goods. When discussed in relation to the society of societies, which views diversity in association and its function as providing valuable services for flourishing, one sees that the common good would maintain a commitment to the propagation of such development. This is how Green proceeds.

Following from this awareness of the need for plurality, Green grounds a good which entrusts individuals with the responsibility of realising themselves in mutuality, rather than forcing upon them an extensive set of values or laws to which they must abide and which the state should enforce throughout society to ensure compliance. Instead, he intertwines his good with a personal, ethical perfectionism, as seen earlier in the chapter, expanding that good so that it becomes the responsibility of each person. To explain this further, consider that Green could opt for a purely political commitment to laws and institutions which can govern us. He, however, rejects such a proposition. He does so because he sees that a common good must have two features. First, it should be orientated around something central to the community, which in this case is flourishing, and which can reasonably be supported comprehensively by its members with a minimum of coercion. He arrives at this position in seeing that our flourishing within community is contingent on those feelings of belonging and the derivation of social benefits. To coerce people into providing such benefits would, in his view, alienate the ability to feel belonging as one is forced, rather than comes to, become part of the social realm. To this end, he asserts the necessity of the internalisation of the good as 'of oneself', meaning that one might meaningfully recognise its value and *fairness* in maintaining a desire for the flourishing of 'everyone', rather than privileging one group or person.

Second, and in relation to this, the good cannot be purely political since it is 'lived' through interaction. For instance, Green emphasises the responsibility of developing one's capacity for compassion, of conscientious judgement, and of mutual respect. To act in ways that amount to the development of these capacities is to uphold a moral character and therefore to support the common good of flourishing. From this, one must recognise that a community cannot rely wholly on a political good alone. Rather, it must be lived, shaped, and enhanced in the social, cultural, and economic spheres. Subsequently, Green's common good is focused on the creation of an equitable and fair society underpinned by a good moral character in its citizens which can facilitate the diverse but coherent development of our persons in line with the society of societies and Higher-self. Such a good, which holds equal worth at its core, is conducive to pluralism and rejects coercion unless citizens attempt to invalidate equal worth.

A Lived Good of Mutual Recognition

The living of the good is important to Green because he sees that the alternative, a political good upheld through state power and legal restriction, can lead individuals to rally against good ethics on the grounds that they justify the state acting to deprive them of something. Such an experience is held to cloud the judgement of the individual and to make it more difficult for them to feel belonging within community. In response to this fear, Green moves to suggest that the good should become the vehicle for the legitimation of public-political institutions because this good, by virtue of representing the interests of the entire society, is free to legislate in a way that is not morally coercive (Green 2008, 202). This leads Green to advocate for a common good based upon mutual recognition, because a lived mutual recognition entails an individual holding certain rights which cannot reasonably be broken unless one is to forsake them for themselves. What he means by this is deceptively simple, following a principle which holds that one should treat others with the consideration that they themselves would expect, which here becomes a right to be upheld when we consider that bonds of equal worth rest upon citizens being held to a common ethical standard. So long as the state can act in accordance with such a good, treating its members with respect whilst seeking to facilitate their development, it can be considered legitimate, whilst it maintains some freedom to restrict those who invalidate this mutualistic flourishing. The result of this, he argues, is to form an interconnected society that cares for its members, with a state that legislates in line with the common good in two senses (1) to support flourishing and (2) to uphold the society of equals. This is to enshrine thoughtful duty and personal responsibility for others at the heart of state belonging or citizenship, as well as to underline that the lived experience of mutual recognition is essential to the maintenance of rights, which can only be infringed upon by the state once an individual has themselves forsaken such bonds. This maintains two important features for the working-class.

Namely, the Greenian good demands respect from other members of society, and within the class itself, to justify it and makes it clear that the community must act as a moral duty to ensure that its members can pursue flourishing.

Nonselfishness and Nonexploitation

Green develops this good further by referring to the supplementary principles of nonselfishness and nonexploitation (Simhony 2014). Although he does define these fully, he posits that the legitimate role of the state would be to curb selfish attitudes, which he sees as leading to greed and the deprivation of both rich and poor alike, and exploitation, which is in no ethical person's interest because it denies the fundamental equality of human beings, essentially reiterating many of the arguments made in Chap. 5, yet presenting state legitimacy as partly founded upon moral rightness. This latter justification for the state acting to limit exploitation is bound up in Green's conception of rights. In his state, rights only exist if citizens recognise that, in applying to them, they must apply equally to others or else the right becomes a privilege and can no longer be guaranteed by mutual respect or recognition alone. To be sure of attaining rights, one consequently has the responsibility of seeing them applied across the board because, in doing so, one confirms themselves as part of a collective which mutually agrees to uphold such agreements. Indeed, what Green suggests is that individual rights are guaranteed on the basis that they are mutually recognised in the community as morally right. They are morally right because they uphold our fundamental desire to flourish, whilst the action of mutually agreeing upon them fulfils Green's hope for "a society of which the life is maintained by what its members do for the sake of maintaining it" (Green 2008, 25).

There is then a civic duty attached to the common good that one, as a citizen, is expected to uphold on the basis that it encourages activity towards growth, as well as stressing the fundamental equality of human beings. This becomes a civic duty, rather than a mere benefit derived from the state because it requires participation in the moral and other codes of society "...[which] can hardly arise while the individual's relation to the state is that of a passive recipient of protection in the exercise of his rights of person and property" (Green 2008, 122). Consequently, Green sees the common good as being more involved than a disinterested mutual recognition of others. Indeed, Green's understanding of rights is essential in his theory of the common good because they provide the conditions that establish a community, which is created by the practice of mutual recognition. These practices are encouraged in a structural sense by state and social institutions, as well as everyday lived social norms, and further act to reaffirm the common good because the practice of mutually recognising rights is demonstrative of one also practising mutual concern (Green 2003, 146). Green says that this practice is of "distinctive social interest" and stresses that it can help to shape the "moral terrain of human connectedness", in which the good of the community and the good of oneself can become unified, in turn becoming a common good because it applies to all members of the community (Green 2003, 230). As such, although on a basic level the common good is concerned with the mutual recognition of all members, it runs deeper than this, entailing civic duty and active involvement in the state and community to guarantee rights and renew the social fabric upon a moral basis. This provides the basis for movement towards the reconciliation of tensions.

Ethical Citizenship

Having said that the common good requires participation as well as state action, Green sets out some of the practical ways we might conceive this. This includes an account of ethical citizenship and of the legitimate role of the state in equalising social provisions.

Ethical citizenship involves those things which we have mentioned, like commitment to mutual respect, self-realisation, the expansion of one's knowledge and reasoning capacity, and participation. However, what does participation necessarily entail, and is every citizen expected to participate in a similar manner? Green's answer to this question provides some basis for a participatory society which is not solely focused on direct involvement in political matters. For example, Simhony (2014, 15) describes Green as adopting a view of citizenship that is not overly monistic. This is best understood as a "my station and its duties" conception of the citizen, wherein one sees themselves as performing some role which, although different to those around them, nevertheless contributes to community. By adopting this stance, which Green does alongside Bosanquet, the Idealists come to a citizenship which is conducive to the integration of diverse dignities. For example, it respects that citizens can have different identities but, through understanding oneself as a member of the community with a distinct purpose, one can subscribe to a shared narrative-based identity in which a society's difference is interconnected so as to ultimately serve the common good.

In line with this "my station and its duties" approach to regard for our citizens, the Idealists suggest that everyone has a purpose which they should pursue because, in developing their capabilities, they improve the community through the skills, knowledge, and expertise which they obtain, so long as they are mutualistic. This is expressed by Bosanquet, who highlights "the illusion that duties which deal with public matters are the only public duties", going on to say, "all duties are public, or at least take us beyond the ordinary self" (Bosanquet 1996, 11). This is expressed by Cruddas, Goodhart, and others as "vocation", the idea that one can find fulfilment in their interests that brings them dignity and yet provides something meaningful to the community through their service—the private interest becoming a public duty to flourish. This is placed at the centre of Idealist thought and reorients our focus towards the recognition of a variety of roles, such as the labourer or factory worker in their time, as being of an essential value to the community that is deserving of recognition in society, as well as within our public discourse. Subsequently, the Idealists understanding of citizenship as related to vocation can be described as diverse, actively encouraging a multitude of activities, and inclusive within a unified narrative that justifies diversity of role on the grounds that it expands our capabilities and, through that, enables individuals or groups to see themselves equally respected (Simhony 2014, 15). Thus, ethical citizenship does not stress conformity. It encourages the development of unique (but coherent) identities and lends itself more specifically to the dignification of previously discounted professions/interests, with significance for Chap. 8 especially.

The Reconciliatory State and the Common Good

Despite his insistence on the diffusion of power throughout the society of societies, Green reserves an integral role for political institutions in fostering flourishing on the grounds that politics is, in an Aristotelian sense, the exercise of ethical principles, of which flourishing is the ultimate one for community (Tyler 2019). In this way, one might consider that our political institutions are legitimated by their responsibility to uphold, encourage, and protect, the progress that is being made towards it. The implication of this is a state which is inherently 'enabling' to its citizens and whose existence is premised on service to its people. As such, he bestows the responsibility for the maintenance of social stability, the provision of services, and the task of moral education upon it.

In this we see Green carve out a role for the state as mediator, primarily because he recognises that political harmony requires deliberate actions to sustain it (Nesbit 2001). Therefore, one of its main roles is to assuage concerns in line with those methods stipulated by its principles, namely those of mutual respect, nonexploitation, and nonselfishness. By making the state responsible for the practice of these principles, Green hopes that it will integrate groups into society in a way that does not diminish their unique identities. In this regard, the Greenian state is responsible for the creation of a "double ontology" of the individual (though no splitting of the self is involved) by providing the grounds upon which one is at once universal (i.e. identical with others) and particular (i.e. unique) in a system of essential human equality and relative social justice (Morrow 2007). As part of this, it should act to create an inclusive narrative, which tends to refer to an accessible national identity in the writings of Green. It is inclusive because every member of the community can find some part of themselves within it, encompassed within a vision for that community which appeals and inspires dedication to the common good. If those responsible for the state can successfully uphold these mutualistic values, assuage concerns, and integrate the members of the community then they will build towards a near future in which the possibility of serious instability within the state is significantly limited, primarily because Green sees that its principles delegitimise most of the views which could cause serious conflict. These views would simply be 'beyond the pale' for an ethical citizen to consider. The nexus that these rights and values create therefore tend towards the establishment of a politics that is ethical and takes account of basic human dignity. This conception of the state might best then be described as the ethical and reconciliatory, with a primary focus on the improvement of human flourishing in line with those principles hitherto established. We return to this understanding in Chaps. 7 and 9.

Conclusions

This chapter has detailed the relevance of British Idealism's principles, namely their focus on the Higher-self and moral character, as well as the society of societies and common good, in relation to alienation.

In discussing the Higher-self we have highlighted how the Idealists sought individual perfection through a commitment to the common. They see the act of seeking perfection improves the lot of others and develops the emotional and intellectual capacities necessary for the creation of a more moral world. This is taken to challenge the dignity component of alienation through the provision of meaning whilst maintaining some influence on the community factor as well through the assertion of moral regard for others. Crucial in this is the sharing of bonds. For the Idealists, these bonds shape our humanity and the faculties which we employ to live and make connections in this world. They help us to realise ourselves as well as the innate value of others. In the search for the Higher-self one, therefore, learns to appreciate others as more than just ends, instead forming meaningful relationships with them that enable us to see mutual growth. This fits with a perspective, popular amongst the working-class broadly that respects community, whilst one cannot deny that traditions, customs, and bonds do shape us as people. It is this aspect of the Higher-self, its relation to others, that has importance in challenging alienation. Indeed, it establishes the importance of equal consideration within community. The realisation that community and individual are interlinked entities in this respect, created by the bonds which exist between peoples, enables one to shape and ground an identity whereby the individual is not pitted against others within a collective but, rather, is a unique part of that entity. In adopting this view, it could well serve to blunt some of the harsh distinctions which are often made between the two, thereby encouraging individuals to conceive themselves as an identifiable part of the collective in a positive way, not subject to its will but informing it as an agent.

The implications of moral character for alienation are two-fold. First, in much the same way that the Higher-self encourages interaction, the moral character focuses on what an individual or community might look towards to govern how they interact with one another, as well as how they might conceive of those around them as equal higher beings. Secondly, at least in the way that Green conceives it, one does not necessarily need to subscribe to a list of established values to become moral. Instead, a person with a strong moral character is defined as someone that is concerned with those around them, treating them as equals worthy of support. The strength of individual moral character arises from the bonds and interactions which they develop in community. To be moral is to feel solidarity and, with that, genuinely attempt to understand others' positions and criticise them if one feels it to be unconscientious, but nevertheless respect their dignity. This emphasis on solidarity and understanding as precursors for moral betterment contains within it the suggestion that members of a society should engage with one another from a position of consideration. This means attempting to empathise so that we might come to arrangements which are mutually beneficial and respective of our dignity. Consequently, the moral character acts to challenge alienation because it leads individuals, and the community, to acknowledge the importance of bonds between equal peoples, as well as the significance of a person's dignity, on a fundamental level.

The society of societies underpins and shapes these notions. The focus of Idealism on flourishing is met within a society where an individual or group has the potential to develop their faculties in a variety of institutions. The importance of diversity within this community cannot be understated. In fact, it is the diversity of societies, or associations, which creates the grounds for improvement, as well as providing impetus for the advancement of the community. This is bound up in a conception of the state wherein knowledge is diffused throughout society, with each institution contributing to communal flourishing. The implication of this for alienation being the further interlinking and expansion of our societies. This would be to help people find acceptance for their uniqueness within associations by recognising them as integral members of the community acting to broaden the knowledge available to it and to better the lives of their members. Consequently, we might consider the society of societies as providing an attractive vision. It builds a narrative wherein our differences expand knowledge and activity in a multitude of directions. It is inclusive and recognises plurality within community which can be bound together through the practical work of civil society associations, as well as a narrative premised on regard for mutual flourishing alongside these shared notions of Higher-self, moral character, and the common good. This focus relates explicitly to that component of alienation which seeks to rebuild community and asserts in relation to this the need to emphasise the mutual recognition of our different talents, experiences, and vocations for the purpose of ensuring dignity and yet also demonstrate our interconnectedness so that we might better appreciate our fellows and overcome our present inter-class and societal divisions. This underlines the importance of both civil society and narrative as tools for the amelioration of alienation, with significance for Chap. 10.

The common good binds these ideas together into a framework focused on rights, citizenship, and state action. It is the common good which offers the most complete vision of the society the Idealists envisage. This is a society which, at its core, requires the mutual recognition of one's innate equality, which underlines an understanding of society whereby one should regard the flourishing of others as akin to one's own. This entails a civic duty to uphold the principles of nonselfishness and nonexploitation which are promoted by Green to ensure fair and ethical action. As such, the good requires participation to maintain it from society and through our interactions. Interestingly, the good relies on the diversity of peoples and professions and is encompassed within the Idealist view of ethical citizenship which promotes a view of the individual as wedded to their own station through which they aid the community. Unlike other theories, however, one identifies their own station depending on what they find they are most effective at, or enjoy the most, and are encouraged to see their position, and that of others, as dignified because it serves community. This is to reaffirm Chap. 5's discussion of vocation as a legitimate and core component of our dignified flourishing, with latter significance for Chaps. 8 and 10.

The common good relies too on the state-political institutions. Indeed, it requires state intervention and education to uphold its principles and maintain stability within the community through the reconciliation of differing groups and the extension of dignity to them. It can be considered a facilitator for social activity, eliminating barriers and at the same time ensuring opportunity, cooperation, and the education of its members, in an intellectual sense, but also according to its own vision of unity and reconciliation. The state here is taken to be legitimised by its actions in accordance with this good and establishes that only a state that maintains the flourishing of its members and respects their rights, so long as they respect those of others, can be considered legitimate. One sees in this the genesis of an ethical enabling state which can reconcile, support, and find redress for its citizens in a way that can be considered fair and inclusive. This finds its expression within Chaps. 9 and 10's focuses on Progressive Nationalism and intermediary associations, respectively.

Taken together, the Idealist philosophy is based upon cooperation and mutual betterment with the express intention of maintaining flourishing. One can reasonably envisage some progress being made in challenging the three core components of alienation in line with this, namely by making individuals, groups, and sub-groups more aware and appreciative of one another, by forging a narrative that restores dignity and cooperation to working-people, as well as bestowing upon them a sense of agency. Naturally, there are issues that must be considered, which the next chapter will deal with, but Idealism provides a philosophical base for the book's challenge to working-class alienation. As such, one adopts the Idealist ethics presented throughout this chapter and will develop them further to address the book's central problem.

Bibliography

Bosanquet, Bernard. *Politics and Philosophy.* Routledge/Thoemmes, 1996.

Bosanquet, Bernard. *Science and Philosophy (Routledge Revivals): And Other Essays.* Routledge, 2013.

Bosanquet, Bernard. *The Introduction to Hegel's Philosophy of Fine Art.* Routledge, 2015.

Brink, David Owen. *Perfectionism and the Common Good: Themes in the Philosophy of T. H. Green.* Clarendon, 2007.

Etzioni, Amitai. *The Common Good.* John Wiley & Sons, 2014.

Evans, Geoffrey, and James Tilley. *The New Politics of Class: The Political Exclusion of the British Working Class.* Oxford University Press, 2017.

Goodhart, David. *Head Hand Heart: The Struggle for Dignity and Status in the Twenty First Century.* Penguin, UK, 2020.

Green, T.H. 'Liberal Legislation and Freedom of Contract, 1861'. Accessed 9 Apr 2023.

Green, T.H. *Lectures on the Principles of Political Obligation.* Cambridge Scholars Publishing, 2008.

Green, T.H. *Prolegomena to Ethics.* Clarendon Press, 2003.

Green, T.H. *Prolegomena to Ethics.* Read Books, 2007.

Guyer, Paul, and Rolf-Peter Horstmann. "Idealism." In *The Stanford Encyclopedia of Philosophy*, edited by Edward N. Zalta and Uri Nodelman, Spring 2023. Metaphysics Research Lab, Stanford University, 2023. https://plato.stanford.edu/archives/spr2023/entries/idealism/. https://history.hanover.edu/texts/green.html.

MacIntyre, Alasdair. *After Virtue: A Study in Moral Theory.* 3rd ed. Notre Dame, IN: University of Notre Dame Press, 2007.
MacKenzie, John Stuart. *An Introduction to Social Philosophy.* Hansebooks, 2017.
Morrow, John. *T.H. Green.* Ashgate, 2007.
Nesbitt, D. Recognizing Rights: Social Recognition in T. H. Green's System of Rights. *Polity* 33 no. 3, (2001): 423-437.
Nicholson, P. P. *The Political Philosophy of the British Idealists: Selected Studies.* Cambridge University Press, 1990.
Rawls, John. *A Theory of Justice.* Harvard University Press, 2009.
Raz, Joseph. *The Morality of Freedom.* Clarendon Press, 1986.
Simhony, Avital. 'The Political Thought of the British Idealists'. In Mander, W.J. *The Oxford Handbook of British Philosophy in the Nineteenth Century.* OUP, 2014.
Tyler, Colin. 'Thomas Hill Green'. In *The Stanford Encyclopedia of Philosophy*, edited by Edward N. Zalta, Summer 2019. Metaphysics Research Lab, Stanford University, 2019. https://plato.stanford.edu/archives/sum2019/entries/green/.
Walzer, Michael. *Spheres of Justice: A Defense of Pluralism and Equality.* Basic Books, 1984.

CHAPTER 7

Developing Idealist-Socialism

This chapter builds on the Idealist ethics of the previous chapter to develop the book's answer to alienation. It will address some of the key ideas of Guild Socialist G.D.H. Cole alongside the related ideas of Harold Laski, discussing the ways in which they drew on Idealism, as well as their ideas which are critical of it.[1] It begins with an overview of Idealist ethics before moving to analyse the socialist and Idealist positions regarding the society of societies, the state, and the capitalist system, before concluding that Guild Socialist and Socialist Pluralist thought builds on Idealist ethics but imbues it with a deeper sense of practicality and social justice, as well as an analysis of the power relations which currently limit flourishing. The chapter concludes by outlining the implications of this for a position which can challenge working-class alienation. This will be labelled Idealist-Socialism.

[1] The link between these two traditions is highlighted in particular by Bevir (1993, 2011), whilst a focus on Cole is found in Stears (1998).

S. Taylor Hill, *Challenging Alienation in the British Working-Class*, Palgrave Politics of Identity and Citizenship Series,
https://doi.org/10.1007/978-3-031-59250-8_7

The Ethics of British Idealism and the Guild Socialist Debt to It

The Guild Socialists, Cole especially, owe much of their understanding of character development to Bosanquet and Green, who envisage our evolution into a Higher-self—defined so as a state of realising our identities, our relationship with each other, our place in the world, and our general purpose within the wider network of human relations (Bosanquet 2015). For instance, Cole focuses upon workplace democratisation because he envisages that by giving individuals responsibility and agency within their work, they will grow as persons. This follows a similar line of argument to that of Bosanquet, who praises "practical socialism" in the form of mutual societies, cooperatives, and credit unions, on the basis that the structures within them, which are participatory and entail the mutual fulfilment of need, form an environment conducive to the creation of a Higher-self (Bosanquet 1889, 46). In fact, they are premised on free peoples, interacting in service of communal goals, such is the basis of these socialist-inspired groups. According to Bosanquet, this gives rise to openness wherein otherwise suppressed voices (in a typical workplace) are treated with dignity because they are held to offer something of potential importance to the collective and its ability to strive towards its goals (Bosanquet 1889). The result is to increase the diversity of opinions to which the workplace community is exposed, which is an essential part of the wider Idealist desire for knowledge, as well as to imbue its individual members with a sense of worth because they have some role to play in the greater development of that collective body.

Cole wholeheartedly buys into this understanding and bases much of his thought on a concept of the Higher-self, though he never says it explicitly. For instance, as we shall see, he advances a plan for the creation of a new society which grants individuals all they require to flourish through "positive self-government" (Cole 1920a, 18). He marries this to a concern for the common, seeing the two as related by virtue of the fact that the collective provides the opportunities and education which one needs to be positive in their own self-government. This is identical to Bosanquet's own discussion of the Higher-self, wherein he sees that a strong social realm, where we form bonds with others and learn from them, is a necessity so that we might come to recognise our individual-collective coherency. (Bosanquet 2013). Subsequently, the Idealist commitment to a Higher-self is pro-social and community focused whilst simultaneously grounding the individual in such a way as to give them purpose, identity, and the means for self-realisation. Cole adopts this as his own and subsequently seeks to have it realised through an interlinked network of intermediary associations.

For Cole this is the Guild system, which represents the most fundamental form of organisation within a community, responsible for numerous services and the exercise of political and social functions. He imagines an interlinked network of intermediary associations which collaborate with each other in service of some specific end. He uses the example of the railways to explain this, suggesting that one could reasonably see a Railways Guild made up of those who work within the industry, which might be split into smaller units based on the role they play or perhaps the region in which they work (Cole 1920a, 47–49). These groups would organise themselves to perform their function but would each have an equal voice in decision-making for the Guild. Thus, if that Guild were to make a decision over a potential change to its own internal regulations, each member could contribute something or elect a delegate to voice their concerns on the particular issue. The changes would then be voted upon by the membership or agreed by the delegates with the consent of those who sent them (Cole 1920b). Internally then, Cole sees the Guild as a social organism in which its members might belong to different groups but perform a function in service of a collective end, in this case the functioning of the Railways, and are consequently afforded a voice in the decision-making process for that 'community'. One can reasonably see themselves as part of that collective and take pride in the work which they do in service of it but also retain some sense of uniqueness since their opinion is treated as essential to the direction of the Guild. Internally then, this system expresses Cole's desire for one to see themselves as at once a member of the collective and a unique entity, which are bound together in an Idealist sense by the common good. We see in this model Cole's belief in the importance of associations in providing the framework for a more agential, dignified existence, as well as the interlinking of these two components to provide the individual with satisfaction in work.

This is underlined by the fact that the Guilds are not standalone democratic institutions. In fact, they exist in parallel with other associations, like say a Railway Users Association(s), that would also have some influence through the mutualistic linking of the two (Cole 1920c). This latter point is important because it demonstrates Cole's underlying ethical intertwining of equality with democracy, seeing that only by extending influence to affected people can one truly be considered equal. In this case, one is equal as a consumer, with the producer, because they both rely on each other for certain ends. As a result of this power-sharing, the groups must come to a mutually beneficial agreement that serves their joint interests. The agreements made through these collective discussions thus represent the physical manifestation of the Idealist belief in the inherent mutuality of the common good society (Green 2003). Here, Cole uses the mechanism of the Guild system to establish mutuality in the minds of society's members simply as the way in which it should naturally operate. This follows his own understanding of the problems of contemporary society as arising out of, and being exacerbated by, the capitalist mode of economic organisation, which we shall discuss in turn. For now, however, we use the example of Guild Socialism and its intended effects as evidence of the underlying Idealist ethics which inspire it, principally those ideas of mutuality and the common good, whilst Cole's Guilds reveal a belief in ensuring working-people maintain agency as a means for the living of the good life.

There are, however, some significant differences in the thought of the Idealists and the two socialist groups which this chapter covers, the most important of which being their views of the Absolute.

This was always a problematic part of Idealist philosophy anyway, which Bertrand Russell critiqued as a severe restriction of diversity on the basis of a monist, objective conception of the good life (Russell 2009, 2). In contrast to this, Russell praises Guild Socialism and Socialist Pluralism for its similar commitment to self-realisation when it is detached from the notion of one Absolute (Russell 2014). Indeed, Cole and Laski do away with this notion entirely, instead focusing on that principle of human flourishing to turn it into an end in itself. For example, Cole writes of the need to create a society which enables the "fullest possible capacity for initiative and self-expression" and to make it "easy for the people feats of self-government and communal expression" (Cole 1920a, 98). This reflects his belief that the 'ultimate' goal of humanity is the realisation of our own flourishing as individuals and as a community of peoples. It, therefore, follows that because we are all subject to different stimuli and other factors, we shall find our happiness in a multitude of diverse activities, which is the job of the community to make available. In this respect then, the Guild Socialists replace the Absolute with a conception of society firmly focused upon flourishing which, in turn, provides others with opportunities for learning and growth. As a result, they reject potential monism in favour of plurality in which the unifying factor is our mutual reliance upon each other for the comprehension of ourselves and the community which shapes us. We still see the Idealist principle of flourishing at the heart of this ethics, but it is raised to a position unto its own as *the* central goal.

This section has sought to demonstrate the compatibility of the socialist position with that of the Idealists. What is evident from Cole's writing is an understanding of society which is like that of the Idealists. This should become clear throughout the chapter, but we stress here the coherency of the two.

Socialist Pluralism and the Society of Societies

Cole, along with the early Harold Laski, develops a theory which can be described as "Socialist Pluralism", which justifies the decentralisation of society by suggesting that it corresponds to the true nature of our humanity as one of unique individuals, finding themselves through the collective, and whose ideas cannot be represented wholesale by political parties (Eisfeld 1996). We thus begin the main bulk of this chapter with an outline of Socialist Pluralism and the socialist society of societies.

The Socialist Pluralists and Guild Socialists largely proceed from an Idealist understanding of society as at once united and diverse (Chap. 6). However, they maintain some important distinctions, which shall be the subject of this section. In fact, in many respects, they interpret this idea to devolve some decision-making power to all citizens who wish to participate in the associations which make up the unified society. Where the Idealists merely prescribed the indirect linking of society through natural social bonds, the Socialist Pluralists assert that this can only occur if power, conceived as relating to influence over all aspects of our lives, i.e. a character of self-government, is institutionally dispersed (Cole 1920b, 41). This finds its most radical expression in the creation of the Guild system and the new local government which is supposed to accompany it. That local government structure, or, more accurately, structures, is best described by Cole, who summarises it in relation to the city of Norwich:

> there will be at least the following bodies possessing important social functions : (a) A number of Industrial Guilds…united in a Guild Council…; (b) a Co-operative Council ; (c) a Collective Utilities Council ; (d) a number of Guilds organising and managing various civic services…; (e) Cultural Council; and (f) a Health Council. All these, not necessarily in the same proportions, have clearly a right to be represented on the communal body. (Cole 1920a, 124–125)

We thus see a decentralised mesh of associations which convene with each other based on ad hoc representation of a community's views. Such views are not limited to one 'political' realm as the civic, cultural, utility, and other associations draw their power from the sovereignty of the people who invest their trust in them. There is no central coercive organisation which promises somehow to represent the entire community but, rather, splintered and ad hoc factions, close to the local people, who can listen to individuals on each separate matter and act in accordance with that single opinion (Cole 1920a, 127). Plurality is maximised here through separation of issues into the realm of the Guild/Association whose function most corresponds to the idea which the individual presents. The relatively equal balance of power which these Guilds/Associations hold subsequently permits each to follow the wishes of its members and to explore potentially divergent routes that another Guild, in another sphere, might do themselves (Stears 1998). In this case, diversity is clearly displayed and any potential conflicts arising out of these divergences are meant to be reconciled in favour of the common good, though the mechanism for this remains unclear and seems to be premised on the assumption that the community believes in mutuality and will thus arrive at the least coercive compromise (Cole 1920a, 122, 125). It is clear from the overview of such a system that Cole especially sees agency as central to a healthy democratic society and associations as key to ensuring it is extended. He emphasises the necessity of belonging within such groups and further asserts that Guilds/Associations can become the embodiment of their members' wills—something imbued with power and able to realise an identity of itself, founded upon the shared work and views of its members.

Building upon this, Socialist Pluralism differs from Idealist Pluralism in two ways. First, it takes a greater note of power relations and sees that only a society rid of its inherent and damaging class inequalities can ever hope to entertain diversity and, second, that plurality comes from the recognition of multiple groups, rather than just multiple mutualistic individuals (Bevir 2011). The Socialist Pluralists here are making an important distinction from Idealism in that, whilst the Idealists see groups as important because they create unique individuals, the Pluralists see that groups create their own identities which are more than just the sum of their individual members and are deserving of consideration because they create their own norms and offer guidance to those who might otherwise have no collective to feel a part of (Eisenberg 2006, 72). The associations thus form an integral part of a pluralistic apparatus. They encourage social interaction between a variety of members, which can open their minds to the possibility of thinking differently and provide options or inspirations which might otherwise have been unavailable to them. These societies unite people actively across society through the organisation of forums for discussion, membership, or other socially conducive activity, whilst their place as active members of the wider Guild system is supposed to fulfil a similar function, bringing people together for their mutual learning and expansion of knowledge, as well as giving their members a place to voice themselves. The multiplicity of associations which one can join is also meant to ensure that opinions either are respected in their current association(s) or can likely find somewhere where they can be positively nurtured. The activities performed by the associations consequently serve to connect the nexus of the community with its individual members, creating a link between them, their direct support system, and the wider community which can engage with them on an ad hoc basis more directly than in the contemporary state. Here one notes the capacity of the associations to provide tangible spiritual and material benefits to their members.

The intended result of this is threefold. Firstly, it provides members of the community with agency in areas which affect them. Secondly, it gives individuals responsibilities, and thirdly, it creates a sense of purpose within something greater not just in the minds of the community but also 'in fact' on an institutional level. The socialist society of societies is thus meant to be realised by taking its liberal counterparts' focus on community and social bonds and creating a deliberate, organised set of institutions to nurture these, directing them towards the extension of the individual's relationship with their community to 'unlock' more effectively their unique capabilities. Here we see the responsibilities of the community, for the community's members' development, shared by the associations which make it up (Cole 1920a, 137). This is the embodiment of the mutualistic and self-reliant ideals which the Idealists first proposed, freed from the problem of overreliance on the centralised state for the provision of even the most basic of services. This latter point, to some extent, also identifies plurality in the way that a society is organised as essential to flourishing.

Indeed, a multiplicity of associations provide belonging, collective agency, and an extension of dignity to its members through shared attachment and cannot themselves be understated.

Consequently, associational pluralism is needed because it tends to 'unlock' the boundaries of society in such a way as to give rise to new opportunities for the development of good moral character, alongside the extension of belonging. Associations here are, therefore, morally educative and provide a core foundation for the dissemination of social benefits, which in turn enhance our collective flourishing.

Taken together, Socialist Pluralism owes much to Idealism in that it wholeheartedly adopts the idea of a society of societies (Carter 2003). Its proponents accept the Idealist argument that compassionate bonds can expand opportunities for mutual self-realisation through the fostering of diversity, which is reflective of a unifying communal spirit dedicated to the betterment of its members and the acknowledgement of our abilities. The Socialist Pluralists see this as intrinsically progressive and premised upon flourishing. However, where it differs is in its attempts at practical implementation. We, therefore, see a Socialist Pluralist desire to connect the social nexus through mechanisms like the Guild system, whilst also grounding an understanding of participation as a right which is conferred by virtue of peoples living within society. Consequently, we see Idealist principles underpinning the socialist society of societies, which seeks to make civil society more important through its interlinking with the apparatus of government in a process of associational expansion (Bevir 1993). This decentralising impetus, matched with the commitment to associational empowerment, seems beneficial in challenging working-class alienation since it affords working-people agency, as well as spaces within the community through which to practise that agency and to connect with others. With some effort, we might use this as a basis to ameliorate issues between constituent members of the class and within our communities, as well as to establish a sense of dignified belonging, or purpose, within their lives. This logic will form the basis for Chap. 10's emphasis on associational expansion, with significance for the working-classes' ability to find belonging, rebuild community, and expand their agential capacities.

The State and Civil Society

Our understanding of Socialist Pluralism and Guild Socialism can be further enhanced by considering their attitude towards the contemporary state, which is one of the primary focuses of both positions. Cole begins *Guild Socialism Restated* (1920a) with an outline of the growth of the state since medieval times, largely in order to demonstrate his belief, akin to the Idealists, that the governmental state should not be one "omnicompetent" force ruling over society but, rather, one association envisaged as playing an important role in cooperation with a diverse range of associations, named so as the 'societies'. Indeed, he notes that the "state was only one of a number of social institutions and associations, all of which exercised, within their more or less clearly defined spheres of operation, a recognised social power and authority" (Cole 1920a, 32). Gradually, however, as society developed and underwent great industrial change, "its turn created the urgent need for intervention; and all alternative forms of communal structure..." have "been destroyed or submerged" (Cole 1920a, 29). That plurality of associations, having been pushed to the boundaries of society left it without the institutions which had anchored and guided it towards the common ends. Replacing this was a behemoth, which promised to do all that the associations had done, represent everyone's interests (virtual or real), and fulfil most, if not all, of their functions. The diversity which had existed previously was, therefore, lost as the state, unable to realistically carry out or fund all the functions which it had inherited, had also accumulated the power to dictate the shape of the new society. Coupled with this understanding of the state as all-powerful but ultimately cumbersome is the idea that it becomes a tool for the stifling of creative impulses. Laski agrees wholeheartedly with the Guild Socialist perspective and suggests in turn that it creates uniformity (Laski 2014a). In fact, in his view state power, when accumulated, could only be self-defeating of "the purpose of social organisation...to secure to each member of society the fullest opportunities for the development of his or her personality, subject only to the impediment of natural aptitude and ability" (Laski in Miliband 1995). This idea of the purpose of the state was, therefore, incompatible with a strong centralised authority, and a correspondingly weak civil society, because it would stifle creativeness and limit the capacity of citizens to exercise communal responsibility in reference to that which they value.

This view of the state as both powerful and cumbersome presents the Guild Socialists with an issue. They deplore the state but recognise that it maintains the power to stifle reform (Cole 1920a). Their answer to this problem is interesting. Cole, for example, suggests that, though the power of the state is considerable, it is the citizenry which legitimises its actions. The citizenry can be considered vital to the continuation of the state's power because they consent to it tacitly by accepting its actions. For example, when the state passes a law, citizens must broadly agree with that law, or the state has a right to make laws, lest it could face unrest. This interpretation of the state's power as ultimately resting on its ability to satisfy a large enough proportion of the population, although not new, underpins the Guild Socialist response to it (Miliband 1995). In fact, on the matter of state power, Cole proposes a form of gradualism in which the few existing associations such as the trade unions, which he sees as having been born out of popular dissatisfaction with the state and its ability to mitigate working-people's concerns, should play an active political role in challenging its legitimacy over certain areas of life in the hope of winning concessions (Cole 1920a, 55). Under this theory, the associations would become places for the transformation of society by providing opportunities for self-realisation, immersing individuals in an atmosphere of equality and respect, and encouraging them to utilise their talent for a common end, as well as creating a social fabric which owes more to a de-facto Socialist Pluralism than that of the society imposed by the state. Although one does not go so far as to deny the legitimacy of the state, Cole's privileging of associations as part of the legitimating apparatus of governance, which expands agency for those citizens who belong to them, is to assert their potential as cultivators for political and social changes.

In raising these points, one accepts that the Guild Socialists do not see the contemporary state as a legitimate entity and subsequently refuse to seek election to offices, which they argue is not fully democratic. Yet, in some respects, this may be a necessary evil since, in the hands of the capitalist, that state apparatus could well become a bastion for the maintenance of the status quo. Indeed, if there is some validity in the arguments of the Guild Socialists that see the state as both over-centralised and encumbered, as well as holding potential as a coercive force, then not controlling that power might simply perpetuate existing inequalities anyway. The Guild Socialist vision, with its critique of the state-as-is, is therefore presented with a challenge with no clear solution. This chapter notes to demonstrate why intellectuals like Laski began to move away from the idea of challenging the state from without, towards a position which one sees as having considerable potential in enhancing working-class agency and grounding a conception of state that aligns with this preference for flourishing (Laski 1925).

The Laskian Model

Laski's view of the state moved from one of deep-seated distrust to a more nuanced view in which the state-as-is was the problem, not the idea of a state more generally. To this end he adopts a two-pronged challenge to the contemporary state, from the associations as before, but also from Parliament. By winning control of Parliament his party, the Labour Party, could alleviate poverty, bring industry into public ownerships, and improve conditions (Laski 2014b, 83). A caveat of this was, however, that it could also use its power to disperse it into a more federal system, somewhat akin to his earlier Socialist Pluralism. Laski thus reiterates his earlier ideas by actively tasking the Labour Party with the decentralisation of power and authority throughout society, in the form of structures which encourage the widest possible degree of popular participation in the exercise of responsibility.

There is an embedded radicalism within this revision of his earlier ideas too as his understanding of the 'widest possible degree' of participation is wide indeed. Laski calls for "ordinary" men and women, through the associations, to be given the power to affect decisions as "producers, as consumers, and as citizens" (Laski 1925, 21). To this end, he argues that the state should act in tandem with the associations, consulting with them, as well as considering their concerns, which are understood to amount to the collected will/s of the citizenry. In this way, he remained true to democratic pluralism, seeing it as the ultimate indicator of an agentially dignified and equal society which could now be arrived at through the use of state power in tandem with an emphasis on those intermediary associations noted previously.

Tied to this is the popularisation of a view of state legitimacy based upon the active consent of the governed. For instance, he asserts that the state is only legitimate when it seriously attempts to find "the maximum of consent on reasonable terms" for its decisions, which requires some level of decentralisation in the first place to even come close to this marker of legitimacy (Laski 2014a, 177). There is no doubt that this is what he hopes will occur and even goes on to say that the popularisation of active consent will safeguard the changes which have already been made, as well as potential future changes because its adoption:

> is to make the task of one's opponents a far more difficult ... when a party puts its policy into operation in terms of an obvious effort to do all possible justice to those whose rights it proposes to redefine, the latter are deprived of an emotional support of high importance. (Laski 2014a, 252)

He, therefore, establishes that a legitimate government must not only govern *for* the people, but also *with* the people (Miliband 1995). It must encourage that flowering of popular responsibility and initiative which are essential to the development of agency. This implies decentralisation to the associations, as well as the evolution of the state towards a situation in which the government must rely on the trade unions, the cooperative societies, and a multiplicity of intermediary associations that consent to act, because these are the closest bodies to the people themselves. Here then the state becomes just one of several actors, requiring consent from the people through their associations. It maintains a significant degree of power, but this power is relational to a number of other groups which hold it to account (Laski 2014a, 252). Consequently, Laski settles on an alliance between the forces at both the top and the bottom. He was uneasily supportive of that alliance but saw that control of the state by progressive forces gave them the ability to effect wide-ranging social, institutional, and economic change. The managed devolution of its power by this force would ensure that the state lost its character as an inefficient behemoth, in turn leaving more opportunities for the associations to make plurality an institutional fact. This action whilst in power would be protected out of power by the popularisation of a viewpoint wherein the state's power was not to be taken for granted. Indeed, if the citizenry could be made aware that the state was reliant on the allegiance of the population, then it would be forced to justify its activity according to some standard, such as the common good of human flourishing (Laski 1922). The state might thus be legitimised depending on its ability to convince its members that their own good was involved in their acceptance of its commands and its wielding of power. How he expects this to happen is somewhat unclear, but the basic solution is a well-intentioned and one for further consideration. This opens space for the understanding of the relationship between state and intermediary associations, which will occur in Chap. 10.

By taking this as our conclusion it, therefore, becomes possible to suggest that the focus from "below" is a noteworthy idea (Cole 1920b, 58). Indeed, just as the Guild Socialists and Idealists saw associations as having an educative, transformative value, there seems some merit in the idea that a coordinated vision of decentralisation, mutualism, and character development could gradually mature and lay the groundwork for a society-wide re-think of our present institutional arrangements. This should not, however, be done instead of trying to win power in the state because, after all, the state has serious "transformative potential" (Laski 2014a, 91). Rather, the network of associations serves as the continual organisers of social change, whether allied to state power or not, and could well serve, in the meantime, to challenge alienation in their own capacity by creating the nexus of communal ties which the Guild Socialists, Socialist Pluralists, and Idealists all see as improving well-being. Thus, through the associations, we might make some, initially small, steps away from overreliance on the state and unlock the "dormant" potential of ordinary citizens for meaningful social evolution (Laski 1931). This diverges from the initial impetus of Guild Socialism and early Laskian Socialist pluralism. However, it nevertheless remains committed to their core principles, seeking a communal pluralism which is based on self-development, character building, identity realisation, and the mutual recognition of collective bonds. This compromises only on the issue of the state to see to it that such changes can be encouraged institutionally, as well as socially through the associations. In addressing working-class alienation then, one sympathises with the expansion of intermediary associations to give voice to their concerns, seeing that the agential action popularised within can offer much to the alleviation of the working-class condition. This, combined with a conception of state legitimacy which enables citizens to demand more of it regarding their flourishing, reorients it towards the recognition of equal worth and dignity, though one will discuss this further in Chap. 10.

Capitalism

Economics does not play a significant role in the Idealist philosophy. There are references to it, like when Bosanquet calls for the creation of mutualistic-socialistic organisations, but this should be seen as part of his desire to develop a good individual moral character in tune with their communities (Bosanquet 1889, 46–48). In fact, this is a common means of discussing the capitalist system, not focusing in on it directly, and instead placing aspects of it in the context of the Idealist vision. This manifests itself in two ways. First, in Green we see a reference to some of the injustices under capitalism in his analysis of poverty and, second, in both his and Bosanquet's writings a clear defence of private property as one of the core foundational elements of the contemporary socio-economic system (Green 2003, 108). Taking these points in turn, we might say that Green is not overly concerned with capitalism provided that its participants accept ethical conditions placed upon it by the Idealist society. As such, we see him criticise the excesses of individuals who exploit the economic system (which is not seen as evidence of flaw in the system itself) for acting immorally in allowing them to "gain by the loss of another" (Green 2003). He supports some state intervention in the economic sphere to maintain its moral integrity by either punishing those who seek to exploit it or remedying the outcomes of misguided activity, though it should be said that this is limited in scope because he sees that "over-enthusiastic or clumsy state intervention could easily...stifle opportunity" (Green in Pandey 2017, 56). Green concludes, in line with this, that the state should only intervene in the economy when an activity is proven to 'enslave' individuals and, seeing as he does not support major intervention, one might infer that most of what happens under capitalism is taken to be acceptable. The implication here is that the fault lies with the individuals who use the economic system and not the system itself. Green too only makes a rudimentary analysis of power relations when he notes the difference between those in poverty and the rich and only seeks to balance the two with some social assistance (Green 2011). It is a position which could be criticised on the basis that it does nothing to change the structural relationship between rich and poor. This is not to downplay social assistance, but it does serve as an example of where the Idealist understanding of capitalism is more structurally limited than that which the Socialists, using Idealist ethics, espouse. In consequence, one sees the Idealist perspective as insufficient in remedying the current struggles of the working-class regarding their work and dignity as outlined in Chap. 5.

The Socialist Ideal

The Socialists begin from a different premise to the Idealists, not treating the capitalist system as the natural order of things in need of reform but, rather, one that inherently promotes vices and degrades our society. The Socialists claim that capitalism ensures that a single class, the Bourgeois, retains significant power protected by the weaving of private property relations into the social fabric (Laski 1950). It is hierarchical by design because its purpose is to maintain the privilege of a social elite, whilst it also follows a corresponding set of norms which are promoted through the order's perpetuation (Laski 1940). Cole cites the accumulation of monetary wealth as one such norm. Here, echoing Sandel (2012), money is seen as a signifier in capitalist society of success and represents an 'end' goal to which someone might aspire. In light of what is perhaps a controversial but nevertheless intuitively plausible claim, to acquire the levels of wealth that capitalism presents as representing one's 'success', one must necessarily deprive someone else of a portion of theirs, due to the stark differences in distribution which are so required to obtain the prestige associated with it (Tawney 1964). Following this illustrative logic, if everyone were to hold the same amount of wealth, then an individual cannot be deemed a success. They cannot be deemed a success because their wealth is not such that it can be envied by others, nor does it confer unto them any power over their fellow human beings, whether that be in the form of becoming a boss, in which case many individuals rely on you for their livelihoods, or in some other respect. The moral bankruptcy of this economic order is clear, prioritising wealth accumulation over human needs, social bonds, and, according to Cole, erstwhile working-class desires for solidarity. The capitalist system thus diminishes us as people and pushes us towards ends which are not of ourselves. This reflects the concerns of Marx (2000) and Sandel (2020), advanced in Chaps. 4 and 5, who assert that capitalism is to alienate us from ourselves, our work, and genuine sociability. In this understanding there is little hope of reforming capitalism. It is, essentially, something that must be eradicated to free humanity to pursue our flourishing. As Cole notes, it is only in eradicating it will "the creative, scientific and artistic impulses which capitalism suppresses" be freed (Cole 1920a, 116).

The Socialists thus view capitalism as fundamentally debilitating. Cole and Laski note its fetishisation of wealth and failure to promote flourishing for most citizens. They take aim in particular at its tendency to impart damaging norms, again reflecting Sandel in Chap. 5, and see this as being perpetuated within a hierarchical system that imparts a "servile character" upon the working-class. This is an important critique, especially post-globalisation, as it asserts that capitalism, which is reliant on stratification for its deification of wealth, exploits working-people with no concern for their dignity or material conditions. One has covered this at length, in Chap. 5, but the Socialists add here that hierarchy is a core element of this exploitation, which is achieved through the stratification of wealth and power and assumes an 'oligarchical nature' under capitalism. The Socialists largely proceed from this basis, seeing the flattening of the economic hierarchy as conducive to the development of a socially healthy set of norms and democratic procedures that can bestow agency, and dignity, upon working-people (Laski 2020).

Cole (1918) and Laski (2020) desire collective ownership over the economy to undermine this hierarchy and institutionally flatten power relations. They argue that collective ownership by the community reflects what should be the purpose of our economy—namely to serve us in pursuit of flourishing. In this view, economics should not be geared towards the deification of wealth and its acquisition by the few at the expense of the many but should be something that we might all benefit from. This benefit takes three forms. First, the Socialists argue that an economy focused on the community can better meet our material requirements with the provision of goods and services, since we have a say in what is produced (Cole 1920c). Second, if the economic hierarchy is flattened, then we free working-people to take control over their work, to organise, and to create in-work systems that are respectful of their members. This involves power equalisation so that wages, working hours, and contracts are mutually agreed upon by workers, thereby undermining the servile state placed upon them by economic hierarchy (Laski 2020; Tawney 1931). Finally, collective ownership is held to break these norms of greed and individualisation by ensuring that the economy is measured according to the flourishing that it provides both to workers through the benefit of vocation and purpose that work can provide and to citizens who rely on our economy for goods and services (Laski 1924). By bringing the economy in line with flourishing, we are seen to abide by the common good and to extend mutuality to this sphere.

This is entwined with an understanding of property relations which itself grounds the necessity of the common good as a fundamental component of our flourishing. In these Socialisms, private property is accepted if one wishes to own their own home, which is seen in the same manner as the Idealists see it as beneficial to personal flourishing (Laski in Sharma 2000, 275). However, ownership where we assume significant power over others, and an ability to exploit them, is denied—which amounts to a denial of ownership over the economy. This is denied because (1) it encourages the distancing of oneself from the community, encouraging a sense of superiority over one's fellows, and (2) it prompts the accumulation of wealth earned on the backs of others as a legitimate and socially healthy end goal (Cole 1920a, 206). Both outcomes undermine the transformation of the economy away from 'capitalist morality' by reiterating the hierarchical norms which underpin it. As such, the Socialists settle on a position which sees that collectively beneficial resources should be placed under control of the community, often understood in relation to the intermediary associations, to maintain fair and equitable control. This is to underline the democratic aspirations of the Socialists and the value that they place on equal agency within the economic superstructure. One takes from this the value of worker representation as part of the moral and practical reshaping of our economy in Chap. 9. In addressing alienation, one establishes that economic democratisation in some capacity offers hope to the redress of working-class concerns over the routinisation of their work, the over-discipline that they face, as well as the injustice and exploitation faced in many jobs.

Although one doubts that this radicalism is achievable at present the basic premise of the Socialists holds, namely, that hierarchy and differential power relations do degrade the working-class. As such, one sees value in the recognition of mutual flourishing as a central indicator of economic success. By proceeding on this basis and emphasising flourishing, one seeks a re-ordering of the economy in favour of the common good and the introduction of reforms that address working-class desires for better pay, conditions, control, and respect. This follows from the critique of our present economic relations in Chap. 5 regarding dignity to suggest that we must re-centre our economy on the moral principles discussed throughout the past two chapters. One builds upon this foundation in Chap. 9 by providing an ethos for our economic relations to promote the dignity of the worker and the flattening of the hierarchies that harm them.

Conclusions

This chapter has demonstrated how Idealism's core ideas were adopted and adapted by the Socialist Pluralists. It has suggested that the ethics of these socialists took inspiration from Idealism (Bevir 1993, 2011; Carter 2003; Stears 1998). Indeed, they maintain a focus on the development of character, the interconnectedness of society, and the importance of a common good in unlocking human flourishing.

The way that they aim to achieve these results, however, differ. We see this in the radicalisation of the 'society of societies' as Cole and the early Laski call for a decentralisation of power which goes beyond the acknowledgement of a wide variety of associations which can shape individual character. Instead, we see power imbued within the associations, which become the apparatus of governance through the creation of a socio-political nexus. Under this, decision-making is opened to those who wish to participate through their associations. One self-realises their purpose and/or identity through their engagement with/in these associations, thus rendering them an important part of the socialist society of societies. Whilst one questions the extent to which the creation of such a radical system might be possible apart from over a considerable period, we have noted that a more decentralised society could serve to encourage agential activity in the name of the common good. The development of a system of interlinked associations, forming a community nexus, does offer hope for the creation of a society, aware of its differences, that proceeds to make decisions with the view in mind of ensuring its members' equal flourishing. For these reasons, an Idealist-inspired Socialism adopts a position which recognises the integral role that civil society associations should play in educating and uniting the community in the common interest and, as a result, seeks to find ways to support the expansion and interlinking of them. One holds this expansion as central in re-creating that sense of community which the working-class see themselves to have lost and which is a key contributor to their continued alienation, as one shall express in Chap. 9.

Related to this is the position of the state under Socialist Pluralism. Cole and the early Laski find themselves in opposition to the state, which has become an ineffective behemoth that prohibits flourishing. In their view, individuals are deprived of their agency since meaningful power belongs to a state that, in its current form, privileges particular ways of living, rather than enables a multitude of diverse activities. The state then is limiting and ineffective in serving the good of the community. This is in sharp contrast to the Idealist interpretation of the state, which sees it not as an organ of class control, but as a powerful force for social betterment, although it cannot use all facets of its power for fear of inadvertently diminishing an individual's ability to enhance their own character.

Such a juxtaposition is striking and, to some extent, outlines the two positions which Laski wished to synthesise into his model. This model acknowledges that it can be used as an organ of class control, but also that it is not inherently like this, and can provide the guidance and alleviation of social evils which the Idealists envisage. By synthesising these models, Laski finds a middle ground in which power is to be won electorally through Parliament and subsequently devolved. This model envisages the integration of civil society associations into the apparatus of governance to ground state legitimacy as based upon its engagement with these groups. Here we see a state that acts to unify its diverse groups and to produce outcomes which are desirable and just. The associations which participate can hold the state to account, and the state would become further legitimised by the community in serving the good. Thus, the model of the state laid down by Laski is designed to provide a route to its realisation through the reiteration of a constant moral and ethical justification delivered within civil society, at the same time as the struggle for an electoral victory which can usher in a political party willing to use state power to transform it for those people who it should serve. Fundamentally, we see in Laski's state the advancement of Socialist Pluralism, the expansion of agency, and a corresponding transformation of the state on Idealist grounds into an organ of communal betterment, guaranteeing well-being, working alongside those who legitimise it, and providing further enablement for flourishing. In consequence, an Idealist-Socialism adopts a Laskian-Idealist model of the state, seeing it as an attractive conception committed to the nurturing of human potential in tandem with the network of communal-intermediary associations. This forms a part of Chap. 10's focus on the expansion of civil society intermediary associations, whilst the reconciliatory state plays a considerable role within Chap. 8's Progressive Nationalism.

Finally, we have explored the differences between the Idealist and Guild Socialist stances regarding the capitalist economic system. We have said that the Idealists do not consider the power relations which arise out of capitalism. This is certainly a weakness in their philosophy as, despite Idealists like Green advocating for some state intervention to alleviate social evils, they tend to ignore the underlying structural causes of societal problems, namely the way in which elites, through the accumulation of wealth and power, effectively limit the ability of the great mass of humanity to develop. This is not to say, of course, that Idealism does not present anything useful when it comes to the economic sphere as Green and Bosanquet both highlight the need for ethical action.

However, the limitations they place on the state to alter structure undermine their commitment to flourishing. Indeed, this is what the Socialist Pluralists essentially suggest. They present a more social justice–orientated view in which strong moral conditions for the economic system are backed by structural change in relation to ownership and property. Capitalism is rejected as inherently immoral in this because of the values it promotes, namely greed, and the exploitation of one's fellows. The argument follows from this that if one cannot exclusively own economic property and cannot, therefore, exert power over others, nor accumulate great wealth, then the values which the economic order promotes shift towards the genuine fulfilment of our collective needs. From this follows the creation of an economic democracy, which provides working-people with agential control. Consequently, from this discussion we come to an understanding of the economy in which it should serve humanity in its quest for scientific, artistic, and creative progress which, under capitalism, has been diminished by the pursuit of wealth. Indeed, the Guild Socialist-Idealist hybrid envisages an alternative economic morality centred on the common good, the bringing in line of the economy with our democratic aspirations, and the equalisation of power to expand working-class agency. It would be too much to ask that capitalism be dismantled at present, but this should not diminish the motivation for flourishing to become the crucial factor in judging economic success. As such, an Idealist-Socialism seeks to address power inequality within the economy, nurture economic democracy, and put forward an argument for the legitimation of our economic institutions based upon their ability to expand dignity and to cultivate the moral behaviour associated with the common good. By looking at the economy from a perspective of human need, we can make significant strides towards ensuring that working-people maintain the agency which they require to secure better working conditions and a dignified existence whilst seeking to challenge those norms identified by Cole, Laski, and Sandel (see Chap. 5) which undermine the capacity of working-people to realise this within our society.

Overall, Guild and Socialist Pluralist thought is more focused on the practical form and function of society than the Idealists before them. In fact, Cole's main focuses have been on the institutions which shall provide society with its democratic character, as well as how to arrive at its creation, namely through the expansion of civil society. Such a commitment to the elucidation of a new set of social institutions, with their innate focus on issues of social justice and democracy, is undoubtedly important. However, the writings of these socialists can be read alongside the Idealists who share their underlying ethics. Where Cole and Laski often neglect to adequately outline the importance of human bonds, these Idealists take much time to explain their value in the potential betterment of society. As such, one considers that the philosophies of the Idealists and Socialists should be combined in such a way that Idealist ethics underpin Socialist practice. By viewing the two as interlinked in this way, one can go beyond the focus on theoretical practicality in the work of the Socialists, as well as the lack of distinct practical features for social justice in the Idealist's works, to create an ideological position which one calls Idealist-Socialism.

This Idealist-Socialist position could be characterised by a commitment to the propagation of good moral character, based upon mutual recognition. This is manifested practically as adherence to a common good centred on flourishing and is coupled with a further commitment to well-being fostered by a socialist society of societies rooted in social justice and the creation of diverse Higher-selves, grounding a need for agency and dignity within the bounds of a reciprocal community. It is in this stead that one continues, expanding upon these core principles to outline position which can diminish alienation.

Bibliography

Bevir, Mark. 'Welfarism, Socialism and Religion: On T. H. Green and Others'. *The Review of Politics* 55, no. 4 (ed 1993): 639–662.

Bevir, Mark. *The Making of British Socialism*. Princeton University Press, 2011.

Bosanquet, Bernard. *Essays and Addresses*. Sonnenschein, 1889.

Bosanquet, Bernard. *Science and Philosophy (Routledge Revivals): And Other Essays*. Routledge, 2013.

Bosanquet, Bernard. *The Introduction to Hegel's Philosophy of Fine Art*. Routledge, 2015.

Carter, Matt. *T.H. Green and the Development of Ethical Socialism*. Imprint Academic, 2003.

Cole, GDH. *Guild Socialism Restated*. Leonard Parsons, 1920a

Cole, GDH. *Self-Government in Industry*. G. Bell and Sons, 1920b.

Cole, GDH. *Social Theory*. Methuen and Co., 1920c.

Eisenberg, Avigail. 'Pluralism and the Politics of Diversity'. In *Pluralism*, edited by Rainer Eisfeld, 1st ed., 59–80. Developments in the Theory and Practice of Democracy. Verlag Barbara Budrich, 2006.

Eisfeld, Rainer. 'The Emergence and Meaning of Socialist Pluralism'. *International Political Science Review / Revue Internationale de Science Politique* 17, no. 3 (1996): 267–79.

Green, T.H. *Prolegomena to Ethics*. Clarendon Press, 2003.

Green, T.H. *Works of Thomas Hill Green*. Cambridge University Press, 2011.

Laski, Harold J. *The State in Theory and Practice*. 1950.

Laski, Harold. 'Socialism and Freedom (1925) | LSE Digital Library'. https://digital.library.lse.ac.uk/objects/lse:qon235yom. Accessed 1 May 2020.

Laski, Harold. 'The Limitations of the Expert (1931) | LSE Digital Library'. https://digital.library.lse.ac.uk/objects/lse:wal303heb. Accessed 1 May 2020.

Laski, Harold. 'The Position of Parties and the Right of Dissolution (1924) | LSE Digital Library'. https://digital.library.lse.ac.uk/objects/lse:guh818hih. Accessed 2 May 2020.

Laski, Harold. 'The State in the New Social Order (1922) | LSE Digital Library'. Accessed 3 May 2020.

Laski, Harold. *A Grammar of Politics (Works of Harold J. Laski)*. Routledge, 2014a.

Laski, Harold. *Democracy in Crisis (Works of Harold J. Laski)*. Routledge, 2014b.

Laski, Harold. *The Decline of Liberalism*. Hobhouse Memorial Lecture, 1940.

Laski, Harold. *The Works of Harold J. Laski*. Routledge, 2020.
Marx, Karl. *Economic & Philosophic Manuscripts of 1844*. Marxists.org, 2000.
Miliband, Ralph. 'Ralph Miliband: Harold Laski's Socialism (1995)'. https://www.marxists.org/archive/miliband/1995/xx/laski.htm. Accessed 16 May 2023.
Pandey, Sadhana. *Western Political Thought*. Horizon Books, 2017.
Russell, Bertrand. *Proposed Roads to Freedom*. Simon and Schuster, 2014.
Russell, Bertrand. *The Philosophy of Logical Atomism*. Routledge, 2009.
Sandel, Michael J. *The Tyranny of Merit: What's Become of the Common Good?* Penguin, UK, 2020.
Sandel, Michael J. *What Money Can't Buy: The Moral Limits of Markets*. Penguin, UK, 2012.
Sharma, Urmila, and S. K. Sharma. *Principles And Theory In Political Science Vol# 1*. Atlantic Publishers & Dist, 2000.
Stears, Marc. 'Guild Socialism and Ideological Diversity on the British Left, 1914–1926'. *Journal of Political Ideologies* 3, no. 3 (1 October 1998): 289–306.
Tawney, R.H. *Equality*. Unwin Books, 1931.
Tawney, R.H. *Equality*. Unwin Books, 1964.

CHAPTER 8

Progressive Nationalism

Utilising the ethos developed over the course of the preceding two chapters, this chapter seeks to develop a Progressive Nationalist vision to challenge alienation. This is a Progressive Nationalism in three parts. First, as we shall see in this chapter, it is progressive in its multicultural orientation and framing for the restoration of a community-derived dignity to working-people. In the subsequent chapters, one will build on this with an economic orientation which stresses the need for worker agency within a context of fairness, and due reward, before sketching out a vision for an expanded civil society which seeks the rooting of community and the provision of collective agency to the working-class.

One posits this against the right-communitarians, who advocate for a populist ethnonationalism which falls between the right-wing ethnonationalism and liberal nationalism described later in this chapter. These communitarians tie to this frame an economic model which leans left in its search for the re-dignification of vocation but which is otherwise insubstantive, and an interest in civil society as the basis for communal belonging, which is also never fully developed unless in reference to the devolution of powers to local authorities (Pabst 2021). One tends to agree with the inclination of these latter points and so seeks to develop them towards clearer ends in Chaps. 9 and 10, yet finds itself in fundamental disagreement over the kind of nationalism that can ameliorate alienation.

S. Taylor Hill, *Challenging Alienation in the British Working-Class*, Palgrave Politics of Identity and Citizenship Series,
https://doi.org/10.1007/978-3-031-59250-8_8

This nationalism begins with a form of patriotism, derived from the common good approach of Maurizio Viroli, before moving in a nationalist direction owing to one's rejection of Viroli's conceptualisation of nationalism as a wholly negative force. Rather, one sees in its multicultural form hope for the creation of a narrative that is pluralistic, respectful of the common good, and which can ensure that our citizens are included in, praised by, and able to shape our shared home. This is significant in the amelioration of alienation for its ability to generate meaning and attachment, to envisage bonds between citizens in support of mutual recognition, and to motivate action for our collective betterment and the betterment of working-people. The chapter will begin with a discussion of common good patriotism, before moving to consider national narratives and culture. From here, one details how a multicultural nationalism might be constructed, before concluding that this Progressive Nationalist framework can serve to justify, inspire, and coordinate those actions which are conducive to the amelioration of alienation.

Why Begin with Patriotism?

One begins here with a theory of patriotism because of the unique nature of Maurizio Viroli's, which is defined in relation to the "common good" (Viroli 2003, 1). This relationship between patriotism and the common good is significant regarding a theory that will become Progressive Nationalism as this identifies a common basis with Idealist-Socialism, which one will build upon subsequently. To this end, it seems appropriate to use Viroli's patriotism as a "base" from which a progressive theory of nationalism can be established given the importance it places upon the good.

Viroli's Patriotism

Viroli develops his patriotism by identifying its historic definition, suggesting that "the love of the *patria* was a sense of compassion as overcoming private selfishness to respect the common good" (Viroli 2003, 25). It was related to a republican idea of virtue as the overriding of sectional interests in the light of the good, defined in accordance with the patria, or nation. This entails a commitment to the personal practice of civic virtue, which is an ideal of duty to one's nation so that we can collectively enjoy our liberty. The ability to enjoy one's liberty, defined by Viroli as the freedom to flourish and to live well, forms the core of his patriotism. He sees that liberty is a collective endeavour for several reasons, not too dissimilar to the way in which the Idealists conceive of it. Indeed, they maintain a similar argument by suggesting that individuals can only achieve their potential when they are part of a community (Green 1997). They cannot, for example, develop their capacity for love if they have no relationships with others and they cannot learn what they wish to learn as effectively without the help of their fellows, whilst we often rely on others constantly to produce that which cannot be produced alone, like our institutions. In many respects, we become the best possible versions of ourselves only when we can interact with, learn from, and rely upon others, and, through the collective contribution of many selves, create things for the nation that we can be most proud of—such as the NHS. Viroli sees that our lives, and the patria itself, as being shaped by our fellows, whilst the relationships that we develop are what provide us with the meaning which makes life worth living, as well as the institutions that guarantee life itself. The realisation of the collective as necessary for the development of liberty, and the ability to live a good life, is consequently placed at the core of Viroli's patriotism and leads him towards a position in which one cannot conceive of oneself as enjoying the fullest life if one does not consider their fellow's life as equal. In this view, we are each guarantors of our fellows and, in line with wishing to live the best life and to express love for country, we must build a patria that is inclusive, enabling, and provides the means for mutual flourishing.

This is a powerful premise for Viroli to base his patriotism upon and is reminiscent of that held by R.H. Tawney and Clement Attlee. In a speech to the Labour Party at Scarborough in 1951, Attlee outlined his progressive patriotic vision for Britain, saying:

> We know the kind of society we want. We want a society of free men and women—free from poverty, free from fear, able to develop to the full their faculties in co-operation with their fellows, everyone giving and having the opportunity to give service to the community, everyone regarding his own private interest in the light of the interest of others, and of the community; a society bound together by rights and obligations, rights bringing obligations, obligations fulfilled bringing rights; a society free from gross inequalities and yet not regimented nor uniform." Before going on to say that we must "[r]emember that we are a great crusading body, armed with a fervent spirit for the reign of righteousness on earth … we will not cease from mental fight, Nor shall the sword sleep in my hand, Till we have built Jerusalem, In England's green and pleasant land. (Attlee 1951)

This is a potent ideal, aligning patriotic duty and obligation with progress towards our flourishing (Bew 2016). Such zeal for a common good-based patriotism, unselfish and loving of "England's green and pleasant land", resonates with what Viroli speaks of, drawing a parallel in which both re-order patriotic duty so that justice is placed at its core, and duty understood as to the national community and one's fellows. In this sense patriotism is a moral, spiritual, and political endeavour in service of the common good, expressing a recognition of the value of equal worth much akin to that of the Idealists, in which "we have to fight against anyone who attempts to impose a particular interest over the common good; we have to oppose discrimination and exclusion … nor to deny civil and political rights to any … patriots" (Viroli 2003, 9).

Such a justice-orientated patriotism is, however, quite different to lay notions of it, which are often bound up in a love for one's country based more clearly along cultural lines (Primoratz 2020). He purports to create an alternative in which the source of the patriot's pride does not stem merely from the feeling of belonging or of being comfortable within the nation, but of duty and the desire to see oneself reflected in it. In line with this, he asks us to consider what we want our country to look like, what we are happy with, and what we would like to change. The patriot, for Viroli, becomes here a political-moral agent who is involved within the shaping of their nation as a labour of love.

The 'shaping' that Viroli places at the forefront of his patriotism is, as we have noted, one that is most fundamentally about the flourishing of people. This focus for patriotism is interesting in that he desires to see liberties and rights extended, and livelihoods protected, to ensure that people are able to love their country. He suggests that part of the patriot's duty is to ensure that one's fellows are "loved" and can express their love of country free from fear, following the logic that "modern citizens too can love their republic, if the republic loves them" (Viroli 2003, 184). This maxim goes some way to describe the patriotism of Viroli, who sees that people can only truly love their country and carry that love into action if it, and people within it, love them back (Viroli 2003, 101). This can become a quest for the patriot who, even having been wronged or having seen their fellows wronged, seeks to remedy such a problem to restore the nation upon a more ethical-principled path. Interestingly, these principles are also considered to be beneficial in both a moral and a pragmatic way, appealing to those who may conceive the nation on different terms than their fellows. For instance, Viroli notes that patriots act in such a way not only because it is morally right and they recognise it as part of the narrative unfolding of their nation but also because it is in the nation's interest to have people love it/to expend effort in support of its flourishing (Viroli 2003, 21). The patriot is, therefore, concerned with righting wrongs because it is beneficial in multiple ways to the common good, whilst the realisation of one's treatment as a dignified member of the community can improve their civic engagement and contribution to the health of the nation. Consequently, the focus of Viroli's patriotism, namely in righting wrongs and expansion of patriotic love through the development of the patria's residents, is centred on a belief that we should be able to embrace our country and feel loved by it, rather than merely expressing love for it. Patriotism is, therefore, taken to be a reciprocal relationship between country, individual, and one's fellows, in which love, and the capacity for human flourishing, is to be continually extended in-line with the common good. Such a logic is supported by the pragmatic side to one's moral duty which seeks to improve belonging, or of dignity, in light of what that may do for the common good. Reciprocity is, therefore, taken here to ensure pride in one's country and to bring others to support it.

This has significance for a Progressive Nationalism because it emphasises that it can well be about more than unconditional loyalty or love for one's country. For Viroli, patriotism comes to involve the expansion of societal unity through the active effort of inclusion, rather than the exclusion of certain groups. Here we see how loyalty is conditional, conceived to rest upon the realisation that one's nation is good to them, and is either deserving, or is potentially deserving, of their loyalty: their love. The impetus for the patriot is subsequently to expand those principles, institutions, and aspects of our culture which tend towards inclusion and make it possible for the residents of our country to flourish. Such an understanding of patriotic duty as related here to the flourishing of the country's residents can be said to fit with arguments made throughout the book in favour of the expansion of equal worth and mutual recognition. If we base our conception of loyalty on conditions of love and betterment, then it becomes necessary to think seriously about what we owe to one-another and how we interact with one-another, and further establishes that, as residents, we may rightly expect our country to act in a particular way to uphold, to enable, or to provide for us. Understood in this way, one might reasonably conceive that much of what Viroli describes is compatible with Idealist ethics and the socialist ideals expressed within the book. One, therefore, finds such a conception of patriotism and related duties as initially appropriate for an Idealist-Socialist-inspired Progressive Nationalism, though we must of course consider this in further detail, especially regarding culture.

Anti-Nationalism

The second component of Viroli's patriotism concerns his opposition to nationalism. This is a curious way to define patriotism but it is one that he supports so as to oppose that which he considers to undermine and devalue the nation itself. In his view, patriotism is synonymous with pride in the country, and the people, as well as the duty to our fellows defined in accordance with the common good. We take deep pride in this and want to see not just any country but one that embodies us, treats us well, and is a moral force. It seeks to appeal to all groups who are *residents* within the country, rather than specific ethnic groups, and is taken by Viroli to be synonymous with a desire to improve the patria through opposition to the "tyranny, despotism, oppression, and corruption", which undermine the good and destroy the civic virtue which we can pride our patria in practicing (Deutsch 1966, 232; Viroli 2003, 1).

He contrasts this with nationalism which he says was forged to reinforce the cultural, linguistic, and ethnic oneness of a people. He argues that the nationalist views the nation in terms of the desire for cultural and spiritual unity, bound by an unconditional loyalty or an exclusive attachment to it. He views this as inherently oppressive and potentially dangerous, citing the examples of Italian Fascist racial and cultural laws, as well as alluding to the persecution of minority groups in the break-up of Yugoslavia, though he notes these are extreme cases (Viroli 2003). More pertinent for Viroli are the results of everyday nationalism, namely the way that it discriminates against groups within one's country if they are seen as outside of the core ethno-cultural group. Indeed, unlike patriotism, which concerns itself with the common good and the moral quest to oppose those things, like tyranny, that undermine human potential, he argues that nationalism opposes cultural contamination, heterogeneity, racial impurity, and "disunion" (Viroli 2003, 86, 120). He argues further that it presents a moral void in which morality—what is good—is defined with the addition of for the nation. In other words, so long as the nation stands strong, almost anything is acceptable, and so long as one seeks to preserve that nation, most actions are permitted. Although this is a strong negative conception of nationalism, it shares some of the characteristics of it that are often defined by scholars. Indeed, a popular contrast made between the two concepts is that attachment to one's country is patriotism, whilst attachment to one's ethnicity and its traditions defines nationalism (Kleinig et al. 2015; Primoratz 2016).

Re-Conceptualising Nationalism

Although Viroli and others condemn nationalism for its tendency to advocate homogeneity in relation to values, culture, and language, he/they go too far in applying such criticisms to all nationalisms. Indeed, he may well be right in suggesting that it is a tendency of nationalisms to do many of the things that he suggests, and one finds it reasonable, as he does, to detest them.

However, what Viroli tends to do is to apply these criticisms wholesale (Viroli 2003). This is problematic because it essentialises nationalism. In fact, there are theories which do not suffer from such issues and are defined upon different bases, including Modood's multicultural nationalism, which breaks with monocultural nationalism and seeks to "allow people to hold, adapt, hyphenate, fuse and create identities important to them in the context of their being not just unique individuals but members of socio-cultural, ethnoracial and ethnoreligious groups, as well as national co-citizens" (Modood 2018).

This constitutes a 'nationalist' theory in the sense that one values the national and wishes to set out a vision for it, considering the nation as "not just another place on the map or workplace opportunity: it is where they belong, it is their country" (Modood 2018; 2019). In other words, it has significance for one's identity, providing a root which ties them to something, tells them about themselves, and forms the basis for interaction with others. It looks to promote a singular shared history which is inclusive in its origin and which speaks to our national sub-groups.

By seeking to make nationalism multicultural, meaning to open it up so that we can create narratives that tie various peoples to the nation and give them a stake within it, we arrive at a position which is different to the form that Viroli despises. In this multicultural nationalism we do not see that same rigid desire for assimilation but, rather, an emphasis on the protection and development of the nation—a privileging of a national identity through means of extending meaning generation, attachment, and belonging. The primary basis of this nationalism is then to engage in a re-thinking of the national story so that it can inspire us and to show us where "we were coming from and where we were going, how history had brought us together and what we could make of our shared future" (Modood 2018; 2020). In theoretical terms then, there are nationalisms which are compatible with Viroli's patriotism. To this end, whilst Viroli defines patriotism in-part as opposing monocultural nationalism, this book marries multicultural nationalism and patriotism together, or at least understands them as inhabiting a similar space.

Progressive Nationalism or Patriotism?

One might wonder why make this step towards nationalism, given that thus far one has advocated for a position which defines itself as patriotic. However, one makes this move to emphasise culture, acknowledging the potential for it to go "too far" to justify injustice, yet remaining steadfast in the belief that it can also do much good for progressives. As such, it may well be more appropriate to label such a theory as Progressive Nationalism.

Indeed, one contends that patriotism does not maintain a strong focus on narrative, nor tends to speak in terms of the nation. This does not always apply and we could find evidence of a patriotism that does make express use of narrative, like MacIntyre's (1984), but this is not the norm. Patriotism does not have an extensive narrative nor one which tends to reference non-political culture in a comprehensive way, as most nationalisms do. In fact, these narratives are often not comprehensive in the same manner, referring instead to aspects of culture or values in a way that is broadly seen as compatible with a vaguely defined sense of who we are. According to Miscevic (2022), patriotic theories also tend to emphasise civil unity and loyalty to the state, rather than reference to the nation and ethno-cultural or cultural-civic communities presented by nationalists. To illustrate this difference further, let us consider the foci of right-wing or populist, and liberal, nationalism, distinguishing these from Constitutional patriotism, as well as Viroli's own conception.

Right-wing nationalism, including populist nationalism, tends to be defined in varying degrees according to a desire for monocultural homogeneity and usually takes on significant ethno-cultural connotations. It is often restrictive and nativist with distinguished 'inside' and 'outside' groups.

These stances are maintained usually to 'protect' the nation's culture from being 'watered down', with groups only allowed into the country on the basis that they assimilate and do not pose a threat to it. Such nationalism can be defined in the way that Viroli (2003) defines it, with his subsequent criticisms of nationalism best applying to this conception, namely as strongly mono-ethnocultural, exclusionary, and discriminative. Associated with the right-wing nationalist position is a strong emphasis on a narrative of national greatness in which the nation is seen to be historically contiguous, maintaining a history in which the dominant ethnic group is seen to be superior. For instance, right-wing and populist nationalism in the United Kingdom makes frequent references to the legacy of Empire, seeing imperial figures such as Cecil Rhodes as admirable because they extended its borders and enhanced its imperial prowess, as well as portraying empire as a source of virtue (Rowland et al. 2017, 72). This reveals one of the central narrative components of right-wing nationalism, which is about conveying to the populace the nation's pre-eminence vis-à-vis other nations, as well as lauding military, economic, and cultural superiority (Edgerton 2021). Although one rejects this position, there is an attempt made to clearly define national identity and to create a narrative identity centred on the excellence of Britain, its organic development, and the need to preserve the homogeneity that 'made' such achievements possible.

In contrast, liberal nationalism tends towards values such as human rights or tolerance and takes on civic, rather than explicitly ethno-cultural, connotations. Liberal nationalists, like David Miller (1995), argue that liberal goals cannot reliably be achieved except in societies whose members share a common national identity. Indeed, these theorists recognise that "the majority of people are too deeply attached to their inherited national identities to make their obliteration an intelligible goal" (Miller 1995, 164). People value the rich cultural inheritance that membership of a nation can bring them and they want to see continuity between their own lives and the lives of their ancestors.

However, they mediate what could potentially become a regressive, right-wing, nationalism by insisting that such attachment be grounded upon those liberal values previously mentioned, altering national identity to recognise that the nation is a cultural group, possibly but not necessarily united by a common descent, that is endowed with civic ties (Miscevic 2022). The focal point here becomes assimilation in-line with such values and ties so that the nation's citizens see themselves as belonging within a mutual community, based upon themes and values which they share. Anyone, regardless of origin, is free to join this nation so long as they embrace these values, which maintain a cultural component whereby one is expected to adopt majoritarian cultural practices (Tamir 1995, 2019).

Liberal nationalism is, therefore, an open nationalism in that it does not seek to outwardly exclude people based on arbitrary factors, though it is unfriendly to ill/anti-liberal traditions or cultural practices and maintains a desire to promote some degree of commonality between peoples. The narrative that arises in liberal nationalist countries is, correspondingly, one in which minorities and new groups are afforded a place but their heritage assumes a private identity. Appeals are made to a liberal-democratic heritage, usually with reference to the search for political democracy, rights, and social freedoms, and is further understood as enabling, and relying upon, an established national culture to create the conditions for liberal flourishing, whilst this continuity enables one to tell of a narrative of continual progress towards the realisation of this dream.

This position shares some characteristics with Constitutional patriotism in that they both emphasise liberal values, though theorists of the latter eschew cultural ideals in favour of a culturally neutral pluralism. Indeed Jürgen Habermas (1999) argues that immigrants to a liberal-democratic state need not assimilate into the host culture but only accept the principles of the country's constitution. This patriotism is consequently devoid of cultural principles and, like Viroli, seeks to emphasise the political nature of our nation whilst downplaying ethnicity, language, or another aspect of culture. This patriotism also does not contain an explicit narrative like right-wing and liberal nationalism. The post-national nature of this patriotism seeks to shift the emphasis from national identity to citizenship identity and is, therefore, highly value-centric, with constitutional patriots distancing themselves further from the cultural-civic nature of liberal nationalism towards a purely civic form, instead embracing pluralism limited only by compatibility with constitutional values (Jan-Werner 2009). Here, we move to a position which can only be labelled as patriotic, given that the characteristics of nationalism described are wholly jettisoned in favour of civic ties. This is further characterised by Primoratz (2020), who defines patriotic theories in general as expressing (1) love of one's country, (2) identification with it, and (3) special concern for its well-being and that of its compatriots, yet often not going further to emphasise the cultural component associated with nationalism.

Taken together, patriotism is a love or attachment and broadly expresses Primoratz's (2016,2020) three characteristics. It may make some appeal to culture, and that may be a driving force behind love of one's country, but it moves further towards nationalism when culture takes a more central role and is expressed in reference to a narrative of the nation or a national culture which we might seek to uphold, improve, or extend. Having established this and considering that one has outlined a theory which considers (multiple) culture(s) to be important, there are at least two reasons as to why this theory is nationalist. First, it enters the bounds of ethno-cultural nationalism by referencing the importance of traditions and customs, and civic nationalism in establishing the need for guiding principles within our society. Second, there is a national narrative one privileges, seeking to tie our cultural heritage together in a way that includes newer groups. This is missing in Constitutional and Viroli's patriotism, whilst it is found in right-wing and liberal nationalism. On this basis it seems reasonable to define such a theory as nationalist. Though, when one says this, one refers to a specific part of the theory, namely the cultural-narrative component, rather than those aspects of it which can be understood as examples of patriotism within their own right. In making this distinction, one thus leaves space for progressive-minded people to adopt characteristics of the approach that one has outlined without embracing the more expressly nationalist parts of it. This would be a multicultural patriotism, made so through reference to our diversity without necessarily linking that to too strong a narrative or sense of culture. Nevertheless, one sees Progressive Nationalism as a stronger vehicle through which to re-introduce ethical language, and objectives, into our national imaginary.

In Defence of Culture/The Importance of Culture

One moves towards this position primarily because one cannot neglect culture, which is a powerful reference point for national attachment. Viroli condemns culture in a non-political sense as inherently exclusionary. It can be, and we have seen how cultural arguments have been used to justify discrimination and exclusion through publicly supported immigration caps, the creation of the "Hostile Environment", and the emphasis on assimilation post-2010, but we also sacrifice a lot if we rule out culture entirely (UK Government 2021; Griffiths and Yeo 2021). Consider, for instance, that culture is something that many people do associate with belonging already. One questions how a patriotism with little reference to non-political culture is meant to capture the imagination to the same extent, whilst the discussion of political ideals alone is insufficient in relating to the people themselves. This is not to say that they are somehow incapable but it is to suggest that such a cultureless patriotism is likely not to be recognised as patriotic but, rather, as something else, likely more akin to good citizenship. This may be effective, but we must consider that the working-class tend to value nation explicitly, and to value the class we must at least seek to adopt a conception of national attachment or belonging which makes sense to them (Surridge 2021; Bloodworth 2018).

To this end, it likely must involve some sense of our nation's culture since it is important to working-people. We may frame good citizenship/patriotism within the context of good nationalism, and therefore include much of what Viroli speaks of, but we cannot disregard culture since it has its own significance. To some extent, we must thus be able to tell stories about our country which refer not only to values but also to those aspects of culture which people recognise as being "British".

The question here becomes, "How does one reference culture and reproduce images of a British culture, whilst remaining inclusive, and encouraging people to feel as if they belong within the country?". One's answer to this is a policy of cultural inclusion alongside relationship-building.

Cultural inclusion asserts that we can discuss culture without resorting to monocultural nationalism, provided that our discussion recognises the value of our nation's residents' culture, as well as their shared sense of attachment to place. This perspective holds that there is a need to be outwardly inclusive, incorporating symbols, tying peoples together, and portraying the full richness of our many sub-cultures so that we might understand that Britain is something that people want to belong to, to identify with, and as representative of them in some way (Soutphommasane 2012). For instance, different communities need to see aspects of Britishness which they might recognise as being representative of them, or as their own distinct contribution to our nation. Our society should be open to additions from new groups, as well as pre-established ones who had hitherto been left out. Contrary to what one might think, this does not mean the replacement of our current institutions or norms in their entirety, but often merely addition to them. For instance, though Britain may be considered as a nation with a Christian heritage, that some of our residents take pride in, it is also home to many other faiths who, at present, lack representation. This does not reflect who we are as a society anymore and is unlikely to inspire our residents. To do so, we must make space within the things that we have cherished/loved so that others may do so too. Echoing Viroli, if the common good requires us to put people first, our institutions need to change to reflect the people that live within that society. It must be able to be shaped by them, be capable of inspiring loyalty from them, and be able to motivate them (Green 2008, 141). In the interests of national belonging and the loyalty that it inspires, it is subsequently necessary to embrace change that both solidifies and strengthens existing institutions, but which is inclusive, and to retain those aspects of our institutions and history that people can most relate to. We might see this as democratisation, the opening of our public spaces so that others can find meaning within them (Green 2008, 202). This involves re-shaping and developing our country in ways that combine age-old sources of identification and of pride with new symbols, institutions, and ways of doing things so that they might be better understood as unified and constitutive parts of one diverse "British" culture. Herein we see references made to many of the things that we have often grown up seeing, possibly relating to, and recognising as being British, whilst simultaneously evolving that to include important aspects of one's heritage or way of life, as well as institutional changes within our society to better recognise its diversity. This appeals to culture in a variety of ways but, through recognition, seeks to tie people together as part of a nation. As one has argued throughout this book, such inclusion is beneficial in challenging alienation, but is taken further here to promote a two-sided integration of minority and majority positions into one, more relatable, Britishness.

Within this understanding of the inclusive attachment that drives belonging, we are seen to recognise Britain as our own, but acknowledge that we see it differently to some extent. In this, attachment and belonging are important motivators for duties and obligations. This echoes the society of societies as it has been established within the book and therefore finds itself compatible with the framework of Idealist-Socialism. However, relationships alone are likely insufficient in defining belonging. People often want more than this; they want to know what Britain is and see reminders within their daily lives. A relationship-only approach is likely too vague and so it seems worthwhile to see to it that our national symbols, our institutions, and our laws come to recognise and represent our peoples, at the same time as fostering relationships. This is a difficult task, as one laid out in Chap. 5, but it is one that is worthwhile to promote belonging across groups, as well as to breakdown the separation which hampers community feelings and, by extension, adherence to a common good. Consequently, one considers it necessary to conceive of a Progressive Nationalism that welcomes people into the nation and inspires loyalty through inclusion and the building of relationships with their fellows.

What Is the National Narrative, and What Is the British Nation?

One has spoken of the need for the national narrative to reflect and appeal to people. However, one has not yet determined what Britain's national story is. What is missing is something to tie these examples of Britishness together, a macro-level idea which we can relate our experiences to to understand them as being British. This macro-level can be a challenge for the progressive, who wishes to be open, but also to unify. Because of this disposition, there is a potential for the Progressive Nationalist to outline a vision which is too disparate to make sense or bring citizens together. Attached to this are several related questions, including how we might determine something to be 'British', how we deal with contestation, and what we use to judge the desirability of something as defining us.

How Does One Determine Something to Be British?

We cannot label something as British without any basis because people are not likely to accept it. For something to be British it must be recognised as such and seen as fitting into the social imaginary. This is a rational and emotional process. Either one recognises that something is British because it feels somehow 'right', perhaps by fitting in with one's ideological inclinations, personal experience, or sense of Britishness, or one can be swayed to consider it as such through historical precedent, amongst other things (McCrone amd Bechhofer 2015). This is significant because it establishes that Britishness can be modified and re-thought to become reflective of the people who we are at present, but roots these experiences so that Britishness maintains a historical tether to its past—a sense that there is precedent for what we come to believe as representing us—or a view to the future whereby our present selves show characteristics which we wish to further embody. This root is important for narrative purposes. Indeed, we could create some vision for Britain which is wholly progressive, with abstract values that we might look towards. However, without tying those values to the present, or to elements within our history, there is a chance that they will not feel fully 'as of us'. One, therefore, prefers to adopt a position in which the working out of our national identity is rooted and can be more tangibly seen as part of an unfolding narrative which we wish to tell. Having established this, let us consider some characteristics of Britain.

Britain is multinational, multicultural, and multilingual with proud sub-national and regional identities and is a union between at least four constituent nations. These are all immediately recognisable aspects of Britain and, whilst there is something worth considering in the rich histories and cultures that each of these nation's/regions hold, as well as some of the things which we have achieved together,[1] we do not often consider these bonds in an emotive way at present and our unity is not often part of the national narrative. This is curious given that what makes us British, rather than say English, Welsh or Scottish, or Northern Irish, is that we belong within Britain, the part-union of nations which exists upon the isles, and the union of the greater part of those isles (Olusoga 2023). We are British because of that fusion of nations into one supra-national entity known as Britain (Lloyd-Jones and Scull 2017). This establishes at the heart of our national identity the possibility of a composite multi-layeredness. For instance, we would likely recognise Tartan as both Scottish and British, although those things are only popular in Scotland itself and that it is 'natural' or comfortable for us to retain composite identities in which someone can well be both British and Scottish, for instance. Commentators like Orwell pick up on this composite identity and highlight that our varied means of attachment have generated a more natural sense of belonging in which we value nation because of 'our' corner of British culture and its life. This is ill-defined by Orwell but one can see a sense that we are united around our nation partly because of the different ways we can connect with it. We need this diversity for our nation to generate loyalty (Orwell 2018, Part 2). In making note of this, Orwell moves towards a position which recognises diversity, acknowledging various things that people do here as examples of Britishness, without asserting that one must also do them to be considered British.

This is a useful example for the creation of a Progressive Nationalist narrative, given that such multi-layeredness suggests that we do not all need to share/do the same things for them to be considered British. If we do it may be easier to realise them as being such, but we might also categorise things as characteristically British if a number of our residents do them, or because we see them popularised in media. Indeed, many of our residents drink tea; it is normal here to queue, whilst others maintain a self-deprecating humour, a tendency to avoid confrontation, and a "stiff

[1] English, Welsh, and Scottish politicians were indispensable in establishing the NHS, for instance, or creating the conditions for the modern welfare state.

upper lip". These things are not imposed upon people as a necessity of being British, but we do often recognise them as being characteristic of our culture and, by extension, our national identity—typified in appeals like "Keep Calm and Carry On". The ways of being British, therefore, differ and are shared by multiple groups within our society who, at times, adopt practices that are niche in comparison to the rest of our populace. In this, one rejects the assertion of an overly totalised Britishness in favour of the recognition of diversity—though such diversity must be able to be understood as of the same nation. This certainly requires a strong emphasis on narrative and a deliberate interweaving of our differences into a cohesive frame. Such a narrative, constituted as an interconnected but multifaceted vision of Britain, would portray it as on a path towards further inclusivity and the realisation of a cultural richness which has been existent since its inception.

However, one cannot reasonably claim that this has been a smooth journey from decade to decade, especially given the fact that a multilayered British identity has often been subsumed by an English-dominated Britishness, much to the frustration of the other nations. Rather, one must say that Britain is a multinational, multicultural, and multilingual nation, potentially built upon foundations of diversity, that is capable of exhibiting recognition, tolerance, and of celebrating its diversity. This is, in part, an exaggeration but it is one which is at least believable and rooted in experience. This is not a story of cosmopolitanism but one in which Britons with cultural differences, and similarities, come to establish the foundations for a culture that is rich and diverse but unified, in which our citizens need not adhere to some totalised Britishness to be considered constituent members of our nation.

Constructing This Identity

In constructing this national identity, and its corresponding vision, we need to be careful because, whilst we have noted that it can be a force for unity, it "can paradoxically also become a cause of its fragmentation and even disintegration" if it becomes exclusive and negatively contested (Parekh 2000, 4). Rather, it must be inclusive and should try to capture the richness of our culture, although any description of what it means to be British, or any vision of Britain, cannot hope to capture it fully. This vision will inevitably involve critical reflection and the determining of which of our qualities are noble and worth cherishing, as well as what we might like to jettison, to come to terms with, or to leave aside. One notes this because, if one wishes to see Britain conceived as what has been described, we need to reckon with episodes in our history which do not reflect such a narrative, given that they cannot be ignored or explained away. Any vision must, therefore, be grounded in reality or in the possibility of a reality that people can recognise as legitimate.

We also need to desire these things to be understood as being part of our national identity, which requires a dialogue about where we are going. For example, one has suggested that something is British if many people either see it as such or engage in it. However, if we were to say that, historically, many British citizens held discriminatory views we likely would not want to define Britishness in accordance with this. This reflects the view that such characteristics are not desirable for us to attribute to our nation and is certainly not a dimension of our identity which we wish to promote as ever typifying us. This requires dialogue and values to relate to, to ask ourselves, "[I]s this something that reflects what we wish to be?". If it is, then we should ensure that there is precedent for it, or at least something rooted that we can relate it to and, if not, then we must evolve. Indeed, if we do not want to have discrimination as part of what constitutes Britishness, we must come to terms with those aspects of our history which evoke such a sense and deal with present inequalities or evidences of discrimination. In either instance, we must attempt to 'root' our sense of something being/not being British by acting in our policy and our narrative to address our concerns. This means holding ourselves to the values and principles which we seek to make characteristic of Britishness.

Our narrative must therefore in part conform to our lives or have space within it to deal with the issues presented by it.

National identity thus involves the careful selection of aspects of culture or history, the coming to terms with contradictions, and the elaboration of historical examples which are at present subsumed, left untold, or told, but never brought together in a cohesive way in-line with our narrative progress. One consequently looks to develop a vision of Progressive Nationalism as one that emphasises a rich, inclusive, history in which our progress towards these British values has been born by a number of groups. Indeed, the desire for democratic rights and dignity was carried forward by the Chartists and their predominately working-class supporters, and then the Suffragettes, resulting in many of the freedoms that we laud and enjoy. Similarly, our socio-economic progress has been fostered by the unions, overwhelmingly backed by working- and middle-class people from the industries of Northern England, Scotland, and the Welsh Valleys, whilst the ability for people to live more equally has been, culturally and socially, advanced by LGBTQ+ peoples and minority advocacy groups. We have a legacy of strong communities, now diminished, but which were proud of their accomplishments, as well as a further sense of national solidarity expressed through institutions such as the NHS. This is not an eclectic appeal to culture or simple diversity but, rather, evidence of a collective endeavour with contributions from across the nation to our shared betterment, across multiple fields. There are tangible outcomes of each of these movements/events/actions and each speak to a desire to live in a country that values its citizens, that involves them, and that is made by them. We see here how citizens have fought for the extension of rights and the equalisation of life chances so that we may enjoy our cultural richness, and our freedoms, in common, rather than as an elite privilege. This is something we do not wish to be associated with anymore and, though it is a part of our history and of us, we have come to terms with it and can see that it has been resigned to the past. In this way then, through our actions, we bring legitimacy to such a positive national narrative. This is not a denial or re-writing of history; it is an acknowledgement of what was, and no longer is, whilst our movement away from this position reflects the journey of our country and of our citizens, which itself can become part of the national story. One subsequently leans towards a vision of a Britain that does not shy away from its mistakes or contradictions, which comes to terms with them, and which, in doing so, shows a renewed strength, maturity, and pride in itself and its citizens. We are a country that is capable of some great things, sometimes slow to recognise our faults and stubborn to change, but with a citizenry capable of righting wrongs, of looking out for one-another, and of creating institutions like the NHS.

In addition to the multi-layered composite diversity laid out previously, one adds to this vision a sense that we are a nation capable of great humanity, solidarity, and an adherence to the good of our fellows, with a sense of purpose that seeks to right wrongs, and to create a more perfect nation, good to its people. Here we also establish some lay tradition of the common good.

Balancing Culture Within National Identity

One, therefore, asserts that the discarding of cultural expressions of nationhood is problematic. For culture is a powerful force and attachment or embeddedness within a particular culture often gives meaning to one's life, provides something to relate one's experiences to, and elicits pride. Culture also forms the bedrock of our patriotic love, whether that be in the form of love for the literature of Shakespeare, the comedy of Monty Python, or those peculiarities which bring up comfort in knowing that they are a quirk of British life. If we solely rely on political-institutional identity in thinking of our national identity, then we would be without in our national identity many things which make people proud to be British or comfortable with belonging here. Indeed, there is also a corresponding worry that we might neglect the richness of our culture and, with that, fail to create a captivating vision for a British national identity which people can relate to and see as representing them. In this way, we need to have some account of culture within our identity, not only to tie people more comfortably to it, and to reflect them, but also because we have a culture and sub-cultures which are rich in heritage and can serve to enhance our identity. In saying this one accepts that we will have to navigate anxieties about the diminishing of our culture on occasion, or the perceived challenges which are made against it by changing circumstances, but one seeks to allay these fears by relating cultural expression to the more political side of our identity. For instance, we need not rule out culture from national identity so long as we recognise that our framing of culture must be respectful and inclusive of our constituent peoples. This will inevitably involve some political direction, including appeal to pre-existing British values, as well as a realisation by those who outwardly shape national identity that inclusivity in the national imaginary is to be desired.

There is, in this, need for a mechanism within our nation which recognises our unity in difference, first born from the inception of Britain in 1707 through the Act of Union, which asserts that our nation is one built upon the recognition of ourselves and others as utilising our talents and enjoying our differences in a way that is 'British'. We need not each become the same as one-another so long as we respect our various means of being British and recognise them as valid. In this view, our fellows make up the nation and its identity and we should be able to see what others do and think that as being somehow British, even if we do not do it ourselves. This links well with a political dimension of national identity, namely through the notions of "respect and tolerance" which successive governments have noted as characteristic of 'us' and portrayed as one of the central "British Values". This is defined by government as "understanding that we all don't share the same beliefs and values. Respecting the values, ideas and beliefs of others whilst not imposing our own".[2] But one might add to this the principle of mutual recognition, that even if we do not share these same beliefs or values, that does not make us or others any less British (Department of Education 2014). In fact, in recognising this, we extend and uphold in-common that principle of respect and tolerance which makes us British in our own right. We, therefore, see here an intertwining of cultural and political Britishness, strengthening both so that, when we for instance see cultural disunity or difference, we might come to recognise its being as in some way congruent with a political identity which is respectful of diversity and sees tolerance as an essential good within our society. This again refers back to the possibility of multilayeredness established as characteristic of Britain earlier on and renders it compatible with this interpretation of British political values. In terms of the macro vision for Britain, in political terms we can chart a path in which our country and its citizens have laboured for the creation of an open and tolerant democracy through various means, though which shape this will take in future is certainly, almost by virtue of these values, up for the deliberation of future generations. We maintain then, as part of this wider vision of Britain, a political component which emphasises these established "British Values" and ties them to the Progressive Nationalism that one promotes.

Culture In-Itself

Having noted the need for political values to become intertwined with Progressive Nationalism to promote a form which can relieve concerns over a cultural dimension of national identity, one now turns to that cultural dimension to suggest that not only should we take pride in our culture for the values that aspects of it promote but we should also seek to incorporate an appreciation for culture itself into our vision.

To illustrate this, consider that the 2012 Olympic Opening Ceremony has been hailed as the pinnacle of British diversity and evocator of national feeling; a performance which exemplified the progressive, multicultural Britain which one promotes (Konstantaki et al. 2019). We saw a celebration of the length and breadth of our culture, and innovation, with reference to "Our Green and Pleasant Land"; the industrial heritage; the

[2] Though one is doubtful that the current government live up to this British Value themselves.

reforming zeal of William Blake; the monarchy; literary and cultural figures like Harry Potter, Mr Bean, Queen, and Pink Floyd; and great institutions like the NHS. The ceremony was idealised but poignant, widely hailed across society as a suitable representation of those who call themselves 'Britons' (Vincent et al. 2018). There was something in it that most, if not all, could relate to as representative of them or of something they believed in. These performances, directed in such a way as to bring together otherwise unrelated parts of 'us' into a coherent, flowing narrative, do much to exemplify the unity in diversity that a Progressive Nationalism would promote. This idea that, through various means, we contribute to our nation, enhance it, and develop its full richness is one that encapsulates well the principles of flourishing and solidarity inherent in a Progressive Nationalist vision. Further, if we are to relate to this vision then we must have some account of the literary and theatrical vibrancy of Shakespeare, Burns, Dickens, or Tolkien; the comedic flair of Blackadder; or any other of those many things which we enjoy and recognise as being 'of us'. These examples evoke pride, but are also things which demonstrate the multifaceted, multi-layered dimensions of our identity. They say something of Britain and are portrayals of parts of our culture, as well as being a part of it in turn. This is significant for a Progressive Nationalist vision because it seeks to go beyond discussion or promotion of values like the common good, for instance, to say that part of our national identity should be that we maintain a culture which we can enjoy and interrelate upon(Llewellyn 2014). Such an addition to national identity may seem strange, yet pride in our country should surely come in-part from a recognition that this is a good place to live, with a culture that has something for each of us to enjoy. This is a fact that we should be able to celebrate for what it does for us.

What Does This Macro Constitute?

The macro of Britain portrayed here is one of collective endeavour, working in/for common to improve the lives of our fellows and, by extension, our nation. It exhibits a cultural richness which does not always avail itself but in some form has existed since our country's inception and has expanded and flourished over time (though not without difficulties) and is particularly salient today. One has added further that this is a country that can take care of its people with services like the NHS, which recognises that we have duties to one-another and which can enhance our lives. This macro also recognises that Britain is a work in progress, capable of mistakes, but equally able to renew itself and to become something more than it was. Many of these things might be overlooked in everyday life but they nevertheless exist, are born of fact, either in our history, in our culture, or in some other thing which constitutes our way of life. This is, of course, but one vision of Britain, yet it is one that draws from our history.

Taken together, a Progressive Nationalist vision for Britain should be one in which it is a diverse union of peoples, bound together by duty and obligation to improve the common good for our mutual flourishing. We are at least the partial embodiment of a cooperative, caring, and just nation built upon a foundation of common liberty, recognition, and tolerance, which may sometimes ebb, but which we remain committed to securing for ourselves and our fellows. This vision is further enhanced by a rich culture, boasting some of the great figures and movements of history, as well as a set of customs, like our characteristic politeness, kindness, awkwardness, and sarcasm, which bind, comfort, and ground us as part of our own national peculiarities. These are not things which we necessarily take pride in, nor which constitute a vision good or bad, but are nevertheless taken here as examples of our uniqueness and as enriching the lives of our citizens. The progressive nationalist vision is thus one of many parts, celebrating a host of different things as part of 'us', yet it maintains a core focus on the common good, grounded by historical precedent, as well as a desire to speak of culture in a way that brings disparate parts together into a narrative of unity and enrichment.

Conclusion: Why Does This Address Alienation?

There are three key benefits that flow from this Progressive Nationalism, namely:

1. Active inclusion and acknowledgement in community.
2. The amelioration of community-tensions through a unified national framing.
3. The rejection of rootlessness and the reintroduction of working-class values into the national imaginary.

On this first matter, a Progressive Nationalism asserts a greater awareness that we belong to one national community. Where one's sense of belonging had perhaps been of an outsider without reference in the national imaginary, this multicultural nationalism intertwines them with other groups within society to suggest that together, through their combined endeavour, we shape Britain. This contributes to the amelioration of alienation in a sense most relating to its dignity component. If one lives in this country, works, learns, and leisure's here but is not recognised by government, in the stories we tell, or by one's fellows, then one is not likely to feel fully of 'us'. In consequence, they might feel distant and isolated. This is reflected in those narratives discussed in Chap. 5. If we do not respect groups and give them a place within our nation that they can use to generate attachment and to understand themselves, then there is every chance that they can become alienated or feel themselves a lower class of citizen. Instead, citizens should have a place and purpose and garner the sense that our society is one of fundamental mutual respect and recognition. Progressive Nationalism looks to achieve this recognition by acknowledging a diverse range of histories, whilst incorporating them into the pluralistic-inclusive narrative presented previously. This has a similar positive impact on the reduction of alienation as point 3, yet here it is presented more fully to integrate different cultural traditions into our sense of national self.

This also speaks to one's second point, that a Progressive Nationalism weaves together narratives that help us to think of one-another as of us. Where we have communities that cannot speak to, nor recognise, one-another, one provides a common framing for identity in which these groups can be represented in our national story, praised for their contributions, and, through this, come to be better appreciated and understood. One seeks to build bridges between people, using a multicultural narrative which can dispel harmful stereotypes and change outlooks. Of course, the power of this narrative alone in challenging alienation is perhaps limited as issues not only arise out of narrative non-recognition. Where issues do persist within communities, relating more centrally to other matters, they must be helped along by those civil society associations advocated for in Chap. 9. However, one holds that this framing, drawing on values of mutual respect and recognition alongside an inclusive narrative which makes explicit positive reference to those groups which one might conflict with in their community, can provide a background against which such issues can be ameliorated and misunderstandings dispelled. In fact, one holds that such a narrative, with serious examples of where our citizens have made their contributions to our shared home, can do much to demonstrate our common frame and the overriding interests of the common good as against self-interest. The proliferation of reconciliation and recognition, detailed in Chap. 6 and beyond, also helps in this.

On a deeper level this nationalism looks to turn politics explicitly to the service of flourishing. One tells a story which can connect and help people to make sense of their lives: to see them as amounting to something. Associated with this are a rejection of rootlessness and the reiteration of working-class values in the national imaginary. For instance, values like duty, obligation, solidarity, and fairness have been noted in Chaps. 4 and 5 as commonly praised by the working-class and its sub-groups. One brings values such as these to the forefront of a Progressive Nationalism alongside a moralising component found in Idealist mutuality and the common good. This links especially to the policies outlined in Chap. 9 wherein we see financial and status redistribution extended into the national imaginary so that working-people can see themselves as active shapers of its core principles. Essentially, where they had been left out previously, undermined, and unrecognised, this nationalism asserts that their values are worthy of recognition, whilst they as citizens are deserving of community-derived prestige, power, and wealth. One thus raises working-people to a position of respect which better reflects their worth as citizens.

With the multicultural vision now set out, one seeks to develop this Progressive Nationalism in relation to our economic life and civil society, seeing the benefits of acknowledgement and inclusion, the amelioration of community-tension, and the development of roots as being fundamentally improved by their extension into other areas of our society.

Bibliography

Attlee, Clement. Leader's Speech, Scarborough 1951. *British Political Speech Archive*. http://www.britishpoliticalspeech.org/speech-archive.htm?speech=161. Accessed 10 Aug 2023.

Bew, John. *Citizen Clem: A Biography of Attlee*. Hachette, UK, 2016.

Bloodworth, James. *Hired: Six Months Undercover in Low-Wage Britain*. Atlantic Books, 2018.

Department of Education. "Guidance on Promoting British Values in Schools Published." 2014. https://www.gov.uk/government/news/guidance-on-promoting-british-values-in-schools-published. Accessed Jan 29 2024.

Deutsch, Karl. *Nationalism and Social Communication: An Inquiry into the Foundations of Nationality*. MIT Press, 1966.

Edgerton, David. *The Rise and Fall of the British Nation*. Penguin Books, 2021.

Green, T.H. *Collected Works of T.H. Green: Works of T.H. Green*. Thoemmes, 1997.

Green, T.H. *Lectures on the Principles of Political Obligation*. Cambridge Scholars Publishing, 2008.

Griffiths, Melanie, and Colin Yeo. 'The UK's Hostile Environment: Deputising Immigration Control'. *Critical Social Policy*, 11 January 2021.

Habermas, Jürgen. *The Inclusion of the Other: Studies in Political Theory*. MIT Press, 1999.

Jan-Werner. *Constitutional Patriotism*. Princeton University Press, 2009.

Kleinig, John, Simon Keller, and Igor Primoratz. *The Ethics of Patriotism: A Debate*. John Wiley & Sons, 2015.

Konstantaki, Maria, Eugenia Wickens, and Feng Yi Perris. "Themes and Content of the London 2012 Olympic Games Opening Ceremony: A Comparison between Pre-Games Perspectives of British Residents and Actual Ceremonial Elements." *Tourism and Hospitality Research* 19, no. 1 (January 1, 2019): 40–53.

Llewellyn, Matthew P. *Rule Britannia: Nationalism, Identity and the Modern Olympic Games*. Routledge, 2014.

Lloyd-Jones, Naomi, and Margaret Scull. *Four Nations Approaches to Modern "British" History: A (Dis) United Kingdom?* Springer, 2017.

MacIntyre, Alasdair. *Is Patriotism a Virtue?*. Department of Philosophy, University of Kansas, 1984.

McCrone, David, and Frank Bechhofer. *Understanding National Identity*. Cambridge: Cambridge University Press, 2015.

Miller, David. *On Nationality*. Oxford University Press, 1995.

Miščević, Nenad. *Nationalism and Beyond: Introducing Moral Debate about Values*. Central European University Press, 2022.

Modood, Tariq. 'A Multicultural Nationalism?' *Brown Journal of World Affairs* 25, no. 2 (June 2019): 233–46.

Modood, Tariq. 'Multicultural Nationalism'. *openDemocracy* 13 August 2018. https://www.opendemocracy.net/en/can-europe-make-it/multicultural-nationalism/. Accessed 23 Sep 2021.

Modood, Tariq. 'Multiculturalism as a New Form of Nationalism?' *Nations and Nationalism* 26, no. 2 (2020): 308–13.

Olusoga, David. "'We Live in a Complicated Country': David Olusoga on the UK's Contested Union, Then and Now." *The Observer*, October 1, 2023. https://www.theguardian.com/tv-and-radio/2023/oct/01/union-with-david-olusoga-bbc-england-scotland-northern-ireland-wales-britain-uk.

Orwell, George. *The Lion and the Unicorn: Socialism and the English Genius*. Penguin, UK, 2018.

Pabst, Adrian. *Postliberal Politics: The Coming Era of Renewal*. John Wiley & Sons, 2021.

Parekh, Bhikhu. *Rethinking Multiculturalism: Cultural Diversity and Political Theory*. Macmillan, 2000.

Primoratz, Igor. *Patriotism: Philosophical and Political Perspectives.* Routledge, 2016.
Primoratz, Igor. 'Patriotism'. In *The Stanford Encyclopedia of Philosophy*, edited by Edward N. Zalta, Winter 2020. Metaphysics Research Lab, Stanford University, 2020. https://plato.stanford.edu/archives/win2020/entries/patriotism/.
Rowland, Atkinson, McKenzie Lisa, and Simon Winlow. *Building Better Societies: Promoting Social Justice in a World Falling Apart.* Policy Press, 2017.
Soutphommasane, Tim. *The Virtuous Citizen: Patriotism in a Multicultural Society.* Cambridge: Cambridge University Press, 2012.
Surridge, Paula. 'Brexit, British Politics and Values'. *UK in a changing Europe*, 30 Jan 2021. https://ukandeu.ac.uk/long-read/brexit-british-politics-and-values/. Accessed 19 May 2023.
Tamir, Yael. *Liberal Nationalism.* Princeton University Press, 1995.
Tamir, Yael. *Why Nationalism.* Princeton University Press, 2019.
UK Government. 'UK Points-Based Immigration System: Further Details Statement—GOV.UK'. https://www.gov.uk/government/publications/uk-points-based-immigration-system-further-details-statement/uk-points-based-immigration-system-further-details-statement. Accessed 9 Aug 2021.
Vincent, John, John S Hill, Andrew Billings, John Harris, and C Dwayne Massey. '"We Are GREAT Britain": British Newspaper Narratives during the London 2012 Olympic Games'. *International Review for the Sociology of Sport* 53, no. 8 (1 December 2018): 895–923.
Viroli, Maurizio. *For Love of Country: An Essay on Patriotism and Nationalism.* Oxford University Press, 2003.

CHAPTER 9

Progressive Nationalism Applied to Our Economic Life

This chapter formulates Idealist-Socialist principles into an ethos which can be used as a normative framework to understand and assess economic policy *intentions* and *directions*. For this purpose the chapter assesses two examples: worker control and pay ratios. One highlights these two illustrative examples because the book has outlined the importance of agency as one of the core components of alienation and developed its ethos based in-part on a distinct socialist perspective which places a significant emphasis on worker control, especially in the case of GDH Cole. Although one does not go as far as Cole in this chapter to advocate for total worker control over the economy, one does first see a clear potential for worker control within the economy as conducive to the amelioration of alienation through primarily its agency component, but also in the provision of dignity to working-people.

Second, one considers pay ratios because they follow a logic which seeks a greater redistribution of material reward and the bringing together of company strata into closer relation so that wage better matches value and does not undermine the dignity of the lowest paid. As such, the chapter considers some of the core policy intentions of worker control and pay ratios alongside relevant case study examples to assess its capacity to ameliorate alienation.

S. Taylor Hill, *Challenging Alienation in the British Working-Class*, Palgrave Politics of Identity and Citizenship Series,
https://doi.org/10.1007/978-3-031-59250-8_9

This step is taken not to specifically advocate for them as such but, rather, as an illustrative example to demonstrate the capacity of Idealist-Socialism to develop principles which work towards alienation's amelioration. This necessarily involves assessing intentions and outcomes of erstwhile 'successful' examples which do challenge alienation, using these to draw general principles which can be used to develop some finer principles for policy consideration. For this purpose, the chapter will not seek to defend at length any component of this illustrative example, seeing the intricacies of policy as both beyond its scope and beside its core purpose in the overarching framework of the book. By taking this approach, however, one establishes a critical ethos which can be used to guide improvements in the working-class position and to bring out the underlying underdeveloped rationale of policies to provide a narrative-vision. This itself maintains a further purpose of demonstrating the ability of Idealist-Socialist theory to evaluate, reform, and justify policies, whilst maintaining the core commitment to narrative-vision which one has suggested is lacking in contemporary political discourses. The chapter concludes by reiterating the general ethos established, as well as these policy points, which amount to a plan for the amelioration of alienation in respect to agency, dignity, and our economic life.

Assessing the Intentions of Worker Control

Worker control is a vast topic which is taken in different directions, and advocated to differing degrees, by various scholars and countries who have implemented it. One makes express reference to two key models of worker control. These are as follows:

1. The German Model. This is centred on the recognition of interest groups and the expression of worker's views through representation on supervisory boards of directors and works councils which are responsible for negotiating pay, conditions, restructuring, as well as acting as the mouthpiece for concerns. This is legally mandated by the Codetermination Act 1976 and other supplementary legislation (Mertens and Schanze 1979).
2. The Swedish Model. This is more loosely legislated but operates on an agreement basis in which trade unions are responsible for collective bargaining, whilst a mixture of union representatives, works councils or committees, and other democratic structures ensures

workers are able to make claims for betterment, contribute to workplace strategy, and pursue improvements in areas like safety. The model relies on strong trade unions, with Sweden's being amongst the strongest in Europe with a membership of 66% of the working population (Logue 2019). This model is additionally underpinned by the idea of the 'social partnership' in which bargaining and worker democracy is framed as a central tenet of the *Folkhemmet*: the narrative-vision for Swedish society based on solidarity, in which citizens treat one-another as "family" (Hedin 2015, 2019).

There are notable differences between the two models. Where we see a more legally mandated worker control in Germany, we see a model in Sweden which maintains similar institutions, but which is also culturally rooted and more reliant on trade union power (Lane and Wallengren-Lynch 2020). These two models demonstrate the different ways in which worker control can become manifest but nevertheless fulfil a core intention, namely the participation in management and organisation of enterprises by those that work within them. One settles on this as a definition of worker control to avoid advocating for a specific model, rather seeing the purpose of this chapter as to assess overarching policy intentions. To do so, one considers three interlinked aims of worker control, including the extension of structural acknowledgement and the development of recognition, solidarity-building, and the extension of autonomy. Each of these aims can be understood to improve working-class agency and dignity and indicates important themes in addressing alienation. One also considers the ownership critique levied by Marx (2000, 2007) and Laski (2020) against worker control, and what that can add to our understanding of the policies which are necessary to challenge alienation.

Recognition and Acknowledgement

Theories of worker control make an express commitment to developing recognition within enterprises. This is often achieved following a two-stage logic in which we first see structural acknowledgement for workers and, from the subsequent interactions which occur, recognition. For example, the Codetermination Act 1976 explicitly recognises workers, employers, the state, and trade unions and seeks cooperation between them for common ends. This distinction between the four, which are understood to be partners, amounts to an official acknowledgement of workers as having a right to co-determine the fate of their enterprise (Mertens and Schanze 1979). This initial framing is important in a symbolic way for working-people because it acknowledges structurally that they are a constituent group which have a stake in, and ideas to contribute to, the running of their enterprises.

In the German Model, there is an underlying assumption of class-cooperation within the framing of the law, which has not always been successful, but which has the advantage of encouraging and facilitating ongoing dialogue and cooperation. The creation of deliberate channels for dialogue between equally acknowledged constituents reflects that part of the agency, and dignity, characteristic of alienation which seeks recognition for the significance of one's role and value (see Chaps. 4 and 5). Indeed, companies which maintain a degree of worker control tend to feel to their workers to be more cooperative, rather than strictly hierarchical, and see themselves as having a place within their enterprise. As Lukes (2005) notes, though hierarchies remain in place, workers are better able to engage across them on a humanistic level and find themselves supported within the frameworks of worker control to challenge what they see as unjust or unfair management decisions. This is to imbue workers with a confidence and ability, rooted in the support of the unions, legal, or institutional procedures, to make claims for their own betterment, and that of workplace practices. This improves the agential capacity of workers within their respective companies and raises their status from employees to a fully constituted group which can express collective desires and act.

There is a wider relevance to the intentions and outcomes of worker control that we might suggest are indicative of the general direction that the economic sphere should move in if the alienation faced by the working-class is to be ameliorated. The intentions of worker control to extend legal and/or structural acknowledgement to provide a space for the working-class to express their interests have integral importance for the provision of agency, as one has already noted. However, we might also highlight its potential as tied to a Progressive Nationalist vision which one has identified as seeking the redignification of the working-class through their inclusion within the nation. Here this is to be achieved in the economic sphere by raising them up to a position of acknowledgement and extending recognition across workplace hierarchies so that they might both share their experiences and participate in the shaping of that which they devote a significant portion of their time to and rely upon for their livelihoods. By focusing our attention on policy which seeks to structurally acknowledge the working-class we can hope to contribute to the amelioration of alienation through the improving of worker agency. One therefore seeks to draw a more general conclusion that policy which extends acknowledgement and builds recognition within the economic sphere is likely to be conducive to the amelioration of alienation.

Fairness, Solidarity, and Equity

The successful development of recognition is intended to make workplaces feel fairer, more equitable, and to improve the workers sense of belonging (Ridley-Duff 2009). This is reflected in a desire for solidarity, which in Sweden is tied to the *Folkhemmet* and in Germany a notion of social partnership. This is to be achieved through solidarity-building, which ranges from the coming together of workers with their employers to set workplace practices, to cooperative goal setting, and to discuss wage and bonus structures. These measures, and bilateral discussion over these issues, is theorised by Cheney (1997) and Luhman (2007, 469) to improve "consciousness of cooperation, and a consciousness of the common good". Such consciousness-building is understood by these authors as a means of bridging gaps between hierarchies and developing a solidarity which extends the bounds of humanistic feeling and regard for one's fellows across hierarchy. In practice, there are issues with this as different groups in the hierarchy maintain varying aims, which sometimes come into conflict (Pateman 1970). However, worker control smooths the edges of such conflict and often leads to compromises which are fairer and do not break the bond between these groups. In fact, Pateman (1970, 2012) suggests that workplaces in which control is shared tend to have considerable support given to employees alongside wages that are more likely to be considered as fair, whilst we also see some evidence in which hardships are shared more equitably (Dahl 1985).

The result of the solidarity-building that worker control seeks to develop is then that corporate elites take on more and are less likely to shift sacrifices onto workers. Gorton and Schmid (2004, n.p.) add to this with their case study of worker control in Germany, which they note as having altered the objective function of businesses "in a way consistent with the aims of workers". This has ensured that "codetermined firms were likely to be more diversified, reducing the risk of the firm failing, and were also less likely to undergo restructuring and layoffs" as management and employees were encouraged to consider one-another, despite divisions between them in terms of their aims.

Essentially, where firms maintain cooperation on important issues and are able to build connections between the various company strata, they are likely to produce workplace policies and practices which share burdens and rewards more equitably, within a wider enterprise that can benefit from diversification of assets and, with that, a stability which is able to provide a decent standard for its employees without increased likelihood of economic dislocation or decline (Dahl 1985; Cathcart 2013).

Solidarity-building as part of worker control then has two relevant contributions to make in the amelioration of alienation. First, there is a material contribution in that the extension of humanistic bonds, alongside acknowledgement and recognition, tends to improve the condition of workers (Siegrist 2002). This is achieved not only by giving them a seat at the table but also by encouraging cooperation for the stability of the enterprise upon which everyone relies, as well as the sharing of burdens and rewards (Arando et al. 2010). This insulates the worker from the worst effects of crisis or provides a welcome improvement in their standard of life, which is to contribute to the dignity component of alienation through the betterment of their material circumstance.

Second, solidarity-building has further relevance to the question of belonging as cooperation in spite of some fundamental differences has been understood by Gorton and Schmid (2004) as evidence of the effectiveness of worker control in building recognition. It might not completely alter the underlying relationship between employees and owners, but it does appear to humanise said relationship, which is what they see as leading to these fairer outcomes and the wider distributions of the benefits of business (Coutinho 2016).

In this sense, the intention of worker control for solidarity-building and the bringing together of owners, managers, workers, and others within an enterprise to inform workplace policy and direction are compatible with the book's central desire to challenge alienation through the extension of agency and dignity if worker control can extend humanistic bonds between these strata, with outcomes that can be considered as fair and equitable. As noted, this does not deny that there will be some conflict over the fundamental aims of each group, yet here we see how cooperation in other areas can smooth the edges of such differences and improve the feeling of belonging and process of recognition within companies, whilst also ensuring that sacrifices and rewards are more fairy distributed.

From this intention, one might also highlight the relevance of solidarity-building in relation to fairness. Chapters 3, 5, and 7 highlighted the working-class regard for fairness and their current frustrations with an unfair and inconsiderate economic and social structure. The value of fairness is then extremely important in the working-class experience of alienation and is expressed at its worst as exploitation, but is also felt more generally in relation to one's pay and conditions, especially when they are precarious, on minimal-hours contract, or on minimum wage as corporate profits and high-end bonuses grow (Equality Trust 2021a). One therefore draws on worker control's desire to improve acknowledgement as a means for the working-class to challenge those aspects of an economic system which they see as unfair and to build an understanding for the circumstances in which they find themselves. As such, one makes note of solidarity-building as part of this wider move towards acknowledgement and recognition as a relevant means to challenge alienation amongst the working-class and sees that a general policy direction which seeks to build bonds between groups and improve conditions in relation to the value of fairness would be worthwhile as a central foci. This intention is thus compatible with the central desire to ameliorate alienation and serves to enhance this aim.

Voice and Autonomy

Bosanquet, as well as Cole (2023, 1920a), and the early Laski (2020) are supportive of worker control as a means to further autonomous action within something which we dedicate a not inconsiderable amount of our lives to. They see that workers should be able to find a sense of value in the work that they do. Although coming from a background that is not directly influenced by the works of these socialists, this value, which amounts to the development of purpose, is a core aim of models of worker control in both the Scandinavian countries and Germany. This is expressed in relation to the central value of autonomy and the related notion of voice.

According to Laski (2020), to have a voice is to be treated not as a "cog" in a machine but as a worker, capable in their role and able to express their ideas and desires. Cole too sees that voice has a quite radical potential because it denies in dehumanisation of the worker, whilst inclusion and stake-giving prevent the transformation of workers into "servile" beings, which he expresses as the uprooting of a hierarchical master-slave relationship in the economy (Cole 1920b, 99). Of course, both go further to advocate for state or worker ownership and the fundamental alteration of our economic system to achieve their ends, yet we see here how the importance that each gave to a sense of control.

They give regard to voice primarily because the ability to direct one's work without exercise of arbitrary authority is both demonstrative of a level of trust in the skill of workers and leaves room for innovation within the remits of the task. Cole (1920b, 56–59) believes such autonomy will "stimulate" and "guarantee liveliness" because it frees oneself from the constraints of authority. This may appear to be a minor concession but, given the time that we commit to work, the ability to be able to work without interference encourages the development of self-respect and belief in one's skill. This is understood to be important because, as Cole (1920b, 58) notes, "workmanship" comes through autonomy, and one can take pride in that which is cooperatively produced or which one achieves by their hand. Cole sees this as liberation from unnecessary stress and considers it to enable esteem-building through the mastery of one's work, perhaps alongside or in support of their fellows. This is summarised by Cole (1920b, 57) as unlocking their "opportunities to use their ability in co-operation with their fellow-workers" and makes work a "centre of self-government". In other words, it frees the worker from fears related to their position at the bottom of the workplace hierarchy, which is itself conducive to problem-solving within a cooperative atmosphere made up of one's immediate fellows. This is important as a means of expressing both oneself and one's frustrations but also contributes to the development of a more positive, and in Marmot's (1991, 2004) view less stressful, working atmosphere. The provision of autonomy within the workplace is then important in improving its atmosphere for employees, putting them in a less stressful and opening space for the development of vocation in their respective roles. It comes together with voice here as an outlet for workers and creates a space for them that is free from arbitrary authority on a day-to-day basis.

The provision of a voice through autonomy thus raises the worker to a position where they can more readily engage in work to give it meaning. This reflects the views of both the Idealists and Socialists who consider work as a place for the development of our skills. Indeed, work is presented, especially by Tawney (1964), as vocation. That is, it can come to be a source of pride for the worker, who sees it as part of their calling; that has purpose which is evocative of dignity. The ability to shape our working practices and to contribute to a myriad of other questions encourages us to think of work in terms of what we wish to get out of it, rather than as something that we must do to survive.

Vocation and Autonomy

However, vocation, which is underpinned by a sense of meaning within, and control over, one's work come together in a substantive way in relation to autonomy, the extension of which is an intention of worker control. Autonomy is tied to this idea of vocation as it assumes trust in one's ability and is understood to improve the self-respect and confidence of workers. However, workplace autonomy is found to diminish considerably the further one gets down a workplace hierarchy, with those at the bottom suffering most in terms of their well-being (Marmot et al. 1991). This suffering is often compounded by issues related to work demands, a lack of balance between effort and reward, and the stresses which result from imposition, including on one's self-respect (Marmot 2004; O'Neill 2010). Cole (1920b, 55–59) was too concerned with "tediousness" and considers work without autonomy as a "prison of boredom and useless toil" because it can lose its cognitive function or feeling of usefulness or purpose, which he suggests can give meaning to tedium so that one does not suffer psychologically. Each of these concerns is likely to be present in non-worker-controlled working-class jobs, such as supermarket work, which is consistent with repetitive action and physical labour, as well as strict discipline, which Marmot (2004) and Siegrist (2002) confirm as having a negative impact on worker well-being. Research by Wilkinson and Pickett (2010) also suggests that the working-class are likelier than any other class to lack autonomy and, consequently, are amongst those who most suffer from mental health problems related to work and feelings of worthlessness. Here, one establishes the value of autonomy and the relevance that it has to the well-being of, perhaps especially, working-people, but also other workers within the economy.

From the outset then, worker control's intention to improve autonomous action for working-people is relevant for the improvement of the working-class condition. Marmot (2004) says as much and observes that the implementation of worker control is associated with feelings of greater agency and is conducive to self-respect, confidence, and the limitation of imposition within hierarchies. In other words, worker control can challenge those factors which cause harm to well-being and deprive workers of dignity. He again singles out how it develops "autonomy … and the opportunities you have for full social engagement and participation" which he says "are crucial for health, well-being, and longevity", whilst autonomous action can be preventative of the "chronic stress" which is caused by lack of control over life circumstances, especially in the context of work, and lack of opportunity for participation (Marmot 2004, 150). Although this a health-focused account of worker control, we do see here how the extension of autonomy and agential control has benefits for well-being and flourishing (Wilkinson and Pickett 2010). Indeed, referring back to the socialistic component of the book, we can draw a direct link between worker control and a Laskian perspective which holds that the workers' life should be "planned by a process of which he [sic] is largely the creator" (Laski 2020, 451), which involves autonomy because it is "the root of freedom" since it gives the worker space to think and room to act, away from the constraints of discipline.

Autonomy and Belonging

Autonomous action has some relevance for the feeling of belonging and of rootedness within work. Laski (2020, 454) is keen to highlight "the general experience that discussion on the plane of comradeship and equality almost always leads to satisfactory compromise". Under a model of worker control, he suggests that workers can begin to feel that decisions are rooted in their experience and that what follows therefore either comes to reflect them or that they are at least recognised as having had a voice in the process. This has special relevance in relation to agency because it prioritises consideration and consent, both of which are said to be undermined within a hierarchical model of decision-making in which change is often imposed from above. In this situation, workers are left subject to the will of higher-ups, with resulting decisions met with either muted relief, indifference, or, in negative cases, frustration or anger, whilst the subsequent implementation of those decisions is often ill-understood. This makes for a more adversarial workplace as workers feel that their ideas are ignored, often because there is no medium through which to make suggestions, and perceive themselves to be powerless, with decisions imposed upon them (Pateman 1970; Marmot 2004). In this situation, regardless of whether one agrees with the decision or not, the worker is likely to have such powerlessness highlighted to them, and hierarchy reinforced so that others are seen to have power over them, their work, and their livelihoods.

The extent of this feeling of powerlessness shifts in the context of different decisions, but Levinson (2000) sees it as being an ever-present feature of the workplace which dehumanises workers and alienates them from the decisions which affect them most. This amounts to a deprivation of their agency and prevents the rooting of workers within their enterprise in a meaningful way, since they lack control over what happens to them.

In contrast, the extension of autonomy and the inclusion of workers in the decision-making process lay the groundwork for belonging. Indeed, as we have noted, autonomy gives space to develop vocation. Part of vocation is appreciation, and trust enough to participate in the decision-making process is supportive of that because it implies that the worker knows their role, their fellows, and their company well enough to contribute to it not only through their endeavour but also with their ideas. Tawney (1964) sees this as empowering and a means of grounding the worker as an important facet of a wider group, with shared purpose. Where autonomy then gives space for the worker to more fully develop a sense of vocation, the mastery of one's work, and the structural acknowledgement in decision-making processes, improves the capacity of that worker to feel that they belong and to contribute to the collective shaping of that which they devote a significant portion of their lives to. In this sense, worker control, and the autonomy and agency that it seeks to develop, has relevance to the development of meaning and purpose, which is itself enhanced by a sense of rooted belonging.

These factors have come together substantively to improve belonging within the workplace. For instance, Levinson's (2000) examination of the Swedish Model found that 82% of employees consulted in his study felt rooted in their workplace, had a positive view of their work, and felt able to influence policy. This, he suggests, helps to build trust, enables innovation, and leads to joint solutions, which are seen by employees to be more legitimate and representative of them, concluding that the result of these practices in Sweden has been to greatly increase "bipartite decision-making" within workplaces (Levinson 2000, 457). Such results contrast heavily with the experience of British workers, where only a third of who feel like they belong at work, are listened to, or are valued (Eltringham 2020). In practice, worker control's extension of autonomy and decision-making to workers has been able to effectively promote a sense of worth through vocation and has had a legitimising effect on workplace policy, which is felt to be of the workers rather than imposed from above. This has significance regarding alienation because it rails against that pressure found within the capitalist economic system which dehumanises workers by enacting changes in their work and conditions without consent.

We can also build on this to highlight a wider significance of autonomy in relation to alienation, as its extension has a positive impact on the agency and dignity of workers. Indeed, we have seen how the socialists considered autonomy as a means to challenge dehumanisation and to promote vocation, which is borne out by evidence from Levinson (2000), whilst it also limits the negative consequences of hierarchy sufficiently to produce a marked improvement in well-being and feelings of worthwhile belonging within work (Marmot 2004). This would suggest that the extension of autonomy is a powerful means by which to challenge alienation across several of its characteristics and could be identified as a significant framing through which to promote its amelioration. With this in mind, one considers worker control's intention to improve autonomy as having a wider policy relevance as a possible to focus for future development.

The Ownership Critique

Thus far one has discussed the intentions of worker control in relation to the amelioration of alienation and suggested that said intentions not only are compatible with this task but also serve to underline the importance of more general directions that our policy should take to see the condition of the working-class improved. However, despite the relevance of worker control to alienation, it is not a panacea. In fact, critiques of worker control do raise questions about the scope of economic reform needed to fundamentally alter the position of working-people, and themselves point towards some worthwhile considerations for alienation's amelioration. It is on this basis that one assesses the critique of a lack of ownership change under the Swedish and German Models of worker control.

Marx (2000, 2007), Laski (2020), and Cole (1918) see the redistribution of ownership as necessary to comprehensively ameliorate alienation. In the classical Marxist view, workers cannot become unalienated unless they have full entitlement to the fruits of their labour, since it is they who have created this value in the first instance through their effort. Although worker control does seek entitlement to some degree, it does fall short of ownership in the Swedish and German Models as the hierarchical separation between employers and employees remains (Mertens and Schanze 1979, 78). What these critics point out are a number of issues related to ownership, including the persistence of hierarchical relationships in enterprise, the value of distributed ownership to working-people, and wealth's intertwining with limited ownership and its effect on social values.

On this first point, Laski (2020, 201–202) sees the hierarchical nature of limited ownership as perpetuating injustices by enabling one group to maintain their wealth whilst the economic condition of the working-class remains that they must sell their labour to survive. Indeed, even if the worker is well-paid, with good employee benefits and conditions, they are still selling themselves for hire and cannot escape the hierarchical nature of this relationship, which Marx (2000) views as fundamentally exploitative because it enables the maintenance of extreme profit by the Bourgeoisie and the influence that comes with it (Tawney 1964; Cole 1920c). He, therefore, draws a link between the acquisition of wealth and the opportunities that one might have, both in terms of their life chances and in terms of agency. The underlying concern here is that, in enabling limited ownership, those at the top of the wealth hierarchy will maintain greater agential power, whilst those who sell their labour are unable to bridge this gap and are afforded limited opportunities.

This, Laski says, is a source of disharmony between labour and capital because there is a "divorce between ownership and work" which will always favour those with the most resources (Laski 2020, 208–210). Indeed, he asserts, "We can make the relationship between manager and machine-tender [worker] an intelligible one if control and decision-making is shared", but "once the element of ownership is introduced the possibility of harmony is absent" because the aims of owners and workers are different, as are the privileges in control that come from wealth (Laski 2020, 203). In Laski's view, ownership only separates people into those that have and those that have not, and though he recognises that some people can contribute to business through investment, he sees that their rewards, including control over enterprise, far outweigh their function—as others struggle but are responsible for the act of production or the servicing of need. Such difference in circumstance is a source of anger amongst the working-class, who perceive the difference in position between owner and worker as being responsible for their agential degradation and the placing of limits on people like them as others prosper (Tawney 1964; McKenzie 2015; Equality Trust 2021c; Marx 2019).

This is, of course, attitudinal, but it also maintains several relevant social effects, including in the way that we value people within our society (Sandel 2012). Although worker control does build recognition across hierarchy and provides the autonomy needed to develop vocation, the difference in wealth between owners and workers remains significant (OECD 2022; CEPR 2023). This is not only a point of contention for workers, but it also has relevance to questions of dignity and social value. At present, Laski (2020) argues that wealth brings privileges in the economy because it secures ownership and, with that, control, without necessitating any duties to others. He sees this as fundamentally wrong, in-part by echoing Marx's concern that those with the greatest wealth maintain undue agential influence because of it, but also because, in a society where some are allowed to become more prosperous than others, to have no duty attached to that is to undermine other values because it transforms privilege into a virtue to be celebrated. As such, he sees that "private prosperity" must "involve an addition to the common welfare" and "must never be so large that its owner exercised power by reason of its sheer magnitude; it must never be so small that it's possessor cannot be himself at his best" (Laski 2020, 217). What he suggests is restraint, and that privilege must come with duty (Laski 2020, 203), but privilege can only be allowed to extend so far, lest it undermines the dignity of one's fellows and unfairly extends one's agency. Therefore, he sees the need for a shared ownership because it turns workers from those selling their labour to partners, with the rights and privileges that flow from it. Here the worker is entitled to a share of the fruits of their labour, whilst those who can serve other functions, like investment, should not be unduly rewarded with greater agential capacity than their fellows, who are vital for enterprise in other ways. In this, ownership changes the nature of hierarchy, with investment turned into a function which is but one of many needed to ensure prosperity. He settles on a position which would give those who invest and who had previously sat at the top of the economic hierarchy a "right to dividend" but suggests that they "must surrender alike profits and control", with the rights of ownership "distributed" (Laski 2020, 208). The core relevance of this to the question of alienation is that it seeks to break the link between wealth and control, seeing that wealth should not entitle one to power over others, nor should it be celebrated as a virtue without the need for duties to be attached to it. Laski sees that limited ownership assumes that those with wealth as owners are deserving of a greater degree of control than others because they can invest more. Wealth here is seen to be the basis for hierarchy as it enables control, which Laski views as "autocratic" (Laski 2020, 210). There are two points that arise out of this. First, wealth is unnecessarily tied to power and the agential actions that one could take on. Second, this assumption that wealth is deserving of greater agential capacity gives no thought to expertise, nor vocation, and essentially limits the worker, who cannot acquire that same level of wealth. This amounts to a degradation of their agency, despite the potential quality of their work, their skill, knowledge, and decency, and is to reinforce wealth as the pre-eminent source of value in our society.

Shared ownership is then seen to break this dominance of wealth and control, which Laski (2020, 210) understands as amounting to a liberation of the worker from an economic "[a]utocracy built upon right of functionless ownership" and the subjugation of vocation and other frames relevant to the extension of dignity and well-being to wealth. In this he sees potential for the radical re-shaping of our economy and, through that, our society by reordering the values and functions which make for economic prosperity. He asserts that shared ownership will create "roots of loyalty" within enterprise and to make the system "a source of moral possibility", where work is transformed from a source of survival for workers, and a quest for pure profit from owners, to one in which "just and discernible purpose (s)" are achieved as vocation, knowledge, skill, and other such frames are not dominated in decision-making by those with greater wealth (Laski 2020, 212–216). This is summarised as the hopeful conclusion that "co-ordination for function makes a plane where all men can meet in common" (Laski 2020, 217) and that an equal distribution leads "citizens to be judged in terms of their social value; to become implicit with purpose as the way to recognition", which is to say that ownership when dispersed is to deny its power to undermine social value and is in fact to unleash it. In Laski's view, if we are all owners, and each holds wealth sufficient to live, then we must look for other, more inherently human, means of understanding ourselves and our value. From this reordering of the fundamentals of ownership within the economy, he hopes for the creation of "a society of deeper spiritual values of which the worst tyranny, that of man over man, will have been extinguished" (Laski 2020, 217), where the worker is transformed from an "animate tool" to a fully-fledged participant in the shaping of the economic sphere (Laski 2020, 476).

Ownership and its distribution are then, for Laski, a central concern. He is not here calling for radical expropriation as one might expect but, rather, the re-shaping of our economy so as to flatten hierarchies based on wealth, which seep into our political life and our culture with consequences for worker dignity and social value. His point here is clear too, namely that ownership by workers transforms their economic position from one of a hired hand to one of an owner able to claim the fruits of their labour. This is potentially a powerful change in circumstance and one which goes beyond the worker control noted above to alter the balance of power in enterprise in a fundamental way. Laski believes that great benefits to well-being and social regard lay in this transformation, including the breaking down of wealth-as-value in favour of more humanistic concerns, as well as the bolstering of the economic system as an example of morality, democratic, and subject to the will of the community through shared ownership. One must be careful not to take such conclusions as the natural result of ownership's distribution, but the Laskian argument for ownership is compelling. It does alter the foundations of the economy and democratises its ownership, whilst the breaking down of autocracy in industry and the limitation of excessive personal profits are likely to reduce the elites' ability to unfairly influence our political system. As a critique of worker control then, its failure to transfer ownership and to reorganise the economy based on function, with a strong focus on relative privileges and the necessity of providing value to the common good, is convincing. Indeed, if our economic system is to be inclusive of the working-class, and crucially to be at its fairest, then ownership seems a stronger way of better guaranteeing their structural equality, of flattening hierarchy ready for the development of recognition, and of ensuring that those in positions of authority are unable to "take advantage" of the community or its citizens (Laski 2020, 524).

Whether such radical outcomes can be realised is, of course, up for debate, but one finds it hard to deny the potential of ownerships distribution and democratisation to challenge alienation. It is on this basis that one suggests the distribution of ownership as a worthwhile exploration for the reformation of an economic system that is fit for, and fair to, working-people.

Conclusion

This section has sought to assess the intentions of worker control in relation to the book's desire to challenge alienation amongst the British working-class. One considers worker control as being compatible with this, and the Idealist-Socialist ethos, seeing its intentions as likely to have a positive effect on working-people. Its central concern with agency, desire to make work more meaningful, and commitment to recognition in both a structural and workplace-social sense seem immediately relevant to the betterment of the working-class position. Furthermore, its intentions, as well as some of the critiques levelled against it, point to further considerations for future policy development and serve as worthwhile aims to potentially assess those policies in light of. Indeed, the benefits of worker control are summarised in relation to four of its core intentions and find themselves compatible with the book's desire to challenge alienation. These are as follows:

1. The extension of acknowledgement and recognition.
2. The emphasis on solidarity-building which looks to extend humanistic feeling across hierarchies.
3. A restructuring in respect to central values like fairness, with resulting workplace policies in the context of worker control seen to redistribute material rewards and reduce feelings of exploitation or otherness.
4. The extension of autonomy.

On this last point, the extension of autonomy is particularly valuable for the working-class sense of dignity and agency, as its expansion as part of worker control demonstrates. Evidence points to autonomy as improving belonging and meaning-generation, encouraging vocation and purpose, and in making the workplace less stressful and more receptive, thereby improving worker well-being.

These positive outcomes are likely to be the result of the myriad intentions of worker control coming together, but it is relevant to note that autonomy plays a part in their positive development, and its expansion is intrinsically tied to the betterment of the working-class position. This is not to say that it is more important than any of the three other points, however. Rather, we should understand these four intentions as mutually beneficial to one-another. Indeed, autonomy is itself strengthened by structural acknowledgement, the recognition derived from solidarity, and better material conditions, the results of the other three intentions. It is, therefore, worth noting here that though one highlights each of these points as relevant goals to direct policy towards or to assess policy aimed at improving the working-class position, alienation might be comprehensively ameliorated by policy which cuts across or seeks to develop more than one of these inclinations. Laski's critique of limited ownership and the unification of wealth with control are also relevant in the development of policy. In fact, if we deem Laski's argument as at least plausible, and there is reason to believe that ownership, wealth, and control are highly concentrated within our economy, then this does raise concerns about wealth as dominating other values which produce dignity, as well as limiting opportunities for agential action within the economic sphere. Worker control does challenge this latter concern somewhat, but the Laskian argument holds that hierarchy and limited ownership still enable unfair agential advantage to be accrued to limited owners, whilst worker control does not go far enough to undo the intertwining of wealth and control which so hamper other values from being realised. In this respect, we do need to think about policy in relation to the values that we wish to see presented within our society. Ownership appears to relate to this, and the reformation of ownership within the economy could well provide a means to improve the social value of much that workers hold dear, as well as to entitle them to the fruits of their labour and break the dominance of capital over agency within our economy. These are all radical outcomes with much promise, and there is no doubt that questions around ownership would generate significant debate in practice. Nevertheless, the Laskian critique of worker control as lacking consideration of the value of ownership has relevance for the future shape of our economy, the values which can help to promote or hinder from realisation, and finally the influence of democratisation, namely in the way that distributed ownership in Laski's view is to reorganise the economy upon the basis of function, with agential power shared, whilst limited ownership cannot but produce "autocratic" control on the basis of wealth. There are contrasting visions for the future of not only our economy tied to this but also our society and extent to which democratisation and agential equalisation should influence the economic sphere.

Pay Ratios and the Question of Dignity

The question of dignity can also be understood in relation to pay and its perceived meaning. In this new Knowledge Economy, where merit has been tied increasingly to a neoliberal cultural perspective which understands the wealth that one can acquire, or the pay that one can receive, as a reflection of their value, we see a situation in which extreme income inequalities do significant damage to worker dignity (Sandel 2020).

Extreme pay inequality is not purely a working-class problem. Indeed, there is often significant disparity between middle-pay workers in companies and corporate elites, which can itself cause frustration and impact upon dignity (Marmot 2004). However, we might underline some of the additional problems faced by low-paid workers which inflict further indignities upon them and which underline the stark inequalities in their pay and perceived value.

One case which can be used to underline this situation is the experience of Tesco workers, their conditions, and their pay vis-à-vis their CEO. At the top of the company, former CEO Dave Lewis received a £1.6m salary in 2020 alongside a £6.24m bonus. In comparison, Tesco shop-floor workers live on an hourly wage, which was below the living wage at £9.55 as of early 2022, with a sick pay which does not pay until day 3 of sickness, and only then at SSP of up to £96.35 per week (Butler 2020; GOV.UK 2021). This is further compounded by the fact that workers face insecure working arrangement owing to the prevalence of minimal-hour contracts. These contracts enable one's working week to be cut down to only 'core' hours, whilst further allowing the company to pay a holiday rate based on one's contracted hours rather than against an average of what they would have worked. This treatment is common within the retail sector and represents a fundamental concern for unions and working-people alike (USDAW 2021). Against this backdrop of insecurity are significant bonuses awarded to CEOs and executives, alongside considerable yearly salaries.

The cumulative result of these circumstances and the comparative wealth of those at the top inflict indignity on the working-class here, as those at the bottom suffer from a mixture of below-living wages, insecure contracts, and precarious entitlements, whilst higher-ups remain comfortable. One might consider the situation to be different if their structural circumstances were better, with higher wages, secure contracts, and guaranteed hours, but even then, 6.42m in bonuses does not constitute fair value for one's contribution, with such bonuses often belied by low-earners themselves as deeply unfair and unreflective of both the value that they have and the work that they do (Churchill 2022; HPC 2022). To underline this point, consider that former Tesco CEO Lewis earned some £1.6m in basic salary and benefits, which alone is 355 times that of the lowest-paid average employee without factoring in this bonus. Taken together with this bonus, this amounts to a pay ratio of 1420:1. Such disparity comes at a time when we see the top earners continue to earn more each year, whilst those on middle and low incomes effectively see their wages, and quality of life, reduced consistently year-on-year and is a frequent source of frustration for workers who feel that they are seriously undervalued and disregarded in their roles (Equality Trust 2021a; HPC 2021).

Within this context, and considering these struggles, it becomes possible to claim that extreme pay inequality undermines working-class dignity sufficiently that we might look towards redistributive policies which can both better the material position of the class and reconsider the link between one's sense of value and the meaning of wage increases.

Policy Direction

The Equality Trust (2021b) propose a fundamental redistributive effort that does not solely rely on government taxation—seeing structural change as a more effective guarantor than tax increases which can be cut by successive governments. In line with this, the Trust have proposed to back 2020 Government regulations which hold that the UK's biggest companies will have to disclose and justify the gap between their company elites and their average worker, whilst going further by demanding measures for its reduction. This is proposed through commitments to reduce pay inequality year-on-year within companies or through the passing of laws regulating a minimum-maximum of pay across the economy. Taken together, this amounts to a year-on-year reduction of pay ratios to a final unspecified point in the future set as a ratio of 20:1. This section analyses this proposal against the ethos developed previously to assess its general implications and develop further principles which we might apply to our economic and workplace policies moving forward.

Assessing Pay Ratios

This policy aims to narrow the gap between the top and bottom of our society displayed here in the microcosm of the workplace. The basic premise that the gap between the worst paid and the highest paid in a company should be reduced is an application of the socialist component of this book. This is not a claim that working conditions for the lowest-paid workers should be improved whilst inequality expands, but, rather, an attempt to ensure that any improvements in material conditions are distributed more fairly than they had been previously. It reflects that component of the ethos which argues for a more equitable distribution so that working-people are better rewarded for their work and that their contribution is sufficiently recognised. In saying this, one establishes that a policy which accomplishes these more generalised effects can be regarded as in-line with the theory of Idealist-Socialism and its proposed amelioration of alienation.

To illustrate this further, let us consider (1) the psychological impact of pay ratios, (2) the material benefits derived from them, and (3) the potential for enshrining obligation as part of one's station. One uses this discussion to draw further implications for policy direction.

Psychological and Social Impacts

In terms of psychological impact, we see in the reduction of executive salaries a reorientation of company priorities so that improvements are made with working-people in mind. According to Wilkinson and Pickett (2010), companies that maintain more minimal pay ratios tend to improve a sense of workplace cohesion. Indeed, Brown et al. (2008), as well as Sandel (2020), note that whilst workers can recognise that those in positions of authority might reasonably receive further reward for their efforts, often due to education level, time-spent at the company, or workload, they reject exorbitant differences on the basis that this constitutes exploitation and belies an underlying assumption that the lowest worker exists in the company to generate rewards for those above them, even whilst they suffer those issues presented above. Following from this logic, one sees a positive psychological impact when pay conforms to lay understandings of fairness as workers in low-pay ratio companies found themselves better able to engage with those in positions above them, owing in-part to the fact that the workplace culture generated was more collaborative (Cohen 2015). This itself has significance in reference to the amelioration of alienation, primarily because such factors as the narrowing of distance between company strata in monetary terms *seem* to have had a corresponding impact on their social capacity, bringing people from different positions into a contact which can be described as collaborative rather than dictatorial or overly hierarchical (Bal 2017). The positive impacts of this can be understood in relation to a study conducted by the New Zealand Government's Fair Pay Agreement Working Group (2023), which found that recognition, and socialisation, between people at different levels of a company tends to create a workplace atmosphere in which power, although remaining in the hands of the same people as before, is 'humanised' so that those in positions of management express greater compassion, understanding, and respect. These results are suitable in challenging alienation and speak to the ethical idea that one should be treated with recognition and respect, regardless of their position. Taken together, one considers that policies such as pay ratios can challenge working-class alienation on a basis of recognition (Laaser and Bolton 2022). Indeed, this research suggests that workers in companies with closer pay differentials tend to form more close-knit bonds to one-another across groups, express greater concern for their colleagues, and are more motivated to engage with them in ways that extend humanistic feeling. On this basis then one asserts that policies or norms that achieve a sense of fairness, like pay ratios, can be a positive force for the extension of dignity because they tend to be conducive to the development of a sense of appreciation for one's station in a given company, as well as laying a groundwork for the establishment of an ethic of fairness and solidarity.

To draw a more general rule from this example, which is of course contingent on other factors aside from the pay ratios themselves, one would suggest that this example demonstrates the need for policy to move in the direction of further workplace recognition in respect to central values such as fairness, with attention being given to the breaking down of distance within workplace hierarchies to facilitate this. Such a direction takes explicit note of the importance of material circumstances, like one's pay and benefits, in shaping the conditions for recognition. Here one asserts that policy aimed at ameliorating alienation must move towards recognition in material and social terms, with care being given to facilitate interaction within existing hierarchies, keeping in mind the importance of 'fairness' as a key element of adequate recognition (D'Cruz et al. 2021).

Material Improvement

One cannot rule out the significance of proposals such as this in improving material-related dignity either. What one means by this is that, where we have highlighted the current insecurity of the worker, the tendency towards further inequality, and the degradation of their social and material conditions, scholars like Herrera (2004), and Szekely and Dossa (2017) point to redistributive measures like pay ratios as a viable means of improving wages and conditions, especially when combined with those methods noted above. These scholars engage in case study analysis to assert this claim, considering the Mondragon Corporation, a sizeable Spanish cooperative which maintains a revenue of around £12bn and employs just over 81,000 people (Szekely and Dossa 2017). They note that the corporation currently has a pay ratio of 5:1 on average which is reaffirmed by democratic vote periodically, though different branches range from ratios of 3:1

to 9:1. According to Herrera (2004), this has resulted in its workers receiving 13% more than the Spanish national average for those employed in similar positions, whilst it has been praised for furthering collaboration and respect between those employed within different roles. Of course, this comes at the financial expense of those at the higher echelons of the company, who do tend to earn less than the average of their peers elsewhere, but Herrera (2004) is keen to note that they nevertheless maintain a good wage, supplemented by respectable employee benefits and, on average, have higher levels of happiness and job satisfaction (Latinne 2014). This is further underlined by the low turnover rate of the corporation, which Szekely and Dossa (2017) take as indicative that the higher echelons of the corporation are satisfied with their working arrangements. Meanwhile, "workers, who get jobs at Mondragon, gain dignity as persons and in their work and participate in economic justice because they receive fair pay and are able to support their families and themselves" (Herrera 2004, 10). In this instance, the redistributive framework, inclusive of pay ratios, has been successful in contributing to the workers' sense of dignity, whilst the distance between employees in various roles has decreased (Redondo et al. 2011). In turn, this has enhanced solidarity and respect, both of which are conducive to workplace participation and the amelioration of alienation more broadly (Bretos and Errasti 2017; Miliband 2021). Although there are several factors which come together here, including a provision for pay ratios, an element of worker democratic control, and a collaborative business model, one can nevertheless point to this restriction of inequality within the corporate hierarchy which necessarily provides workers with a significant increase in wages vis-à-vis those in similar positions elsewhere. Such a situation fulfils this emphasis on material improvement, whilst simultaneously offering a pathway to greater cohesion through a lens of common dignity.

From this we can suggest that material reward must enable workers to better care for themselves and their families, placing the ability to live decently for all workers above the desire to expand profits at the top. How this might translate into policy is partly unclear, but one nevertheless stresses that policy must move in a direction of worker improvement with a view to the restriction of growing inequality at the top with a redirection of wealth further down the workplace hierarchy so that economic gains benefit these lower groups considerably more-so than at present. We may consider that changes can be justified if they benefit the worst-off group and that such change must also be restrained at the top within pre-defined limits, perhaps set by government, unions, or some cooperative agreement, to protect the *meaning* of such wage increases/improvements, though the mechanism by which we achieve this is beyond the scope of the book.

Social Obligation

Finally, those corporate elites, under policies like pay ratios, which place conditions on their wealth, are essentially required to consider their workers and practice obligations. This can be considered in-part as an application of the common good ethos within businesses so that those who have risen to positions of authority are required to act in ways that are more conducive to the betterment of those 'below' them within the company hierarchy. One has touched upon this in discussing psychological and material benefits but reserves space here to draw attention to that component of the ethos which holds that those who are mobile should accrue additional social obligations owing to their improved station, which has consequences for their own moral flourishing. The moral component ensures that this social obligation is associated with a personal obligation and the recognition of one's station as inclusive of greater responsibilities to others. This is a difficult form of obligation to understand because its more personal nature means that one cannot simply be satisfied with a faceless redistribution of wealth in the form of, for example, taxation, which is effective in material terms but only requires passive acceptance of the state's right to tax (Pabst 2021; Lasch 2018). Pay ratios enforce a similar logic by redistributing wealth before the individual has seen what their pay could have been, which goes some way towards highlighting the need for other measures to encourage the development of the moral character outlined in Chap. 6.

However, where they do somewhat branch into a more morally compatible area is regarding the development of workplace strategy. They do not fully fulfil this obligation because decisions can still be made here based primarily on the 'numbers', but the active inclusion of worker well-being and material improvement in decision-making processes does require an effective obligation in some respects because it so necessitates this consideration. What one means by this is that, even if the spiritual/moral component of social obligation is lacking, the result is nevertheless an improved practical consideration of factors conducive to worker fulfilment. More procedural measures such as pay ratios are, therefore, adequate for grounding a need for obligation from the company hierarchy, yet do not fully encourage the moral activity expressed within the ethos. In this respect, pay ratios can be considered as beneficial, though partially lacking, given that they do not inspire a re-definition of station to include an ethical-moral obligation towards those who are not so lucky; instead setting out a technical obligation to consider as part of workplace strategy. Nevertheless, this is a positive step in redressing pay inequalities and in bringing company strata into further consideration.

One sees in this example a direction which favours the inclusion of material measures which increase obligations amongst those at the top of our society to redress issues of indignity and inequality. This, however, must be matched with the development of a narrative element which is conducive to the establishment of 'fellow-feeling' best understood in light of the principle of moral character as outlined in Chap. 6 primarily.

Other Factors

However, whilst one supports pay ratios on this basis, one must recognise that many of these studies also consider that other factors have themselves played an important role in facilitating this more positive workplace structure. In fact, given that pay ratios were often at their lowest extents in Denmark, Sweden, and Germany, one cannot rule out the importance of unions, worker representation, and other forms of worker control/consultation in creating this sense of workplace community, each of which are common across these nations in different forms (Miliband 2021; Taylor 2018). This is worth considering in-itself on the basis that there are no national laws stipulating the need for pay ratios specifically but, rather, a network of institutions which have been historically successful in ensuring that disparities do not grow too much between company strata.

For instance, the Swedish Model of economic participation makes use of strong unions, inclusive of some 66% of the working population, and has been developed in a context of a large (according to Western European standards) Public Sector (Pierre 2016; ETUI 2021). This is underpinned by the vision of the *Folkhemmet* or 'peoples' home' which involves a conception of the national community in which we act to maintain a common good of all under the guise of the "national family" (Hänninen et al. 2019). Taken together, these kinds of factors combine to create a situation in which, even with a lack of laws regulating executive pay or stipulating a national minimum wage, the success of this network can be expressed in relation to multinational companies usually typified by low pay, who are compelled to pay far more to their workers than in other countries. Indeed, McDonald's maintains a rate of pay in the Swedish context which stands at £11.32, above the UK's living wage as of late 2023 (HRF 2021; GOV. UK 2021). This stands as a particularly useful and relevant example of the positive power of such networks, which reserve space for workers and their associations, both at a national and at an individual company level, to improve their own position and to form agreements/compacts with employers for a decent standard of living.

In fact, the World Happiness Report (WHR) points to this network explicitly as a key factor for the development of a life satisfaction that is amongst the best in the world (Martela et al. 2021). Indeed, it notes that "quality Institutions" and a "strong civil society" help to build "community, trust, and social cohesion", wherein we see a recognition which can help to shape a sense of one's dignity (Martela et al. 2021). Material security is combined with institutional and social recognition to ensure that working-people retain control over their being, either through the unions or within companies through their own modes of worker-engagement (Miliband 2021). This is understood within the narrative of the *Folkhemmet*, which provides a background against which one can better understand their obligations, as well as their function/station. Thus, although one highlights pay ratios as being a positive force in challenging alienation, we see in this complex model a more robust challenge to its effects, branching into those questions of community and agency, as well as dignity. However, it is beyond the remit of this book to assess each of these contributions. Nevertheless, one does point to this nexus of institutional, social, and workplace arrangements as being more comprehensive in its challenge to alienation, though it is worth noting that recent years have seen an upward trend towards inequality, which itself might reassert the importance of legislation to arrest this movement.

This again raises a more general point, namely that policy must look to the strengthening and expansion of civil society intermediary associations and the trade unions in particular, who form a core component of a national-corporate strategy which imbues working-people with the agency to obtain material and institutional improvements, including decent pay, democratic representation, and recognition within a national narrative. In line with this, and as developed in the subsequent chapter, one establishes a primacy for intermediary associational expansion and the passing of legislation which bestows upon them power to democratise our economy with the guidance of working-people.

Conclusion

In considering policy ideas, expressed here through the examples of worker control and pay ratios, one has noted their intentions as relevant to the amelioration of alienation, namely by seeking:

1. The extension of acknowledgement and recognition.
2. An emphasis on solidarity-building which looks to extend humanistic feeling across hierarchies.
3. A restructuring in respect to central values like fairness, with resulting workplace policies in the context of worker control seen to redistribute material rewards and reduce feelings of exploitation or otherness.
4. The extension of autonomy.

In relation to alienation, both worker control and pay ratios can be understood as being successful in their function. Indeed, by their nature they seek to shrink workplace hierarchy, which has been found to produce important social benefits, including greater confidence amongst the lowest paid, increased inter-hierarchy communication, and institutional 'closeness'. Such benefits fulfil in themselves the further necessity of bridging gaps between peoples by bringing them into closer relation. Here we see a positive move in the direction of recognition, whilst diminishing wealth in favour of more 'human' ties. Material redistribution has also been secured in companies that either enact pay ratios or follow the first point of the ethos. In outlining this success, one notes that those companies which have broadly taken actions which align themselves with the first and second points of the ethos have tended to enhance the livelihoods of their workers with express benefits to their sense of happiness and workplace cohesion. It is in light of these successes that one stresses Idealist-Socialism as capable of ameliorating alienation relative to our economic life, though it is worth noting how questions remain over the relevance of ownership to alienation, as well as the value of social obligation. In this sense, there is scope to explore further questions and to determine how specific policies and aims contribute to the Progressive Nationalist narrative established in Chap. 8.

One has highlighted this assessment not only to demonstrate the capacity for Idealist-Socialism to be used to evaluate policy intentions and their outcomes in reference to alienation but also to aid the development of policy guidelines. Indeed, where one has discussed the material, psychological, and ethical improvements offered by policies like worker control and pay ratios, one has been further able to formulate a more specific direction, adding to the aims outlined above a further commitment to:

1. Move towards recognition in material and social terms, centred on values such as fairness.
2. Establish that one of the core goals of work should be to ensure that the worker can live decently at the same time as restricting the growth of inequality at the top of the workplace hierarchy.
3. Match legal and procedural obligation with a narrative that can encourage ethical obligation conducive to the development of moral character.
4. Enact comprehensive measures to promote associational expansion and the creation of a network with an express place for working-people to influence both specific workplace and more general economic policy. One will say more on this in relation to agency in subsequent chapters.

Thus, we can move beyond this illustrative example to suggest that many of those things which flow from these policies are goods that we should consider as integral parts of the Idealist-Socialist attempt to ameliorate alienation, primarily by ensuring the working-people are encouraged to feel belonging within their enterprises and to assert some control over them. As such, what is important to consider within this chapter is that the general policy direction should be towards the achievement of those ends that one has made explicit note of, namely movement towards recognition, obligation, and a material and social betterment.

Bibliography

Arando, Saioa, Mónica Gago, Takao Kato, Derek C. Jones, and Fred Freundlich. "*Assessing Mondragon: Stability & Managed Change in the Face of Globalization.*" SSRN Scholarly Paper. Rochester, NY, November 16, 2010.

Bal, Matthijs. *Dignity in the Workplace: New Theoretical Perspectives.* Springer, 2017.

Bretos, Ignacio, and Anjel Errasti. 'Challenges and Opportunities for the Regeneration of Multinational Worker Cooperatives: Lessons from the Mondragon Corporation—a Case Study of the Fagor Ederlan Group'. *Organization* 24, no. 2 (1 March 2017): 154–173.

Brown, Gordon D. A., Jonathan Gardner, Andrew J. Oswald, and Jing Qian. "Does Wage Rank Affect Employees' Well-Being?" *Industrial Relations: A Journal of Economy and Society* 47, no. 3 (2008): 355–389.

Butler, Sarah. 'Tesco Chief Executive Handed £6.42m Pay Package'. *The Guardian*, 13 May 2020, sec. Business. https://www.theguardian.com/business/2020/may/13/tesco-chief-executive-handed-642m-pay-package-dave-lewis.

Cathcart, A. Directing democracy: competing interests and contested terrain in the John Lewis Partnership. *Journal of Industrial Relations*, 55, No. 4, (2013) 601–620.

CEPR. 'Wealth and Its Distribution in Germany, 1895–2018'. https://cepr.org/voxeu/columns/wealth-and-its-distribution-germany-1895-2018. Accessed 6 Jan 2023.

Cheney, George, and Craig Carroll. 'The Person as Object in Discourses in and Around Organizations'. *Communication Research* 24, no. 6 (1 December 1997): 593–630.

Churchill, Francis. 'Average Supermarket Boss Earns More in Two Days than Shop Floor Staff in a Year, Research Finds'. https://www.peoplemanagement.co.uk/article/1751828?utm_source=website&utm_medium=socia. Accessed 20 Dec 2022.

Cohen, A. *Fairness in the Workplace: A Global Perspective*. Springer, 2015.

Cole, GDH. 'Guild Socialism (1918) | LSE Digital Library'. https://digital.library.lse.ac.uk/objects/lse:sug908yob. Accessed 17 May 2023.

Cole, GDH. *Chaos and Order in Industry*. Methuen and Co., 1920a.

Cole, GDH. *Guild Socialism Restated*. Leonard Parsons, 1920b.

Cole, GDH. *Self-Government in Industry*. G. Bell and Sons, 1920c.

Countinho, James. *Workplace Democracy, Well-Being, and Political Participation*. PhD Thesis, University of Manchester, 2016.

D'Cruz, Premilla, Ernesto Noronha, Carlo Caponecchia, Jordi Escartín, Denise Salin, and Michelle Rae Tuckey. *Dignity and Inclusion at Work*. Springer, 2021.

Dahl, R. *A Preface to Economic Democracy*. University of California Press, 1985.

Eltringham, George. 'Fewer than One-Third of UK Employees Feel a Sense of Belonging'. *Workplace Insight*, 11 June 2020. https://workplaceinsight.net/less-than-one-third-of-uk-employees-feel-they-belong/.

Equality Trust. 'Fair Pay FTSE | The Equality Trust'. https://equalitytrust.org.uk/fair-pay-campaign/fair-pay-ftse. Accessed 2 Dec 2021, 2021a.

Equality Trust. 'How Has Inequality Changed? | The Equality Trust'. https://www.equalitytrust.org.uk/how-has-inequality-changed. Accessed 19 January 2021, 2021b.

Equality Trust. 'The Scale of Economic Inequality in the UK | The Equality Trust'. https://www.equalitytrust.org.uk/scale-economic-inequality-uk. Accessed 19 Jan 2021, 2021c.

European Trade Union Institute, The. 'Trade Unions / Sweden / Countries / National Industrial Relations / Home—WORKER PARTICIPATION.Eu'. https://www.worker-participation.eu/National-Industrial-Relations/Countries/Sweden/Trade-Unions. Accessed 16 Mar 2021.

Gorton, Gary, and Frank A. Schmid. 'Capital, Labor, and the Firm: A Study of German Codetermination'. *Journal of the European Economic Association* 2, no. 5 (2004): 863–905.

Hänninen, Sakari, Kirsi-Marja Lehtelä, and Paula Saikkonen. *The Relational Nordic Welfare State: Between Utopia and Ideology*. Edward Elgar Publishing, 2019.

Hedin, Astrid. 'Before the breakdown of the Saltsjobaden spirit of labour market cooperation: The Swedish Employers' Confederation and Workplace Democracy in the 1960s'. *Scandinavian Journal of History* 44, no. 5 (20 October 2019): 591–616.

Hedin, Astrid. 'The Origins and Myths of the Swedish Model of Workplace Democracy'. *Contemporary European History* 24, no. 1 (2015): 59–82.

Herrera, David. Mondragon: a for-profit organization that embodies Catholic social thought. *Review of Business,* vol 25, no. 1, (2004): 56-68.

High Pay Centre. 'About High Pay Centre'. https://highpaycentre.org/about/. Accessed 4 Dec 2021.

High Pay Centre. 'It Would Take the Average Supermarket CEO Less than Two Days' Work to Earn the Annual Salary of a Colleague on the Minimum Wage High Pay Centre'. *High Pay Centre* (blog), 14 March 2022. https://highpaycentre.org/it-would-take-the-average-supermarket-ceo-less-than-two-days-work-to-earn-the-annual-salary-of-a-colleague-on-the-minimum-wage/.

Hotelloch restaurangfacket (HRF). 'Minimilön För Lönegrupp 1'. https://www.hrf.net/lon-och-villkor/din-lon/minimilon-for-kvalificerat-yrkesarbete-lonegrupp-1/. Accessed 6 Dec 2021.

Laaser, Knut, and Sharon Bolton. 'Absolute Autonomy, Respectful Recognition and Derived Dignity: Towards a Typology of Meaningful Work'. *International Journal of Management Reviews* 24, no. 3 (2022): 373–93.

Lane, Linda, and Michael Wallengren-Lynch. *Narratives of Social Work Practice and Education in Sweden*. Springer Nature, 2020.

Lasch, Christopher. *The Culture of Narcissism: American Life in an Age of Diminishing Expectations*. W. W. Norton & Company, 2018.

Laski, Harold. *The Works of Harold J. Laski*. Routledge, 2020.

Laski, Harold. *Trade Unions in the New Society*. Routledge, 2021.

Latinne, Amanda. *The Mondragon Cooperatives: Workplace Democracy and Globalization*. Intersentia, 2014.

Levinson, Klas. "Codetermination in Sweden: Myth and Reality." *Economic and Industrial Democracy* 21, no. 4 (November 1, 2000): 457–73.

Logue, John. "Trade Unions in the Nordic Countries," February 18, 2019. https://nordics.info/show/artikel/trade-unions-in-the-nordic-region. Accessed 29 Jan 2024.

Luhman, John. "Worker-Ownership as an Instrument for Solidarity and Social Change?,". *ephemera* 7, no. 3 (2007): 462-474.

Lukes, S. *Power: A Radical View*. Palgrave Macmillan, 2005.

Marmot, M. *Status Syndrome: How Your Social Standing Directly Affects Your Health*. Bloomsbury, 2004.

Marmot, Ml. Health Inequalities Among British Civil Servants: The Whitehall II Study. *The Lancet*, 337, no. 8754, (1991) 1387–1393.

Martela, Frank, Bent Greve, Bo Rothstein, and Juho Saari. World Happiness Report. 'The Nordic Exceptionalism: What Explains Why the Nordic Countries Are Constantly Among the Happiest in the World'. https://worldhappiness.report/ed/2020/the-nordic-exceptionalism-what-explains-why-the-nordic-countries-are-constantly-among-the-happiest-in-the-world/. Accessed 6 Dec 2021.

Marx, Karl. *Das Kapital*. Synergy, 2007.

Marx, Karl. *Economic & Philosophic Manuscripts of 1844*. Marxists.org, 2000.

Marx, Paul. 'Anti-Elite Politics and Emotional Reactions to Socio-Economic Problems. Experimental Evidence on "Pocketbook Anger" from France, Germany, and the United States'. *The British Journal of Sociology* 71, no. 4 (2019) 608-624.

McKenzie, Lisa. *Getting By: Estates, Class and Culture in Austerity Britain*. Policy Press, 2015.

Mertens, Hans-Joachim, and Erich Schanze. '*The German Codetermination Act of 1976*'. 1979.

Miliband, Ed. *GO BIG: How To Fix Our World*. Random House, 2021.

New Zealand Government Fair Pay Agreement Working Group. 'Fair Pay Agreements | Ministry of Business, Innovation & Employment'. https://www.mbie.govt.nz/business-and-employment/employment-and-skills/employment-legislation-reviews/fair-pay-agreements/. Accessed 15 Dec 2023.

O'Neill, M. The facts of inequality. *Journal of Moral Philosophy*, 7, no. 3, (2010) 397–409.

OECD. 'Inequality—Income Inequality—OECD Data'. http://data.oecd.org/inequality/income-inequality.htm. Accessed 16 Dec 2022.

Pabst, Adrian. *Postliberal Politics: The Coming Era of Renewal*. John Wiley & Sons, 2021.

Pateman, Carol. *Participation and Democratic Theory*. Cambridge University Press, 1970.

Pateman, Carol. Participatory Democracy Revisited. *Perspectives on Politics*, 10, no. 1 (2012) 7–19.

Pierre, Jon. *The Oxford Handbook of Swedish Politics*. Oxford University Press, 2016.

Redondo, Gisela, Ignacio Santa Cruz, and Josep Maria Rotger. 'Why Mondragon? Analyzing What Works in Overcoming Inequalities'. *Qualitative Inquiry* 17, no. 3 (1 March 2011): 277–283.

Ridley-Duff, R. 'Co-operative Social Enterprises: Company Rules, Access to Finance and Management Practice'. *Social Enterprise Journal*, 5, no. 1, (2009) 50–68.

Sandel, Michael J. *The Tyranny of Merit: What's Become of the Common Good?*. Penguin, UK, 2020.

Sandel, Michael J. *What Money Can't Buy: The Moral Limits of Markets*. Penguin, UK, 2012.

Siegrist, J. Effort-Reward Imbalance at Work and Health. *Historical and Current Perspectives on Stress and Health*, 2, (2002) 261–291

Szekely, Francisco, and Zahir Dossa. *Beyond the Triple Bottom Line: Eight Steps Toward a Sustainable Business Model*. MIT Press, 2017.

Tawney, R.H. *Equality*. Unwin Books, 1964.

Taylor, Matthew. 'Good Work: The Taylor Review of Modern Working Practices'. 2018. https://www.gov.uk/government/publications/good-work-the-taylor-review-of-modern-working-practices. Accessed 15 Dec 2021.

USDAW. 'USDAW—Campaigns'. https://www.usdaw.org.uk/Campaigns. Accessed 15 Dec 2021.

Wilkinson, Richard & Pickett, Kate. *The Spirit Level: Why Equality is Better for Everyone*. Penguin, 2010.

CHAPTER 10

An Ethos for Civil Society

This chapter develops the associational inclination of the book. We have already said that the working-class historically had strong associations that were conducive to developing agency, dignity, and sense of community and that their decline corresponded to the decline of these goods.

Considering this, this chapter emphasises the continued value of associations in challenging alienation, drawing on the Idealism and Socialism of the preceding chapters to identify how they come to support and/or provide four key benefits to citizens, namely:

1. Improving belonging
2. Acknowledgement in society's processes
3. Recognition
4. Symbolic inclusion

These benefits can also be considered as a kind of ethos against which we can assess civil society expansion, seeing it as effective if it subsequently fulfils any of the four.

In outlining these benefits, one will touch upon the associations' relationship with the state to assert the need for it to govern *with* the people and in the interests of inclusive reconciliation. This understanding combines aspects of the Greenian (2003, 2008; Chap. 6) state with the Laskian

S. Taylor Hill, *Challenging Alienation in the British Working-Class*, Palgrave Politics of Identity and Citizenship Series,
https://doi.org/10.1007/978-3-031-59250-8_10

(2020; Chap. 7) model of social federalism to underline the necessity of inclusion and recognition within the institutions and narrative of this nation. Taken together, one asserts the need for the expansion of civil society associations to facilitate the development of these benefits and the corresponding movement of the state towards an active and considered reconciliation, to be achieved in collaboration with the people through their intermediary associations.

Membership-Belonging

The communitarian tradition maintains a position that overlaps with Bosanquet's (2008) and Green's (2008) desire to see the expansion of civil society to provide opportunities for our flourishing and the Socialist desire to see relationships expanded. Indeed, although we have criticised communitarians like Etzioni (1996, 2014a) for their moral rigidity and sought to replace that with a framework of Idealist ethics, this tradition maintains a commitment to belonging and agential generation within the bounds of the association (understood as a microcosm of community), alongside relational development and, through that, enhanced flourishing in specific associations—by engaging one's fellows politically or in the workplace or by providing a more apolitical good in the form of attachment and support for individually defined interests. One will refrain from giving an account of membership-belonging that focuses on its potential to allow flourishing in highly specific personal terms, however, since such flourishing is contingent on factors that are in part down to the way that associations are individually organised. Rather, one wishes to assert a broader point in relation to alienation which sees that the associations and membership, active or not, provide two goods: namely, (1) a personal sense of membership-belonging and (2) a relational belonging capable of enhancing moral character. These two goods come together to challenge alienation through the provision of symbolic-agency and a sense of community, perhaps made deeper by interaction, as well as a relational belonging in which one can engage with others, form bonds, and, depending on associations, cultivate other-consideration, which is necessary for a democratic society that dignifies its members (Green 2008; Taylor 1998).

On this first point, critics of civil society expansion often argue that working-people do not have the time for associations (Vidal et al. 2019). One, in part, accepts and agrees with this criticism. In fact, devoting time is a difficult proposition for many working-people given the insecurity of their work, their unsociable hours, or any of the many issues which demand their attention (Bloodworth 2018). To add to these with a further obligation to take a *consistently* active part in association would then be quite unreasonable and set the ethos of civil society expansion back in much the same way that it has done for broadly related plans in the past, like Cameron's 'Big Society' (Vidal et al. 2019).

In response to this one highlights unions because, often, its members do not have to engage in overly time-consuming processes to derive material and psychological benefits. Indeed, union members often can pay their dues and receive the protection of the union without going any further to seriously engage with its campaigns in a way that is perhaps overly demanding (Barling et al. 1992). However, the act of joining and being part of a union, something imbued with collective power, can bestow a kind of dignity on the person without necessitating further action. Indeed, this sense of collectivity is a communal good because, just by being part of that union, one adds to its collective strength, which itself presents the union with a greater capacity to act in its members' interests through negotiated settlement, pressuring government, or, in more pressing circumstances, strikes (Barrows 2017). Interestingly, this is a consideration which has been advanced by both former President Barack Obama (2020) and Michael Sandel (2020), who desire an active citizenry but recognise the challenges of participation in an economy especially which needs substantive work-life reform. Both recognise an "essential truth" that "most of us just want to belong" and to "feel like others have our backs" (Sandel 2020, 107). As Sandel notes, this feeling can be guaranteed through associations without the need for a demanding participation, noting how unions bring their members together to fight for common causes without demanding much "heavy-lifting", whilst Obama (2020) notes, drawing on his experience as a community organiser, that the act of paying union dues and seeing that union fight for oneself is empowering and fulfils some notion of solidarity. From this we can see the benefits of belonging and a greater degree of agency bestowed upon the individual without a greater corresponding demand for time under normal circumstances, though a strike or other special actions may require further commitment in return. One stresses here that participation in most cases does not have to place significant strains on an individual with other commitments, especially in comparison to the psychological impact of their commitments to those civil society associations which provide them with support and psychological foundations for solidarity and belonging (Mogollón et al. 2021).

Participation may develop these goods further, but here one recognises that such goods can still be derived to pose a challenge to alienation without substantial time-constraints being imposed upon individuals. On this basis, we can dismiss the criticism that such plans rely on extensive participation. Rather, there is a normative benefit to simple membership-belonging, especially perhaps in those associations which have a political function to alter circumstances in favour of its members. Presented in this way, membership within association can be seen as a good in itself.

Relational-Belonging

Further, one sees that associations provide space for the cultivation of relationships because they are organised around points of shared interest. For Walzer (1984) this is important because it premises individual-belonging on a core similarity, which can then be expanded to understand difference between members. This is a move that ultimately tends towards the Greenian mutual recognition of others on an individual level, which does not itself go far to ameliorate community tensions or rooted distrusts but makes an individualised difference as an opportunity for personal enrichment and the practice of moral character. Indeed, Walzer (1967) asserts that associations create the space that one requires to feel that they belong when they interact in that space to create relationships. For example, he notes how association have the potential to become significant support structures in our lives because they encourage basic goods such as friendship and reciprocity. For him this is an important and often undervalued benefit of association. In fact, he notes that relationships and the support that they provide are so foundational to the living of the good life that we tend to overlook them. Just as in Macintyre's (2013) thought, they are the basis of community because they move beyond a transactionalism to underline the relevance and positivity of interaction, support, respect, and selflessness—which each considered as virtues and can be understood as relational to the common good as established in Chap. 6. The development of these feelings/principles helps to tether us to one another so that we are better able to deal with a wider society that can feel like it has lost its meaning (Macintyre 2013; Standing 2019). Understood in this way, associations create the space for a foundational element of non-alienation in which we are encouraged to form relationships, to practise mutual support, and to develop a sense of community-belonging. This perspective, advanced here in reference to Walzer, but equally relevant in

Sandel (2012, 2020) and others, connects with first an Idealist-Socialist desire to see us better able to flourish, in which the interconnected bonds we create with others is conducive to that in a foundational way, and second that component of working-class alienation which we identified in Chap. 5 that highlights community breakdown and structural decline as a key contributing factor to their present state. Here one reasserts the relevancy of associations in challenging this by extending that feeling of community and by providing space to form the relationships that we so rely upon for the living of the good life.

Pluralism and Belonging

Relationships are also important because they can root a lay form of unity in difference, as advanced in this book in reference to the Idealist-Socialist focus on a pluralism backed by mutual recognition (Green 2008; Bosanquet 2008). As Walzer (1967) notes, the character of associations usually means that their membership base maintains some similarities, which had encouraged them to join in the first instance, yet the nature of our society and people as diverse and intersectional leads one to consider the positive benefit of associations in creating this tangible sense of unity and fellow feeling with respect of difference. For example, they can bring together people with different life experiences around that which they share and within a space that is positively integrative (More in Common 2022a). This is to do some work for our wider community because, in developing personal relationships in respect of differences, we fulfil in part that characteristic of democratic equality which requires that "the members (of our society) must know one another, listen to one another, and understand one another. If they are not mutually acquainted, or if they cannot really understand one another, how can they truly engage in joint deliberation?" (Taylor 1998, 144). Associations become a way of practising this mutuality through the integration of peoples within spaces that they feel they collectively 'belong' to. Here, and as Chin asserts, "to belong to a community is to participate in the life of this community, to understand and be understandable to other members of it, and to be able to recognize and be recognized by fellow members" (Chin 2019, 717–718). Associations achieve this is in different contexts depending on their purpose, but they should impact the feeling of "horizontal belonging", which is that form which "concerns the relations of mutual identification and recognition amongst various individuals and groups within the state" (Chin 2019, 717–718) since they seek to draw people together and, in doing so, encourage the development of those relationships which cut across ideational boundaries. We are not seeing a challenge to alienation in a definitive sense, but what we do see is a movement away from isolation/separateness towards interaction with, and the understanding of, our fellows which is conducive to moral character and other-consideration. This is, in turn, referenced by Chin as essential to democratic membership and recognition in asserting a form premised on the mutual acceptance of one's belonging. In fact, in many respects, the creation of space for relationship-building and interaction is conducive to the breaking down of misrecognitions on behalf of diverse participants, is demonstrative of their similarity in difference as members of the same association, and tangibly encourages the belonging and solidarity which is desired by most citizens (More in Common 2022b).

The visibility and tangible belonging, expressed through one's relationships with others in association, is therefore important in challenging the community component of alienation which highlights isolation and separateness, exacerbated by misunderstanding and misrecognition of our fellows as belonging within our society. Ultimately, the foundational relationship-building which associations can provide maintain that most basic of benefits that we see each other not as ideas or abstractions but as people, deserving of the opportunity to live the good life, with hopes and dreams, and concerns that we can navigate together. Understood in this way, membership and relational belonging provide a kind of solidarity and space for understanding that is conducive to relationship, and therefore community, building.

The Good of Acknowledgement

Matched with the goods of membership-belonging and relationship-building is the more institutional-structural good of acknowledgement. Tully (2008) highlights this good, which suggests that by being heard and hearing others in turn, citizens come to identify with the community without necessarily being dependent on the success of their claims. This amounts to a form of inclusion in the processes of our society, defined here in relation to a notion of political equality which rests on one's ability, either personally or through their association, to be 'acknowledged' as having a stake. What we see here is a preference for the inclusion of one's voice, as an agent, in the decisions which shape our society and, with that, an act of acknowledgement from our fellows to listen to our perspective. This involves "acknowledging citizens in ways that are appropriately responsive to their status as free and equal persons or members of the polity" (Tully and Owen 2007, 266). The acknowledgement of one, or one's group, as an active and equal member of our society, deserving of a 'place at the table' to some extent aligns with the perspective of Cole, who sees that this act of inclusion, again regardless of outcome, is a core benefit of associational life, since it is within these frameworks that one is able to practise agency and "self-expression", both within association and in wider spheres as part of a collective body (Cole 1920, 20). What is important to note here in relation to alienation is that the status of groups is made procedurally more equal, not only by giving citizens a stake in the process, but also insofar as the process itself establishes the necessity of other-consideration in our debates, even if that is only on a more limited procedural level. Indeed, Levey describes acknowledgement as "modest" since it does not promise change, rather seeing inclusion in the processes that define and determine societal change as practising an "awareness and acceptance that there are others…in our political community" (Levey 2006, 363) and that their presence is legitimate—that they belong. This is not only to ascribe agency to the relevant party through the provision of a stake, but also a degree of dignity from one's procedural acknowledgement as constituent members of debates. Whilst this is not a deep-rooted socially determined dignity, it nevertheless identifies how acknowledgement can improve at least two of the three characteristics of alienation.

Understanding this in the working-class context, this position asserts that they should be considered in the processes of change within our society, which requires the inclusion of representatives from that class who are recognised as such, like perhaps the Labour Party and trade unions were historically. Here we see the importance of stake raised so that working-people feel that they have been seen to have one in the future of our society and have the potential to shape it in line with others. This is a modest expression of belonging and highlights the working-class as a constituent group that *deserves* to have a 'seat at the table'. To underline the relevance of this move we can affirm the strength of the "left behind" narrative and the related "politics of resentment" (Eatwell and Goodwin 2018). This is a powerful narrative that is born out of a loss of agency, either as the Labour Party has shifted to become a more middle-class-dominated party, with a lack of consideration for the voices of working-people themselves, or by the decline of the trade unions, which have suffered draconian legal restrictions and, apart from within a few sectors, now struggle to win concessions for the class (Goodhart 2020; Bloodworth 2018). We can refer to examples which speak to this narrative and of the classes' lack of acknowledgement. For instance, the Parliamentary Labour Party only has around 10% of its MPs from a working-class background, down from 37% in 1964, whilst Keir Starmer has sought to overturn popular proposals for the nationalisation of the railways and the strengthening of trade union and labour rights as part of his centrist programme (Coman 2022). Within government itself, the rhetoric of levelling up has not been backed by a concerted effort to see it through in practice, whilst there remains a rooted distrust of the Conservative Party amongst working-people, and recent outcry from the class, who have suffered because of the cost-of-living crisis and yet have been told not to ask for wage increases (Surridge 2021; Dastidar 2022). This serves as evidence for such a narrative that working-people are not effectively acknowledged as constituent members of society and are effectively sidelined or ignored institutionally, with little tangibly done to alleviate their circumstances. In line with arguments made in Chap. 5, such a reality is only likely to breed further resentment and to produce radicalism or apathy within the class. This is a theme that is identified by the populist and communitarian right, as well as trade unionists like RMT leader Mick Lynch, who received some popular acclaim for calling out a "government of billionaires who tell people to tighten their belts while they're raking it in", singling them out as out of touch and dismissive of "ordinary working-class people" (Lynch in Strick 2022). In fact, he speaks to this sidelining and a corresponding institutional lack of acknowledgement or agency for the working-class and their associations in stating, "What the rest of the country suffers from is the lack of power, the lack of the ability to organise and the lack of the wherewithal to take on these employers that are continually driving down wages and making the working class in this country poorer year on year on year." This rhetoric encapsulates working-class concerns about the decline of their agency and its corresponding connection to their degradation in the economy and its impact on their dignity. Where they at present believe that there is nobody that listens to them or is willing to support them, acknowledgement seeks to ensure that the working-class is represented across a range of issues, can utilise their voice, and is at the very least a constituent member of debates about the future of our society.

As one has noted, associations represent a potential source of this representation for members of the class. However, important intermediary associations with historic links to the class like trade unions at present suffer procedural limitations in their capacity to project working-class concerns. The Thatcher era passing of no less than six trade union laws and the Labour Party's restructuring of its own internal voting structure have contributed, alongside other factors, to the weakening of such associations and a corresponding decline in membership and reach across sectors (Towers 1989). There is not necessarily a clear solution to such challenges, but the present circumstances of the unions are one that we might draw a general point from. Namely, where in the past unions were legally 'freer' to act, and acknowledged by the government in part because of this, they tended to maintain higher membership rates and satisfaction from those members, who could more tangibly see what it could do for them to improve their circumstances. This would indicate the need to re-think the structural limitations that have been placed on historic working-class associations, which have a track record of enhancing agency and satisfaction for them (Evans and Tilley 2017; Edgerton 2021). A policy aimed at further acknowledgement of the class through these associations as a constituent member of debates would undoubtedly go some way to improving that agency, as well as the classes' sense of belonging within the national frame, with corresponding implications for their dignity. This likely requires some deliberation on how to include them better within our decision-making processes, and the associations which are part of them, as well as what might be done to ensure those associations which they imbue with their trust are better able to share the voices of their members. In expanding civil society and its capacity to challenge alienation, we can highlight the need to acknowledge and procedurally include the working-class and their representatives—to take the sting out of the left behind narrative and to restore a sense of agency to the class.

The second point that one considers is that the working-class itself must be able to practise acknowledgement, or to be acknowledged, in its associations. In Chap. 5 we raised the problem of community distrust, often felt in working-class areas between sub-groups that do not understand one another as equals. This is a difficult problem to overcome and one which is multifaceted, born out of a series of issues around misrecognition, racism, structural and cultural insecurity, and more. However, whilst these issues might each require their own consideration, one notes here how relevant working-class associations must make space within their frameworks for the acknowledgement of an expanded membership which encompasses the working-class in its various sub-groups. This is to identify that they maintain similarities between them in terms of their class, but also to demonstrate the diversity of its membership more so than groups like the right-communitarians give credit for. The acknowledgement of this within associations, in which equality and respect go hand in hand with the explicit bringing together of citizens for common ends, is understood by Walzer (1967), Sandel (2020), and Obama (2020) as a conducive place for the integration of difference into the working-class self-understanding since it emphasises their shared features. One maintains too that the Labour Party struggles in the acknowledgement of its working-class base[1] as an association with significant historic links to them, the breakdown of which we referenced in Chap. 5 as worsening this state of alienation in the first instance. Thus, where broader associations should pursue acknowledgement internally in order to see that their members are integrated and better able to practise agency, one raises the point here that historic working-class associations like the Labour Party have failed to acknowledge working-people, not just in their rhetoric but also in their processes. This is partially consistent with the right-communitarian argument that Labour could better acknowledge working-people, who maintain 'tribal' links to the party, but broadens this to be inclusive of a variety of working-class sub-groups rather than the white working-class alone (Kaufmann 2018; Goodhart 2020; Surridge 2021).

Understood in this way, one identifies acknowledgement, and the associations value in promoting it, as a relevant means of challenging alienation. By including the representatives and intermediaries of the working-class in discussions over the future of our society, we are better able to connect with them and to explicitly realise their legitimacy and value as constituent members of our society.

Associations can also help in this through an internal process of acknowledgement to bring a multitude of overlapping and specific concerns to the forefront, building understanding between their members whilst committing to the advancement of the working-class position.

[1] Keir Starmer identified one of Labour's goals as to re-connect with working-people during his leadership campaign.

Recognition

In considering the value of recognition, it is first worth identifying Markell's (2003) critique of acknowledgement alone, which can be applied to identify how the working-class have a significant degree of procedural equality in the form of voting rights, are able to form parties, and can develop associations already, but continue to struggle, not only because such procedural rights do not extend far enough and require a more concerted form of acknowledgement in, say, the economic structure of our country through a strong trade union legal framework, or worker representation, but also because their views are more easily dismissed. Young (2002) builds on this criticism to underline that the status of groups is important because unequal status implies unequal citizenship, with consequences for one's sense of belonging within community and one's ability to feel the benefit of procedural inclusion.[2] In the context of the working-class, the rise of the Knowledge Economy has been matched with that value shift discussed in Chap. 5 which has been to harm their status with respect to their dignity and ability to find prestige in a society where wealth[3] has become further intertwined with the notion of success (Sandel 2020). This is compounded by the fact that some identities are marked by negative differences around culture, religion, race, language, or ethnicity, as well as class, which can seriously hamper minority working-people's agency especially. In this we see those with lower status suffer in that their identities, values, histories, and norms are outside *the* norm, and so are either ignored or denigrated (Moosa-Mitha 2016). This is to undermine social relations and democratic agency when a group has lower status and can, as a result, largely be dismissed in the political mainstream, which is a key assertion of the right- and left-communitarians and which one agrees with in Chap. 5. Associations can challenge this through self-assertion to some extent, which is part of the historic birth of the working-class trade union movement, as well as associations centred on the advancement of women's equality, LGBTQ+ rights, or minority consideration, and progress has been made in advancing the equal status, legal and social, of these groups (Virdee 2014). However, more important to note is that the recognition that these associations often pursue emphasises the necessity of

[2] Equal status refers to the recognition of others on their terms, inclusive of their perspectives, both as an absence of misrecognition and the extension of understanding and the inclusion of positive aspects of identity.

[3] That they cannot acquire in the jobs that they work.

extending genuine understanding within our society for the purposes of improving belonging and of seeing meaningful agency generated for our citizens. The pursuit of recognition, once achieved, is then a great equaliser and enabler of enhanced agential activity (Green 2008).

As Markell (2003) and Tully (2007, 2008) assert, recognition entails achieving equal dignity within the sphere of formal citizenship through the cultivation of respect for social identities. This moves beyond acknowledgement to suggest something more radical—namely an acceptance of one as belonging and an understanding that not only does one get a 'seat at the table', but also that they are worth listening to because they are 'of us'. This is to build on procedural inclusion towards an understanding of one's social identity as valid and legitimate in an altogether more intimate way. Of course, procedural acknowledgement is important and must be a part of this recognition, but Young identifies how this often falls short because of a socio-cultural element that undermines the effectiveness of structural sources of acknowledgement alone. Indeed, she notes how "citizens sometimes find that those still more powerful in the process exercise, often unconsciously, a new form of exclusion: others ignore or dismiss or patronize their statements and expressions" (Young 2002, 55). This would indicate that our society, whilst affording equal rights and capacity to citizens and their associational representatives as part of acknowledgement, often perpetuates inequality because we do not adopt an actively integrative stance where we seek to understand one another on *their* terms. Here, citizens can be ignorant of others, primarily by not adequately understanding *their* perspectives. This is perhaps why Levey (2006) understands such recognition to be a more radical proposal than modest acknowledgement, because it requires some legwork to be done by each group to understand one another in a way that is mutualistic in its intentions, echoing that component of Green's (2008) thought that is explicitly about recognition and other-consideration. In fact, as Chaps. 6 and 7 established, mutual recognition is an integral part of the common good because it is the recognition of others as different but equal to ourselves that is the foundation for our rights, duties, and obligations to one another as co-citizens (Green 2008; Laski 2020). If we cannot view one another in this light, then those elements which bind us together as a political community become fractured, and distrust is likely to be the result. Here one connects with that tendency within the working-class that establishes a desire for interdependence and notes that recognition facilitates this in identifying the grounds upon which a pluralistic and unified society can better be realised, tied together by duty and obligation.[4]

This highlights the relevance of Idealism in providing a challenge to alienation through the process of recognition as part of the common good. Within this, we see a particular importance for the development of moral character as citizens should be encouraged to see others as belonging to the same community and act to learn about them and from them. One has already noted how associations partially achieve this through relationship-building, referencing how bonds across difference help to encourage that willingness to understand people on their own terms (Walzer 1967, 1984; Sandel 2020). The relational character of associations therefore has a role to play in challenging alienation, albeit directly on a more individualised level with potential repercussions indirectly within wider society. Nevertheless, the provision of space for this relationship-building is crucial to the extension of belonging and the positive development of community premised on equal mutual recognition.

Recognition and Education

We can stress the significance of associations further in developing recognition. In fact, we can highlight the importance of those that carry out an explicit educative role. This is what associations like More in Common aim to do. Often these associations know what it is they want to achieve, and how to achieve it, enabling them to take on responsibilities and to craft initiatives that go beyond what government might seek (More In Common 2022a). More in Common, as an example, has commissioned several reports since its founding in 2016 that challenge established narratives and key points of division and has worked with 'thousands' of citizens for each of its studies. Although this is perhaps a limited reach, its associational network has provided support to recent scholarship and governmental research, whilst personal feedback from citizens who participated in the workshops has been overwhelmingly positive. Moreover, these workshops and the reports drafted from them have been able to uncover areas of particular tension, and places of commonality, between citizens, as well as identifying specific narratives that require attention. For instance, they highlight a distorted narrative of trans-exclusion when most citizens are accepting of trans-equality, whilst narratives around the

[4] Which is the subject of one's Progressive Nationalism.

so-called culture wars highlight divisions that are often much exaggerated where there is significant common ground between citizens (More In Common 2022a, b).

This demonstrates the necessity of publicly educative associations as an important part of civil society because they look to reconcile conflict and to promote understanding, especially in the face of these divisive narratives that come to dominate popular discourse. As More in Common (2022b) expresses, "we are losing trust in each other and in the future. Feelings of frustration, powerlessness and a loss of belonging are making us vulnerable to 'us versus them' stories, which turn us against each other" and, in place of this, we do require a means "to understand the forces driving us apart, to find common ground and help to bring people together to tackle our shared challenges". In the search for understanding, these associations consequently help to bridge divides by fulfilling at least three important functions. Namely they:

1. Challenge established and damaging narratives.
2. Build trust by overcoming misunderstandings between individuals and groups.
3. Press for institutions to become more satisfactory for citizens—whether that be in the form of promoting a more inclusive curriculum in schools to cover the breadth of, for example, British history or by identifying ways that institutions can build trust with specific groups.

Having identified these benefits, we can better understand the relevance of civil society expansion in support of such associations which maintain a positive educative role. These associations help to educate the public and to bridge differences, healing areas of conflict at the same time as drawing citizens together on those areas which unite them. This provides an essential component in challenging alienation by dispelling misrecognitions, false and distorted narratives, and rebuilding trust between citizens. For this reason, it is necessary to consider both the benefit that recognition can bring to the amelioration of alienation, as well as how associations facilitate and extend it, and seek a policy direction which is capable of perhaps supporting them in this role.

The Reconciliatory State

Such support might reasonably come from the state, although this could mean embracing its reconciliatory potential more so than at present. Indeed, Green (2008) calls for the creation of an ethical-reconciliatory state to provide the basis for our flourishing, to which end the book is committed as a means of challenging alienation. In this he sees the necessity of drawing together our citizens through the cultivation of the national frame, as well as what amounts to a pluralistic desire for inclusion. This, combined with his commitment to the creation of a society of societies, tends towards a position in which the state is to work with civil society to meet the needs of its members. One builds on the basic tenets of this position to suggest that alienation can be challenged if government takes seriously this role of reconciliation and cooperative link that it can establish with those civil society associations that act as intermediary for the concerns of their members.

This notion of the reconciliatory state is developed by Laski, who sees the potential for government to recognise the pluralistic nature of its society and bonds people together using symbols, narratives, and tangible improvements in their position. For Laski (1925, 2020), this means embracing a system of cooperative social federalism in which government seeks support, advice, and critique from the relevant intermediary associations both as a matter of procedure and, more importantly, for the purpose of carving out a place within the national decision-making apparatus for citizens to exercise their collective agency—echoing the desire for acknowledgement detailed earlier. He sees that intermediary associations bring alive this concept of government *with* the people primarily because they enable a wider net of participation. They succeed in doing this by moving government policy away from more limited internal discussions towards the recognition of explicit bodies which can exert their members' will far more effectively than most can as individuals—in effect 'scaling up' their agency to push, in our example, for working-class improvements or to express their concerns. In this, we refer to the relevancy of the associations given that citizens cannot participate widely and consistently and so this role often comes down to their representatives, which requires a multitude of associations to be effective because of the sheer scale of our society. Here we see the necessity of a pluralistic civil society as government need not only to collaborate with membership-based associations like trade unions, but also to collaborate with identity or issue-based ones who look out for particular interests.

Together, this plurality of associations serves the function of what Bosanquet (2006, 290) calls the "necessity of civilised societies exercising their wills through the state in order to encourage progress in the condition and quality of its members' lives" by expanding the capacity for citizens to engage with, and work alongside, the state to see their interests met. This orientates the state around a more cooperative, reconciliatory model that explicitly seeks to ensure that groups are acknowledged in a Tullian (2008) sense and enabled to better practise the goods of internal recognition and belonging creation, but also seeks fairness in its judgement by integrating groups into its representations of nation—so that no one group can claim that acknowledgement has failed and that they are 'left behind'. This is the pluralistic, socialist influence of social federalism over the Greenian model of the ethical-reconciliatory state to ensure that this is both an imagined and a practical process. We, therefore, require a concerted effort on behalf of government and civil society associations to stress the similarities and common goals that we share whilst making space for the recognition of differences and their symbolic inclusion in a positive light. This will undoubtedly involve cooperation and consideration over a range of issues and is going to be an ongoing process, much like the shaping of one's Progressive Nationalism in the preceding chapters. What is important to stress, however, is that a government policy of recognition and reconciliation would be aided by cooperation with a range of associations, which itself has significance for the renewal of lost agency on behalf of working-people by creating a necessary space for their inclusion and consultation, through their associations, for the purposes of shaping our future. If such a model is effective, then one sees potential to rebuild trust in a state that has felt distant for working-class people in recent times, which is undoubtedly a necessary and self-identified step if the working-class are to feel that they are regarded in our society (More In Common 2022a, b).

Symbolic Inclusion and the State

As one has noted, part of this recognition involves the symbolic inclusion of groups within the state and society. Chin and Levey (2022) advance the claim that symbolic inclusion is an integral component of belonging and is a form of recognition and acknowledgement that can be pursued by the state, necessarily with the assistance of intermediary associations. Although this is a multifaceted idea, let us highlight how a symbolic inclusion privileges to some degree identities and their physical manifestation, rather than direct participation, and seeks to ensure that our community is made more reflective of its members. For example, we might imagine symbolic inclusion to include the erection of a monument because even without direct personal participation in the creation of that monument one can view that action as being representative of them if it speaks to *their* values and that which they consider to be important. This provides a feeling of inclusion within the bounds of the community because it is a resonant attempt to represent them and is visible to other members (Nagel 2003). This latter point is especially important when we consider that national recognition is often crucial to the meaningful extension of belonging to individuals, especially those of the working-class who we have noted as having a particular preference for nation (Eatwell and Goodwin 2018; Kaufmann 2018). To this end, we can assert the necessity of the state taking on the duty of symbolic inclusion in the way that it looks to interact with our citizens and shape our collective future. Such recognition does not have to be practical but must reflect symbolically the class. This means creating space for people like them, and associations like theirs, within the framework of our society, which necessitates to some extent the recognition and acknowledgement noted previously.

To push this point towards a more general policy direction, one would highlight the relevance of associations in bringing to the government or state's attention important facets of their identity, or claims that they have for recognition, and would go further to suggest that government actively seeks to demonstrate that it will 'listen to their opinions and take them seriously'. This means considering the proposals of associations themselves, but it can also mean the extension of 'greetings' to groups as identified by Young (1989), which could be understood as a reference to, in our case, the working-class or one of its sub-groups within a speech, government contact with an intermediary association or its members, or, alternatively, any act which can be understood as inclusionary in its intent. One sees in this symbolic inclusion a general benefit for the working-class in the addition of their values, heroes, and symbols into the national imaginary in a way that corresponds to their sense of dignified place and contribution, echoing the main thrust of the Socialists in Chap. 7. One also notes how Chin and Levey (2022, 19) see symbolic inclusion as an essential good for the integration of minority, and in the case of this book minority working-class, groups into wider society so that they can "enjoy the same level and sense of belonging as majority communities." On this basis, one identifies the importance of associations as potential representatives for the values, concerns, and beliefs of their members and implores government to develop its capacity for interaction, cooperation, and the inclusion of these groups into its narratives, in which symbolic inclusion has a role to play. This has an implication for dignity within the class if they are included in our frameworks and fellow citizens can come to understand them and their experiences and share public space for the celebration of 'their' contributions.

Conclusion

This chapter has sought to identify the ethos upon which civil society should be regenerated. We have laid out four ideas which are beneficial in different ways to the amelioration of the community and agency components of alienation. The chapter has identified how each of these benefits can be enhanced by civil society associations. Indeed, we have seen how associations, in the view of Walzer and Sandel, create a space for the foundational development of relationships whilst encouraging belonging without the necessity of participation. This is especially relevant for working-class people who are under significant structural pressures and yet who require spaces that they can feel they belong to and are supported in.

However, associations can also provide the basis for the extension of moral character and mutuality on an individual level as they provide positive integrative space for people of different backgrounds to form bonds based at first on a shared focus and then proceed to understand one another as a complex web of identities and as people with hopes, dreams, and concerns for our future. Such bonds are taken here as a fundamental element in shaping a more open and pluralistic community, in which the democratic aspirations of our citizens are understood better by their fellows and collectives better constituted so as to enhance their agency to fulfil common ends. Understood in these ways, belonging as promoted by associations challenges that part of alienation from community which relies on us being isolated from one another and de-humanised by the transactionalism which can be felt to dominate our society. Associations are insulation against this and provide support and space for the positive cultivation of bonds—literally the foundational elements of community.

This latter point finds a link to acknowledgement, which sees that citizens and their representatives must be given space within our decision-making processes so that they have procedural equality and are better understood to be legitimate actors within our social imaginary (though this can be undermined by pursuing acknowledgement alone). Here one draws attention to the left behind narrative and asserts a need for historical working-class associations to speak to as well as with those who had placed faith in them, in addition to its emphasis that the government and state must see that the working-class and its sub-groups can place trust in them again by giving them a stake in the future of our society. Acknowledgement expresses the need for the working-class and its civil society intermediaries to benefit from procedural changes to ensure that they are structurally included within our decision-making processes in a way that is representative of them. This refers to decision-making within the wider community but also implores associations themselves to seek inclusion for the broadest possible range of members, so that non-majority groups and sub-groups are given space for the practice of their agency.

Yet, whilst acknowledgement is undoubtedly necessary for improving working-class agency in a structural sense, Tully and Markell demonstrate how social identities and their status can undermine such agency as certain groups can be ignored, often consistently over an extended period of time.

We see this again linked to the left behind narrative and draw on this to suggest that associations have an important function in recognising their members and building understanding between them, as well as pressing government for recognition. This is underlined as a fundamental necessity for the extension of democratic equality, and with that agency, whilst the act of recognition itself has a corresponding positive impact on belonging, the importance of which has already been discussed. Building on this, equally as important to the amelioration of alienation and the extension of equal belonging is that component of recognition which can be tied to public education, especially that part of it which seeks to break down areas of misrecognition, misunderstanding, and distrust, fomented by false or distorted narratives and a simple lack of awareness. Associations have a key role to play in this regard too in repairing these divisions and finding ways to bond citizens together across differences so that they might better understand one another and see themselves in common. This has a poignancy for a working-class that has many areas of shared concern yet struggles to connect its white majority with the multitude of minority working-class sub-groups for common ends.

For these benefits to be expressed, there is a sense that government and the state also have a role to play, both in enhancing and supporting the associations that provide such benefits and in practising these principles themselves. Laski's and Green's stances find some common ground on this and together can be used to build a framework for a state that practises recognition, and acknowledgement, within a desire to see government *with* the people, reconciling interests for the purposes of the common good and the extension of flourishing for our nation's members. In this, one reserves space for the practice of symbolic inclusion, which we have said can be manifest in diverse ways, but is taken here to refer to that practice which actively looks to bring different groups into the community in tangible, practical, and imaginary or symbolic ways. Associations have a vital role to play in this as they are often the bodies which are most capable of making claims for recognition, whilst they themselves are collective symbols of their members that the state/government can cooperate with and work alongside. This also underlines the importance of symbolic inclusion as a means for a reconciliatory state to tie its members together for the purposes of legitimising a sense of equal belonging and of challenging that component of alienation from community that pertains to exclusion from it as a kind of second-class citizen.

To draw a wider point from these discussions, civil society expansion as an ethos and general policy direction can be orientated around these four benefits, with government and relevant actors implored to seek a means to extend such benefits to the working-class. The associations appear to be a natural ally of this impetus and, in line with this, one maintains a commitment to their development, though the chapter reserves space for this to be established practically by policy experts in accordance with the ethos developed. One now turns to the overarching framework which is inclusive of some of these moves and the means by which we might turn to a Progressive Nationalism for the purposes of recognition, acknowledgement, and symbolic inclusion.

Bibliography

Barling, Julian, Clive Fullagar, E. Kevin Kelloway, and K. Kevin Kelloway. *The Union and Its Members: A Psychological Approach*. Oxford University Press, 1992.

Barrows, Thomas S. *What Do Unions Do?: A Twenty-Year Perspective*. Routledge, 2017.

Bloodworth, James. *Hired: Six Months Undercover in Low-Wage Britain*. Atlantic Books, 2018.

Bosanquet, Bernard. *The Philosophical Theory of the State*. Read Books, 2008.

Chin, Clayton, and Geoffrey Brahm Levey. 'Recognition as Acknowledgement: Symbolic Politics in Multicultural Democracies'. *Ethnic and Racial Studies* 0, no. 0 (17 May 2022): 1–24.

Chin, Clayton. 'The Concept of Belonging: Critical, Normative and Multicultural'. *Ethnicities* 19, no. 5 (1 October 2019): 715–739.

Cole, GDH. *Guild Socialism Restated*. Leonard Parsons, 1920.

Coman, Julian. 'Labour May Think It's Moving on, but Working-Class Voters Aren't Following'. *The Guardian*, 10 May 2022. https://www.theguardian.com/commentisfree/2022/may/10/starmer-working-class-voters-labour-leader-brexit. Accessed 21 May 2022.

Dastidar, Sunita Ghosh. 'The Cost of Living Crisis Has Been Going on for Decades – Just Ask Families like Mine'. *The Guardian*, 13 April 2022. https://www.theguardian.com/commentisfree/2022/apr/13/cost-of-living-crisis-working-class-families. Accessed 20 May 2022

Eatwell, Roger, and Matthew Goodwin. *National Populism: The Revolt Against Liberal Democracy*. Penguin, 2018.

Edgerton, David. *The Rise and Fall of the British Nation*. Penguin Books, 2021.

Etzioni, Amitai. 'A Moderate Communitarian Proposal'. *Political Theory* 24, no. 2 (1996): 155–71.

Etzioni, Amitai. 'Communitarianism Revisited'. *Journal of Political Ideologies* 19, no. 3 (2 September 2014a): 241–260.

Evans, Geoffrey, and James Tilley. *The New Politics of Class: The Political Exclusion of the British Working Class*. Oxford University Press, 2017.

Goodhart, David. *Head Hand Heart: The Struggle for Dignity and Status in the Twenty First Century*. Penguin, UK, 2020.

Green, T.H. *Lectures on the Principles of Political Obligation*. Cambridge Scholars Publishing, 2008.

Green, T.H. *Prolegomena to Ethics*. Clarendon Press, 2003.

Kaufmann, Eric. *Whiteshift: Populism, Immigration and the Future of White Majorities*. Penguin, UK, 2018.

Laski, Harold. 'Socialism and Freedom (1925) | LSE Digital Library'. https://digital.library.lse.ac.uk/objects/lse:baz942hap. Accessed 1 May 2023.

Laski, Harold. *The Works of Harold J. Laski*. Routledge, 2020.

Levey, Geoffrey Brahm. "Symbolic Recognition, Multicultural Citizens, and Acknowledgement: Negotiating the Christmas Wars." *Australian Journal of Political Science* 41, no. 3 (September 1, 2006): 355–370.

Macintyre, Alasdair. *After Virtue*. A&C Black, 2013.

Markell, Patchen. *Bound by Recognition*. Princeton University Press, 2003.

Mogollón, Durán, Lía, Olga Eisele, and Maria Paschou. 'Applied Solidarity in Times of Crisis: Exploring the Contexts of Civil Society Activities in Greece and Germany'. *Acta Politica* 56, no. 2 (1 April 2021): 308–329.

Moosa-Mitha, Mehmoona. *Reconfiguring Citizenship: Social Exclusion and Diversity within Inclusive Citizenship Practices.* Routledge, 2016.

More In Common. 'Democratic Repair'. https://www.moreincommon.org.uk/our-work/research/democratic-repair/. Accessed 5 Jul 2022a.

More In Common. 'Navigating Uncertainty'. https://www.moreincommon.com/navigatinguncertainty/. Accessed 7 Jul 2022b.

Nagel, Joane. *Race, Ethnicity, and Sexuality: Intimate Intersections, Forbidden Frontiers.* Oxford University Press, 2003.

Obama, Barack. *A Promised Land.* Penguin Books, 2020.

Sandel, Michael J. *The Tyranny of Merit: What's Become of the Common Good?.* Penguin, UK, 2020.

Sandel, Michael J. *What Money Can't Buy: The Moral Limits of Markets.* Penguin, UK, 2012.

Standing, Guy. *Plunder of the Commons: A Manifesto for Sharing Public Wealth.* Penguin, UK, 2019.

Strick, Katie. "How RMT Boss Mick Lynch Became the Star of the Rail Strikes—and All His Top Moments." *Evening Standard*, June 26, 2022. https://www.standard.co.uk/lifestyle/rmt-boss-mick-lynch-rail-strikes-kay-burley-piers-morgan-b1007619.html.

Surridge, Paula. 'Beyond Binaries: Understanding the Fragmentation of British Politics'. *Political Insight* 12, no. 4 (1 December 2021): 32–35.

Taylor, Charles. 'The Dynamics of Democratic Exclusion'. *Journal of Democracy* 9, no. 4 (1998): 143–156.

Towers, Brian. 'Running the Gauntlet: British Trade Unions under Thatcher, 1979–1988'. *Industrial and Labor Relations Review* 42, no. 2 (1989): 163–88.

Tully, James. *Public Philosophy in a New Key Vol. 1: Democracy and Civic Freedom.* Cambridge University Press, 2008.

Tully, James. *Redistribution and Recognition: Two Approaches.* Cambridge University Press 2007.

Tully, James and Owen, David. Redistribution and Recognition: Two Approaches. In, Laden, A. and Owen, David. *Multiculturalism and Political Theory.* Cambridge University Press, 2007: 265–291.

Vidal, Matt, Tony Smith, Tomás Rotta, and Paul Prew. *The Oxford Handbook of Karl Marx.* Oxford University Press, 2019.

Virdee, Satnam. *Racism, Class and the Racialized Outsider.* Bloomsbury Publishing, 2014.

Walzer, Michael. 'On the Role of Symbolism in Political Thought'. *Political Science Quarterly* 82, no. 2 (1967): 191–204.

Walzer, Michael. *Spheres Of Justice: A Defense Of Pluralism And Equality*. Basic Books, 1984.
Young, Marion. 'Polity and Group Difference: A Critique of the Ideal of Universal Citizenship'. *Ethics* 99, no. 2 (1989): 250–74.
Young, Marion. *Inclusion and Democracy*. Oxford University Press, 2002.

CHAPTER 11

Conclusion: Building a Community of Equals

This book has sought to address the potential for alienation within the British working-class. It has done so by, first, examining the nature of alienation, identifying it as a nexus of characteristics which, if lacking, constitute alienation. To assert this one has drawn on Hegel, Marx, and Macintyre, utilising them to assert that alienation is constituted in relation to a lack of:

1. Dignity—defined as a sense of respect or recognition, and one's inclusion within a wider social activity.
2. Community—inclusiveness, a sense that one can form attachments with others, expand their capacities, and feel part of something larger than oneself. This speaks to the notion that we can find purpose within the commons and improve as individuals through the relationships which we form with others.
3. Agency—a sense that one is their own master, able to control one's life to some extent and to participate in those representative and personal structures which shape our community.

This triad of characteristics becomes the basis for the book's subsequent exploration of the working-class position.

S. Taylor Hill, *Challenging Alienation in the British Working-Class*, Palgrave Politics of Identity and Citizenship Series,
https://doi.org/10.1007/978-3-031-59250-8_11

One has framed this discussion in reference to an emerging right-communitarian literature which partially acknowledges the issues faced by the class across these three characteristics. As Chap. 5 examined, these right-communitarians understand the issues faced by the class with respect to their declining dignity within the emerging Knowledge Economy and its ties to neoliberalism which intertwines the notion of success with that of wealth, the sundering of community upon a structurally insecure and socio-culturally factitious basis, and the degradation of working-class agency both in work and within a political system in which many feel that they have been 'left behind' by the transformation of our society and, in particular, that of the trade unions and the Labour Party. However, in this one also identified areas of concern over the right-communitarian discourse, including the way in which decline was characterised in reference to the multicultural society whilst at the same time doing little to acknowledge the diverse nature of the working-class itself, which maintains minority sub-groups that would struggle unaided or in worse circumstances because of their proposed remedies. While challenging these implications, one has asserted the basic adequacy of their analysis and underlined it with reference to Bloodworth (2018), McKenzie (2015, 2017), Cruddas (2015, 2021), Sandel (2020), and others. It is indeed the case that the working-class are alienated, even if some do not recognise their alienation as anything but 'normal', as the class retain a sense of who they are, and what values they hold dear, desiring something 'more' for them and the country. In this we have rejected the diagnosis of anomie and asserted the general inadequacy of a social capital understanding of their position.

Having concluded that the working-class is alienated, the second half of this book has endeavoured to determine how we might address this by adopting a theoretical approach which is lacking from contemporary solutions provided by the right-communitarians, which one has criticised for their tendency to enhance its effects. Part of this book's originality stems from the source of this. It presents a theory which is drawn from essentially forgotten work, considering alienation in relation to Idealism, which itself went out of fashion after the First World War, Guild and Socialist Pluralism, both of which rose and fell in the interwar period, and an Ethical Socialism which remains alive, but has been pushed to the margins of the Labour movement. In resurrecting these traditions, one seeks to increase the perspectives available to us in coming to understand and address contemporary social issues.

Policies and Principles

As part of this one has outlined a theoretical perspective dubbed 'Idealist-Socialism'. This Idealist-Socialism can be characterised according to its adherence to a common good of mutual flourishing which is underpinned by a commitment to the development of dignity, community, and agency through the nurturing of a reciprocal moral character. This takes place within an expanded network of intermediary associations. These are themselves understood as providing space for the cultivation of our talents and the utilisation of collective efforts for common ends, either as key players in a system of social federalism or as active spaces for our movement towards a state of Higher-selves.

Within, one provides a privileged place for nation, seeing our national community and the vision that it can inspire as wholly conducive to the reconciliation and recognition of our constituent peoples, with significance for our unity.

In creating space for this position, one has identified the place of Idealism as between, on one side, a liberal-individualism that looks to remain neutral in the pursuit of human flourishing/perfection through its propagation of a thin conception of the good life and a communitarianism that can often subsume individual conceptions of that good life in a monistic-thick understanding of it. Idealism charts a path between the two with its notion of the common good and in particular the mutual recognition and other-consideration that underpin it. Here one asserts the necessity of challenging a thin conception of the good life that does little to alleviate the problems of greed, selfishness, and exploitation that so hamper the working-class, at the same time as defending a pluralism which is conducive to multiple individually defined good lives so long as they practise those duties and responsibilities attached to the common good, understood in its simplest form according to Green's (2003, 248) proviso that one should not "gain at the expense of another". This ethical orientation, and the values which flow from it, ultimately underpins a socialist critique of the capitalist system that views the excess accumulation of wealth, strict hierarchy, and inequitable distribution of resources and products, as fundamentally degrading working-people.

What follows from this theory are a set of principles, constitutive of an ethos, which challenge the three components of alienation in such a way as to enhance our ability to flourish. Taken together, one makes three general policy suggestions which are capable of reducing alienation within the working-class, whilst simultaneously presenting a kind of roadmap for national renewal according to the Progressive Nationalist vision outlined here.

Rooting Agency and Dignity in the Economy

The first way that one has sought to challenge alienation is by addressing an economic model that degrades working-people and pushes others towards a state of selfish individualism. To reverse this degradation, one has sought to detail two policy examples that have the potential to help bring us into closer relations with our fellows in cooperative enterprises and to render material and spiritual dignity to the working-class. Such an answer is based around the dual themes of narrative-belonging in work that dignifies one's contribution in spirit and materially, as well as bestowing upon workers control over their own destiny, thus fulfilling that component of non-alienation which requires agency.

This can be helped along by policy which:

1. Seeks the extension of acknowledgement and recognition.
2. Places emphasis on solidarity-building which looks to extend humanistic feeling across hierarchies.
3. Proposes a restructuring with respect to central values like fairness, with resulting workplace policies in the context of worker control seen to redistribute material rewards and reduce feelings of exploitation or otherness.
4. Looks to the extension of autonomy.

However, one does not stop at these suggestions, going on to highlight the need to pursue policies which achieve the following:

1) Movement towards recognition of the working-class in material and narrative terms, centred on important lay values such as fairness, with care being given to facilitate interaction within existing hierarchies as a good in itself.
2) Establishing that one of the core goals of work and workplace strategy, including its pay and bonus structure, should be to ensure that the worker can live decently at the same time as restricting the growth of inequality at the top of the workplace hierarchy.

3) Matching legal and procedural obligation with a narrative that can encourage ethical obligation conducive to the development of moral character.
4) Enacting comprehensive measures to promote associational expansion and the creation of a network with an express place for working-people to agentially influence both specific workplace and more general economic policy.

Taken together, the pursuit of these ends amounts to a reorientation of our economy towards ensuring that working-people are respected and fairly rewarded in their roles, with a sense of agential power. Here one asserts the need for fair material reward, narrative recognition, and the reassertion of working-class control over aspects of their economic circumstance, whilst there is scope for further development around the question of ownership.

Civil Society Expansion

One has outlined the value of civil society associations in providing four core benefits to the working-class, understood as the following:

1. Belonging, in both its membership and relational forms.
2. Acknowledgement, both meaning acknowledgement of the classes' associations as having a stake in the future of our nation and within these associations as an inclusion of different sub-groups in their development.
3. Recognition, by government as part of the ethical-reconciliatory state and by our fellows within society as equals, perhaps different but nevertheless of fundamental worth and deserving of respect.
4. Symbolic inclusion, understood as those acts which speak to a particular group within our society and seek to include them, their symbols, or their values, amongst other things, within our collective national spaces and institutions.

The chapter determined that a policy of civil society expansion should focus on enhancing these benefits. In this one identifies a potential role for the state, drawn out of a synthesis of the Greenian and Laskian understandings of it, which bestows upon it a duty to 'enable' citizens through a process of ethical action and active reconciliation. This is to enshrine a need to pursue recognition and acknowledgement as fundamental guiding principles for the state, to be achieved through the tangible and symbolic inclusion of groups in our national narrative and institutions and by working alongside, and listening to, the demands of the people through their respective intermediary associations. It is in this stead that one sees the potential for the agential enhancement of the working-class through the expansion of associations which encourage these four goods, and which seek the classes' representation within our nation. As part of this one recognises a need for procedural and socio-cultural development and ties this to the wider ethos established in Chaps. 8 and 10.

The Propagation of a Tangible Progressive Nationalism

The book has sought to tie this together within a frame that is inclusive and can re-forge the bonds of the working-class. One advocates in favour of a nationalist position, rather than a patriotic one, to achieve this, seeing the latter as lacking the ability to construct a coherent national narrative that actively recognises and ties together our disparate groups, with consequences for their mutual recognition. This nationalism is itself underpinned by the common good of flourishing advocated for throughout the book and stresses the importance of recognition for the purposes of collective betterment through mutual ethical duty and obligation to one's fellows. One sees this as essential if we are to be able to realise our fundamental worth alongside other citizens, with significance for the present distrust and segregation that has undermined our communities. Fundamentally, one holds that nation is a collective work of many selves and is the embodiment of 'us'. We should be able to feel pride in our country and see ourselves reflected in its progress, narrative, culture, and institutions. In line with this perspective, the book asserts that the working-class and its sub-groups must be able to celebrate themselves as Britons and be understood in their different ways as contributing to this greater whole. Policy which achieves this purpose can be judged to be a success against the ethos provided here, which is valuable to the restoration of dignity within a class that privileges the national frame and belonging, acknowledgement, and recognition within it.

To this end, one advocates for:

1. Active inclusion and acknowledgement in community.
2. The amelioration of community tensions through a unified national framing (in tandem with Chap. 10's associational expansion).
3. The rejection of rootlessness and the reintroduction of working-class values into the national imaginary.

One has outlined in part how these objectives can be achieved but leaves space open for government or relevant groups within civil society to add to, expand, and alter the national narrative, seeing it as in a constant state of evolution. Progressive Nationalism is then an ongoing process that requires commitment to it to challenge the exclusivist populist nationalism advocated for by the current government and right-communitarians alike, which is only likely to cause further discord.

A Contribution to Contemporary Debate

Reflecting on the book, when one began this process, there was very little that dealt with alienation explicitly. However, in the past couple of years, especially post-2020 with the publishing of works by Goodhart, Sandel, and Cruddas, there seems to be a growing understanding that our present social structures are unstable in the current political climate and detrimental to our citizenry. One has sought to acknowledge and engage with such literature by both supporting this main thrust and offering a proposal for a more connected, perhaps even post-Liberal, future. One can, therefore, understand this book as a part of an emerging political current, one not yet fully developed, which seeks to provide the grounds upon which further debate and research can be conducted. More specifically, one makes special recommendations for theoretical research, which currently lacks in comparison to practical awareness of contemporary class issues.

One has moved beyond this established work in laying down a theoretical framework for understanding these issues, defined so as alienation. No scholar currently goes so far as to do this, which presents an opportunity for further debate, defence of this position, and the academic development of this emerging current. In a similar vein, many of the positions that this book has consulted are also light on theory, either referencing it in particularly broad terms such as in the work of Cruddas or largely neglecting it as in Goodhart. Here, one presents a proposed solution found via a deeper understanding of theory and thus goes beyond established literature to provide a framework which can be used to conceptualise contemporary issues. The book maintains a theoretical relevance in that it seeks to be part of a re-consideration of alienation as a valid and accurate characterisation for the issues faced by the working-class within contemporary Britain.

Finally, one's Progressive Nationalism makes express intersections with Modood's Multicultural Nationalism to advance its position. It follows in a similar vein to that which has been developed by the Bristol School of Multiculturalism, sharing an emphasis on recognition, inclusion, and the importance of narrative. Although one does not wish to claim that this Progressive Nationalism is new, the attempt to construct a comprehensive vision of what Britain is is an important step in trying to transform a Progressive Nationalist narrative from theory to reality. This has significance for the development of the debate moving forward, with attention to be paid in particular to the way we come to conceive of something as being constitutive of 'us', how we might move to recognise and intertwine our sub-cultures in a cohesive way, and what this might require of government in policy and on an institutional level. These are all questions which need to be considered if Progressive Nationalism is to challenge its populist counterpart.

Opportunities for Further Research and Recommendations

The book uses a secondary literature which does not engage with the framework of alienation explicitly. In fact, though one has used these works extensively to demonstrate the nature of alienation within contemporary Britain, this has been done by examining how social commentary and scholarly works identify themes which themselves reflect one of its three core characteristics. This secondary research could well reveal a more limited understanding of alienation in practice because these studies do not engage with its framework, though it is worth acknowledging that the book would not have had space to conduct its own primary research. This presents an opportunity to explore alienation further by utilising the framework theorised by this book within future studies.

This also identifies a point of originality as the framework is not a common way of conceptualising the issues faced by the working-class. In this respect, the book demonstrates in a unique way how contemporary issues can be understood within this conceptual framework, hopefully prompting some consideration over its usage in future scholarly works, with the potential for these subsequent works to fit within a schema that broadly resembles the one outlined here. As such, though one could not directly engage with much scholarly work that explicitly recognises alienation as impacting the working-class, the book has been able to develop and support its conceptualisation, with significance for further study and debate.

There is also some scope to develop the theory of alienation as one has presented it. Indeed, given that this book has sought to conceptualise a form that can understand the experience of the working-class within Britain, one questions the extent to which such a framework could be expanded upon and developed. Indeed, though one has touched upon the fact that these characteristics are often impacted by similar events, for example, how agency, community, and dignity have been challenged by trade union decline, one would like to further examine the relationship that each characteristic has with one another, for example, whether agency be utilised to restore dignity.

Similarly, though one has mentioned the potentially disproportionate impact of the community component of alienation on minority workers, one wonders how other intersections, like gender, play a role and the extent to which an intersectional lens can help develop the Progressive Nationalist position further.

Indeed, to explore this somewhat, work was heavily gendered in many of the historic working-class industries and some of the most important, but critically undervalued, work is now disproportionately done by women, many from minority backgrounds, on minimum wage, with long hours, and precarious contracts (Topping 2023). In this Progressive account of work we therefore require an awareness of gender in conjunction with the factors already considered, both so that we might garner a better understanding of the role and struggles of women (and others) in the economy and to fix the 'pink collar' sectors most focused on care, teaching, and nursing work which suffer from critical underfunding, a lack of pay, and, in spite of these issues, increasing demand. In fact, evidence suggests that it is these low-pay sectors that are most responsible for in-work poverty and a more general poverty rate which is now at some 14.5m (JRF 2010; TUC 2023). The TUC (2023) indicates that a poverty-free Britain would require better wages, paid at the living wage or above, across these sectors alongside new forms of social support, including the provision of free hygiene products and, crucially, more equitable access to childcare (Brown 2022). UNICEF (2021) too highlights how lack of access to childcare compounds socio-economic inequality as parents, disproportionally women, are forced to stay at home to care for their children and are subsequently unable to obtain a wage—which is often the most effective way to escape poverty. At a time when the cost of living is rising, and many are unable to heat their homes properly, this can also have a series of ramifications, including pushing parents into food, fuel, and other forms of poverty. A Progressive Nationalist position would need to be aware of these nuances in order to better formulate policy which is capable of ensuring that citizens maintain dignity and to offer reforms to those sectors of the economy which continue to reproduce poverty and prevent working-people from escaping alienation. The interplay between these characteristics and the relevance of identity intersections in contributing to alienation looks to be a fruitful opportunity for additional research and one which can help to make a Progressive Nationalism more tangible.

There are also further opportunities to develop the Idealist-Socialism presented within this book and the questions that arise out of its synthesis. The intertwining which takes place within the book is unique, bringing together positions which, as far as one is aware, have not explicitly been combined either as an ideological position or as a solution to a political issue. In this stead, there is an opportunity to continue this process of philosophical intertwining, whilst it should be noted that the Idealist contribution to the propagation of Progressive Nationalism might well be significant. Indeed, both Green and Bosanquet saw great value in promoting education as a means for mutual flourishing. They saw that it was through education that we might create good and dutiful citizens who are both aware of the structures in which they live, and can engage with them, and have the necessary critical and empathetic skills to engage with their fellows within community. To this end, subjects like Ethics, History, Politics, and English might well be fit to teach different aspects of citizenship, narrative, inclusion, obligation, and those critical and other skills necessary to be able to better engage within our society. It may then be of interest to scholars, particularly those who value the Progressive Nationalist perspective outlined in this book, to look to the Idealists to inform a reform of our education system to create more capable and inclusive citizens. This example serves to reinforce the continued relevance of Idealist thought to contemporary society whilst simultaneously encouraging us as scholars to consider the ways in which hitherto 'forgotten' thought can be synthesised to produce solutions to complex problems in our present.

Final Thoughts

The book has sought to develop a theoretical framework for the understanding of the working-class position, which is increasingly challenging, often frustrating, and difficult to categorise for scholars. In the process of coming to an understanding of the class position as one of alienation we have challenged the remedies proposed by the right-communitarians and reasserted the relevance of the left in supporting working-people. This has been achieved by turning to contemporaries like Sandel and Cruddas and by reconsidering the legacy of the Socialists, combining this with an Idealism rooted in the philosophy of Hegel and the early Marx that connects with working-class concerns about the values present within our society, of the common good, and of interdependent duty and obligation to one another.

In the development of this theory, one has sought to advance a corresponding Idealist-Socialist ethos that is capable of ameliorating alienation across its three characteristics, asserting a fundamental need for us to recognise the present agential, economic, and socio-cultural degradation of the working-class, the structural limitations that have been placed on them and their associations, the indignity inflicted upon them by their lack of inclusion in the processes that govern our society, structural insecurity, and limited respect for the work that they do or their contributions to this nation. These circumstances have fed a politics of resentment that has contributed to the rise of the populist-right, which has itself exacerbated tensions within the class to the detriment of its sub-groups, and left working-people continuing to struggle.

The state of the working-class is thus one that we should express concern over. Indeed, this resentment is only likely to build if nothing is done to address it. We are likely to see the continued shift of working-people towards apathy or populism, unable to reach their potential in this country or to flourish as citizens. Such an outcome is not morally permissible within the theory of Idealist-Socialism, which seeks a dignified Britain, aware of its constituent members and their value, where working-people are rewarded materially and in narrative terms for their contributions, and in which we might overcome our present divisions to create a fairer, more receptive, and dutiful society for all—truly a community of equals. This book goes some way to outlining that vision and asserts fundamentally the need to address the continued degradation of the working-class position, defined here as constitutive of alienation.

Bibliography

Bloodworth, James. *Hired: Six Months Undercover in Low-Wage Britain*. Atlantic Books, 2018.

Brown, Gordon. "A Poverty Time-Bomb Is Ticking Across Britain." *The Big Issue*, August 8, 2022. https://www.bigissue.com/opinion/gordon-brown-a-poverty-time-bomb-is-ticking-across-britain%EF%BF%BC/. Accessed 15 Feb 2024.

Cruddas, Jon. 'The Common Good in an Age of Austerity'. in Geary, Ian, and Adrian Pabst. *Blue Labour: Forging a New Politics*. Bloomsbury Publishing, 2015: 87–97.

Cruddas, Jon. *The Dignity of Labour*. Polity Press, 2021.

Green, T.H. *Prolegomena to Ethics*. Clarendon Press, 2003.

Joseph Rowntree Foundation. "The Low-Pay, No-Pay Cycle: Understanding Recurrent Poverty," November 17, 2010. https://www.jrf.org.uk/work/the-low-pay-no-pay-cycle-understanding-recurrent-poverty. Accessed 12 Feb 2024.

McKenzie, Lisa. 'The Class Politics of Prejudice: Brexit and the Land of No-Hope and Glory'. *The British Journal of Sociology* 68, no. S1 (2017): 265–80.

McKenzie, Lisa. *Getting By: Estates, Class and Culture in Austerity Britain*. Policy Press, 2015.

Sandel, Michael J. *The Tyranny of Merit: What's Become of the Common Good?*. Penguin, UK, 2020.

Topping, Alexandra. "Exploitation and Low Pay Causing Poverty among Care Workers, TUC Finds." *The Guardian*, August 29, 2023, sec. Society. https://www.theguardian.com/society/2023/aug/29/exploitation-and-low-pay-causing-poverty-among-care-workers-tuc-finds. Accessed 19 Feb 2024.

Trades Union Congress. "A Strategy for the Care Workforce," August 28, 2023. https://www.tuc.org.uk/research-analysis/reports/strategy-care-workforce. Accessed 12 Feb 2024.

UNICEF. "Affordable, Quality Childcare Inaccessible in Many of World's Wealthiest Countries." 2021. https://www.unicef.org/press-releases/affordable-quality-childcare-inaccessible-many-worlds-wealthiest-countries-unicef. Accessed 8 Jan 2024.

Index[1]

[1] Note: Page numbers followed by 'n' refer to notes.

S. Taylor Hill, *Challenging Alienation in the British Working-Class*, Palgrave Politics of Identity and Citizenship Series, https://doi.org/10.1007/978-3-031-59250-8

The manufacturer's authorised representative in the EU is Springer
Nature Customer Service Centre GmbH, Europaplatz 3, 69115 Heidelberg,
Germany. If you have any concerns regarding our products, please
contact ProductSafety@springernature.com

Printed and bound by CPI Group (UK) Ltd, Croydon, CR0 4YY
28/09/2026
02224083-0003